THE
INDUSTRIAL RAILWAYS
OF
ST HELENS, WIDNES
AND
WARRINGTON

Part One - St Helens

(Including the development of the canals and the main line railways)

by

C. H. A. Townley

and

J. A. Peden

Industrial Railway Society 1999

The Industrial Railways of St Helens, Widnes and Warrington
Part One St Helens

© C.H.A. Townley, J.A. Peden and the Industrial Railway Society, 1999

ISBN 1 901556 10 7

Published in 1999 by the Industrial Railway Society, 18 Osprey Close, Guisborough, Cleveland TS14, 8HN

Available from IRS Publications
1 Clifton Court, Oakham, Rutland LE15 6LT

Typesetting and artwork by the Industrial Railway Society and the authors
Printed by A B Printers Ltd, 33 Cannock St, Leicester LE4 9HR

CONTENTS

CHAPTER 1   INTRODUCTION   5

CHAPTER 2   THE CANALS AND THE MAIN LINE RAILWAYS   15

                     RAILWAY CHRONOLOGY   55

CHAPTER 3   AROUND RAVENHEAD JUNCTION   77

CHAPTER 4   PILKINGTON BROTHERS SHEET WORKS   103

CHAPTER 5   SUTTON AND LOWER RAVENHEAD   136

CHAPTER 6   RAVENHEAD   159

CHAPTER 7   THE ECCLESTON BRANCH   183

CHAPTER 8   PEASLEY AND SUTTON   197

CHAPTER 9   ST HELENS TOWN CENTRE AND POCKET NOOK   217

CHAPTER 10   AROUND GERARD'S BRIDGE   242

WINDLE photographed at Pilkington Brothers Ltd's Sheet Works on 17th October 1961, on the occasion of its presentation to the Middleton Railway Preservation Society. WINDLE was one of around 50 similar locomotives built by Edward Borrows and Sons of the Providence Foundry at St Helens Junction and its successor, H.W. Johnson and Company. The majority of these locomotives were employed at works and collieries in and around St Helens. Water was carried beneath the boiler in well tanks between the frames and, as a consequence, the valve gear had to be placed between the frames and the wheels.

(C.A. Appleton)

4

CHAPTER ONE

INTRODUCTION

Previous volumes [1,2,3,4] have covered the central and eastern parts of South Lancashire and in our final study we turn our attention to the industrial railways of St Helens, Widnes, Warrington and surrounding districts. To the west, we stop short of the boundary of the City of Liverpool. Our southern limits are the River Mersey and the Manchester Ship Canal but we have also included Runcorn, where the history of the chemical industry is virtually inseparable from that of Widnes on the north bank of the river. In the east and the north we link up with the areas dealt with in the earlier books. We have attempted, as far as possible, to bring our story up to date to the beginning of 1997, when the present text was completed.

Our main purpose is to trace the development of the various industrial railway systems and the locomotives which worked on them. To understand the subject properly, however, we need to know something of the history of the mines and works which they served. We hope that what we have written will prove of interest to the industrial archaeologist as well as to the railway historian.

We start our story at St Helens, a town founded on coal, glass, copper and chemicals. The development up to 1900 of these industries and of the town itself has been fully described by Barker and Harris in *A Merseyside Town in the Industrial Revolution* [5]. *The Glass Makers* by Professor Barker [6] covers the history of the flat glass industry, with the main emphasis on Pilkington Brothers' works. Both have provided much background material for the present book.

The initial impetus for industrial expansion came with the opening of the Sankey Brook Navigation in 1755. The canal gave access to the Mersey and the port of Liverpool and, as well as being able to compete with coal from Prescot and Whiston for the Liverpool market, the St Helens collieries were able to meet the demand from the Cheshire saltmakers for cheap fuel. Indeed, many of the salt proprietors became colliery owners, while many of the colliery owners entered the salt industry. Coal output continued to rise throughout the nineteenth century to provide fuel for the local glass and chemical industries as well as to supply customers further afield and this led to the sinking of larger and better equipped collieries to the south of the town. The last colliery, Sutton Manor, did not close until 1987.

The modern glass industry also had its origins in the late eighteenth century, influenced more by local supplies of good quality sand and cheap coal rather than by the transport facilities offered by the canal. Ravenhead Plate Glass Works was founded in 1777 and a number of glass bottle works were also in operation by that date. The early years of the nineteenth century saw the establishment of crown glass manufacture together with several more plate glass works. By the end of the century the flat glass trade was dominated by the firm of Pilkington Brothers which had changed over from crown glass to the less labour intensive production of rolled glass as well as setting up its own plate glass works at Cowley Hill. The manufacture of glass bottles, always a separate business, was latterly in the hands of the United Glass Bottle Manufacturers Ltd and Forster's Glass Co Ltd.

The chemical industry was founded on the Leblanc process to produce carbonate of soda for use as a detergent and as a starting point for the manufacture of soap. An intermediate product, soda ash, was extensively used by the glass industry. Later, hydrochloric acid, originally allowed to go to waste, became important in the manufacture of bleaching powder. One of the main raw materials, salt, was readily available as was the coal needed as fuel. Sulphur and pyrites, required to produce the sulphuric acid for the first stage of the process, were imported via Liverpool.

The first alkali works at St Helens was established at Gerard's Bridge around 1830. Following the opening of the St Helens and Runcorn Gap Railway, a multiplicity of firms sprang up, many of which lasted only a few years before becoming bankrupt. With a few minor exceptions, the survivors joined the United Alkali Co Ltd, which was set up in 1890 to bring together all the major producers using the Leblanc process. The least viable works were closed immediately as the centre of alkali production moved first to Widnes and then Northwich. The five remaining works at St Helens ceased production in the period between 1920 and 1928.

Copper smelting began at Blackbrook in the early 1770s and at Ravenhead around 1780, taking advantage of the cheap local coal and the Sankey Brook Navigation for the transport of the ore. Although the Blackbrook works had a relatively short life, a number of other copper works were established in the nineteenth century as an adjunct to the alkali industry. These used imported pyrites, much of it from Spain and Portugal, to provide the sulphuric acid needed for the Leblanc process as well as producing copper. Those copper works having strong links with the chemical industry also joined the United Alkali Company in 1890 and one survived until 1928.

By contrast, industrial development at Widnes did not get under way until the middle of the nineteenth century, with John Hutchinson building the first alkali works in 1847. Widnes offered several advantages compared with St Helens. It was nearer to the River Weaver and thus to the Cheshire salt fields, which supplied one of the principal raw materials. Sulphur and pyrites could be imported through either the West Bank Dock or the Railway Dock at Widnes and were not subject to further transport costs. Land was also readily available as large areas had been purchased by John Hutchinson to let out to firms setting up works in the district.

By 1890, more than twenty chemical and copper works had been established at Widnes, the majority of which were absorbed into the United Alkali Company. Widnes had now overtaken St Helens in terms of alkali production and was fast becoming one of the country's main centres for the manufacture of heavy chemicals. A further amalgamation in 1926 led to the formation of Imperial Chemical Industries Ltd, which acquired the United Alkali Company's properties at Widnes and St Helens. The full story is told in Hardie's *A History of the Chemical Industry in Widnes* [7] which we have used extensively for background material. Although there was some rationalisation of production under the United Alkali Company Ltd and later by Imperial Chemical Industries Ltd, the chemical industry dominated the scene in Widnes until well after the second world war. Now the majority of the works have disappeared.

Both St Helens and Widnes attracted a number of ancillary industries, such as ironfounding, general engineering and the manufacture of casks and drums for the transport of chemical products. A development unconnected with the chemical industry was the iron works which was built at Ditton in 1868. There was a serious explosion in one of its blast furnaces in 1876 and the works closed shortly afterwards.

On the Runcorn side of the river several soap works were opened in the early years of the nineteenth century, which later had their own plant for the manufacture of alkali. Other alkali works followed in the 1850s and 1860s although the town was still probably better known for shipbuilding and stone quarrying than for chemicals. The Castner Kellner Works at Weston Point was constructed in the 1890s to produce alkali using an electrolytic process to decompose brine brought by pipeline from mid Cheshire. There followed an almost continuous expansion of the chemical industry with two major plants, at Rocksavage and Randle Sluices, being built and operated by Imperial Chemical Industries Ltd on behalf of the Ministry of Supply during the second world war. Although many of the works have now been dismantled, those at Weston Point and Rocksavage are still in production.

Warrington, in contrast to St Helens and Widnes, was an old established town, situated at what for many years was the head of navigation on the River Mersey. Glass manufacture was recorded as early as 1696 [6] and continued in a small way until the 1930s. Copper smelting was also carried on during most of the eighteenth century. It was not until around 1800 that the foundations were laid for developments which turned the town into a major industrial centre. The first wire drawing works was set up by Nathaniel Greening in 1799 [8], while Joseph Crosfield's soap works was established in 1815 [9].

Manufacture of wire and associated products expanded rapidly in the period between 1840 and 1860 and works were built at Dallam and Sankey Bridges to supply the wrought iron bar which was needed. With the decline of heavy industries, starting in the 1960s, most of the works associated with wire manufacture have closed; only those belonging to Rylands Brothers are still at work.

Crosfield's soap works went from strength to strength in the nineteenth century. Before the first world war land on the south bank of the Mersey was developed, linked to the other side of the river by the only two privately owned transporter bridges in Britain. Taken over by Lever Brothers Ltd in 1919, the works now produces detergents and other chemical products.

Irlam, where we conclude our book, was virtually non-existent until the Manchester Ship Canal was built. Coal shipping facilities were provided when the canal was opened and, during the early years of the present century, a number of factories were erected nearby. These included several tar distilleries and chemical plants as well as margarine and soap factories for the Cooperative Wholesale Society. The district was dominated by the Partington Steel and Iron Company's works which came into production just before the first world war. Under a succession of different owners, this remained in production until 1979 and was then demolished. Most of the other industries have disappeared as well and only one of the tar works still remains, now used for the bulk storage of liquid chemicals.

By way of background, we have provided a chapter summarising the history of the canals and the public railways. Without improved transport facilities, industrial development would undoubtedly have taken a very different course. Our treatment of this topic is necessarily brief. For those wishing to study the story of the canals in greater depth a comprehensive treatment is given in Hadfield and Biddle's *Canals of North West England* [10]. *The St Helens Railway* by John Tolson [11] and *Waterways and Railways to Warrington* by Peter Norton [12] provide a wealth of information about the main line and industrial railways in the area covered by our book. The early history of the Liverpool and Manchester Railway is described in three publications which appeared around the time of the 150th anniversary of the line [13,14,15], while developments on the west coast main line are described in Brian Read's *Crewe to Carlisle* [16]. The history of the railways of the Manchester Ship Canal Company are featured in a publication by Don Thorpe [17].

In addition to the books mentioned above, we have made reference to numerous other primary and secondary sources. Much useful information relating to colliery history is to be found in the list of coal mines provided from the mid 1850s until 1881 in the Mineral Statistics published by the Geological Survey and from 1883 onwards in the Annual Reports of the Inspectors of Mines. Documents relating to colliery leases, where they exist in the archives, provide further evidence for the dates of opening of the various collieries and their transfer to new ownership.

Local newspapers have proved an invaluable source for all aspects of industrial activities - the opening of mines and factories, bankruptcies, sales of plant, new owners and final closure. Sometimes there are references to industrial railways, perhaps the opening of a new line but more usually an accident on an existing one. Much can also be learned from the *London Gazette*. Before the days of the Limited Liability Company, most firms operated as legally constituted partnerships and the changes which took place as partners retired or died are recorded in this publication.

Without access to archive material it would have been impossible to put together our story. We should specially like to thank Pilkington plc for granting us access to the firm's records, now held at Information Management and Storage Ltd, and to acknowledge our debt of gratitude to Ms Dinah Stobbs for the time and trouble that she took helping us to find the documents which would be of value.

Equally important has been the help which we have received from members of staff at the many libraries and record offices which we visited in our search for material. We should like to record our very grateful thanks to:

The staff of the St Helens Local History Library and particularly to Mrs Hainsworth and Mr Sargeant
The staff of the Warrington Local History Library
The staff of the History Shop at Wigan
The staff of the Map Department and the Official Publications Department at the British Library
The staff of the Map Department and the Official Publications Department at Cambridge University Library
The Chief Archivist and the staff of the Cheshire Record Office
The Chief Archivist and the staff of the Greater Manchester Record Office
The Chief Archivist and the staff of the Lancashire Record Office
The Chief Archivist and the staff of the Wigan Record Office
The Librarian and his staff at the National Railway Museum at York
The Trustees of the National Galleries and Museums on Merseyside and the staff at the Modern Business Records Centre
The Archivist and staff at the Catalyst Museum at Widnes

Through the courtesy of the Estates Surveyor, British Rail Property Board, North Western Region, we have inspected the complete set of Line Plans for the area. These were produced by the railway companies and show details of the track layout, including that at the various private sidings. Notes about the agreements relating to the sidings are often included as well as information about land ownership. We have also been able to refer to some older issues of the Line Plans which are available in the Greater Manchester Record Office and in the Cheshire Record Office. Further information about private sidings has come from the special diagrams which were prepared by the main line railway companies. Those for the London and North Western Railway have been lent to us by the Librarian of the Manchester Locomotive Society.

For our locomotive information we have relied heavily on data contained in those locomotive manufacturers' records which have survived. We have also referred to lists compiled by organisations such as the Industrial Locomotive Society and the Industrial Railway Society, but omitting some information which could not be verified independently. Additional material comes from the notes which we made from the 1940s onwards, during our conversations with the older generation of employees whom we met when visiting various works and collieries. Often their memories went back to late Victorian times. Finally, much of the later history, from the mid 1930s onwards, comes from personal observations by the authors and their colleagues.

We must also express our gratitude to all our friends who have assisted in the preparation of the book. John Tolson allowed us to use extracts from material, much of it unpublished, which he has put together relating to the St Helens Railway and associated matters. Ken Plant made information available from his extensive collection of locomotive builders archives. Rodney Weaver and Harry Jack brought their expertise on early locomotives to bear on the complicated history of the engines used at Haydock Colliery. John Ryan provided much useful material from Working Time Tables and other documents in his possession and Roy Etherington cleared up many queries about the movement of National Coal Board locomotives. Finally we wish to acknowledge our special debt to Mike Pain, who has provided a superb set of maps from our very rough drafts, and to Cliff Shepherd who painstakingly read the draft text and helped to prepare the manuscipt for publication.

Those who so generously made available photographs from their collections are acknowledged individually in the captions. Some of the illustrations are copies of rather faded and damaged originals. We trust that readers will appreciate that they have been included for their historical importance rather than their artistic merit.

As in previous books, we are conscious that our research is far from complete and that much more information, at present buried in the archives, still remains to be discovered. We hope that others will be inspired to undertake a more detailed investigation of some of these topics.

A last point concerns the spelling of place names, always a contentious subject. We have tried, as far as possible, to keep to the spelling contemporary with the time that we write about. Thus we have Fidler's Ferry as shown on the first edition of the 6 inch Ordnance Survey map and Fiddler's Ferry in more recent times.

Locomotive Summaries

A summary is provided at the end of most of the chapters giving, in tabular form, details of the locomotives referred to in the text.

The tables are set out in order of name or number; type of locomotive (wheel arrangement, position of tanks, position of cylinders); maker; maker's number (where known); cylinder dimensions (bore and stroke); and diameter of driving wheels.

The Whyte system of classification has been used to describe the wheel arrangements of the locomotives, with the addition of 4w and 6w to indicate four or six wheels with gear or chain drive.

The position of the water tanks is denoted by ST for saddle tank, T for side tank, WT for well tank, BT for back tank and FT for front tank. Tk indicates that we lack information, other than knowing that the locomotive in question had a tank rather than a tender.

Cylinder position is denoted by IC for inside the frames and by OC for outside the frames. VC indicates vertical cylinders. A vertical boiler is indicated by V and a geared drive, on a steam locomotive, by G.

Diesel locomotives are identified by a D after the wheel arrangement, with M added for mechanical drive, H for hydraulic drive and E for electric drive.

In the case of electric locomotives, OHW denotes current collection from an overhead wire system and Batt shows that the supply came from storage batteries on the locomotive.

We have used the conventional abbreviations for the locomotive builders, with a few extra which are relevant to our own area. A full list of the abbreviations is given below.

AB   Andrew Barclay, Sons & Co Ltd, Caledonia Works, Kilmarnock
AE   Avonside Engine Co Ltd, Bristol
AK   Alan Keef Ltd, Cote Farm, Bampton, later Lea Line, Ross on Wye
AtW Atkinson Walker Wagons Ltd, Frenchwood, Preston
AW   Sir W.G. Armstrong Whitworth & Co (Engineers) Ltd, Newcastle upon Tyne
Bg   E.E. Baguley Ltd, Burton on Trent
BH   Black, Hawthorn & Co Ltd, Gateshead
Bs   Barclays & Company, River Bank Engine Works, Kilmarnock
CF   Chapman & Furneaux Ltd, Gateshead
Ch   Alexander Chaplin & Co Ltd, Cranstonhill Engine Works, Glasgow
DA   Daniel Adamson & Co, Dukinfield
DC   Drewry Car Co Ltd, London (suppliers only)
DK   Dick Kerr & Co Ltd, Preston
EB   Edward Bury & Co, Clarence Foundry, Liverpool
EBS Edward Borrows & Sons, Providence Foundry, St Helens
EBW E.B. Wilson & Co, Railway Foundry, Leeds
EE   English Electric Co Ltd, Preston
EEV English Electric Co Ltd, Vulcan Works, Newton le Willows
Fbn   William Fairbairn & Sons, Manchester
FH   F.C. Hibberd & Co Ltd, Park Royal, London
FW   Fox, Walker & Co, Atlas Works, Bristol
GB   Greenwood & Batley Ltd, Leeds
GH   Gibb and Hogg, Airdrie
HC   Hudswell, Clarke & Co Ltd, Railway Foundry, Leeds
HCR Hudswell, Clarke & Rodgers, Railway Foundry, Leeds
HE   Hunslet Engine Co Ltd, Leeds
HH   Henry Hughes & Co, Falcon Works, Loughborough
HKP H.K. Porter Inc, Pittsburgh, USA
HL   R.& W. Hawthorn, Leslie & Co Ltd, Forth Bank Works, Newcastle upon Tyne
Hor   Lancashire & Yorkshire Railway Co, Horwich Works
HWJ H.W. Johnson & Co, St Helens and later Rainford, successors to Edward Borrows & Sons
IWB Isaac Watt Boulton, Ashton under Lyme
JCK J.C. Kay & Co Ltd, Bury
JF   John Fowler & Co Ltd, Leeds
JSW John Scarisrbrick Walker & Brother, Pagefield Ironworks, Wigan

K	Kitson & Co, Airedale Foundry, Leeds
KS	Kerr, Stuart & Co Ltd, California Works, Stoke on Trent
L	R.& A. Lister & Co Ltd, Dursley
Long	London, Chatham & Dover Railway, Longhedge Works, London
LE	Lowca Engineering Co Ltd, Whitehaven
MD	Mather Dixon & Co, Liverpool
MR	Motor Rail Ltd, Simplex Works, Bedford
MW	Manning, Wardle & Co Ltd, Boyne Engine Works, Leeds
NBL	North British Locomotive Co Ltd, Glasgow
NG	Nasmyth, Gaskell & Co, Bridgewater Foundry, Patricroft
NW	Nasmyth, Wilson & Co Ltd, Bridgewater Foundry, Patricroft
P	Peckett & Sons Ltd, Atlas Locomotive Works, Bristol
P&K	Pearson & Knowles Coal & Iron Co Ltd, Dallam Forge, Warrington
RH	Ruston and Hornsby Ltd, Lincoln
RS	Robert Stephenson & Co Ltd, Newcastle upon Tyne, later Darlington
RSH	Robert Stephenson & Hawthorns Ltd, Newcastle and Darlington
S	Sentinel Waggon Works Ltd, Shrewsbury, later Sentinel (Shrewsbury) Ltd
SS	Sharp, Stewart & Co Ltd, Atlas Works, Manchester. Later Atlas Works, Glasgow
StHR	St Helens Railway Company, Sutton Works, later St Helens Junction Works
TH	Thomas Hill (Rotherham) Ltd, Kilnhurst
VF	Vulcan Foundry Ltd, Newton le Willows
VIW	Vulcan Iron Works, Wilkes-Barre, USA
WB	W.G. Bagnall Ltd, Castle Engine Works, Stafford
WCI	Wigan Coal & Iron Co Ltd, Kirkless Workshops, Wigan
WkB	Walker Brothers & Co Ltd, Pagefield Works, Wigan
Wpn	Great Western Railway, Wolverhampton Works
WR	Wingrove & Rogers Ltd, Liverpool
YE	Yorkshire Engine Co Ltd, Meadow Hall Works, Sheffield

Also mentioned are :

Brassey	Thos Brassey & Co, Canada Works, Birkenhead
Daglish	Robert Daglish & Co, St Helens Foundry, St Helens
Cross	James Cross & Co, Sutton Engine Works, St Helens Junction
Jones & Potts	Viaduct Foundry, Newton le Willows
Jones, Turner & Evans	Viaduct Foundry, Newton le Willows
Haydock	Haydock Foundry of Richard Evans & Co
Lewin	Stephen Lewin, Poole
Melling	John Melling & Sons, Rainhill
Mordale	Mordale Ltd, Little Woulden, Glazebrook
Robinson & Cooks	St Helens and Widnes
Tayleur	Charles Tayleur & Co, Vulcan Foundry, Newton le Willows, later Vulcan Foundry Co (qv)

References

References to the background literature are given at the end of each chapter. The following abbreviations have been used:-

BMB	Bolton Metropolitan Borough Local History Library and Archives
CRO	Cheshire Record Office
GMRO	Greater Manchester Records Office
IM&S	Information Management and Storage Ltd
LeiRO	Leicestershire Record Office, Wigston
LRO	Lancashire Records Office, Preston
NMGM	National Museums and Galleries on Merseyside
NRM	National Railway Museum
WRO	Wigan Metropolitan Borough Record Office, Leigh
StHLH	St Helens Local History Library
WLH	Warrington Local History Library

BC	Bolton Chronicle
BLN	Branch Line News
CG	Colliery Guardian
CJ	Contract Journal
HayRep	Haydock Reporter
LC	Leigh Chronicle
LG	London Gazette
LMerc	Liverpool Mercury
MG	Manchester Guardian
MJ	Mining Journal
MM	Machinery Mart
PC	Preston Chronicle
StHNews	St Helens Newspaper
STHRep	St Helens Reporter
WEx	Wigan Examiner
WO	Wigan Observer

Maps

The maps following Chapter Two show the main line railways as they existed immediately before the amalgamations of 1923 and will assist the reader in identifying the locations which are mentioned in the text.

The maps in subsequent chapters present a picture of the various industrial railway systems as they existed at selected dates and are based on large scale maps, works plans, estate plans and similar material. While we have attempted to illustrate the complexity of the sidings at individual sites it would have been impossible to record every piece of track and every crossover and spur.

Those dated 1948 and later contain information from Ordnance Survey maps which is still in copyright. We wish to acknowledge the permission which has been given to us to make use of this material.

For all railways which were less than the standard 4ft 8½in gauge we have adopted the symbol :

$$\vdash\!\!+\!\!+\!\!+\!\!+\!\!+\!\!+\!\!+\!\!+\!\!+\!\dashv$$

On the maps themselves we distinguish between the early tramroads, which used animal power to haul the trucks, and the later tubways on which pit tubs were drawn by chains or ropes, powered by a stationary engine.

References to Chapter 1

1 *The Industrial Railways of the Wigan Coalfield - Part One - South and West of Wigan*, C.H.A. Townley, F.D. Smith and J.A. Peden, Runpast Publishing, Cheltenham, March 1991

2 *The Industrial Railways of the Wigan Coalfield - Part Two - North and East of Wigan*, C.H.A. Townley, F.D. Smith and J.A. Peden, Runpast Publishing, Cheltenham, November 1992

3 *The Industrial Railways of Bolton, Bury and the Manchester Coalfield - Part 1 - Bolton and Bury*, C.H.A. Townley, C.A. Appleton, F.D. Smith and J.A. Peden, Runpast Publishing, Cheltenham, 1994

4 *The Industrial Railways of Bolton, Bury and the Manchester Coalfield - Part 2 - The Manchester Coalfield*, C.H.A. Townley, C.A. Appleton, F.D. Smith and J.A. Peden, Runpast Publishing, Cheltenham, 1995

5 *A Merseyside Town in the Industrial Revolution - St Helens 1750 - 1900*, T.C. Barker and J.R. Harris, Revised Edition, Frank Cass & Co Ltd, London 1959

6 *The Glassmakers*, T.C. Barker, Weidenfeld and Nicholson, London, 1977

7 *A History of the Chemical Industry in Widnes*, D.W.F. Hardie, Imperial Chemical Industries, General Chemicals Division, 1950

8 *A History of Greenings 1799 - 1949*, S.P.B. Mais, Guardian Press, Warrington, nd

9 *Enterprise in Soap and Chemicals - Joseph Crosfield and Sons Ltd 1815-1965* A.E. Musson, Manchester University Press, 1965

10 *The Canals of North West England, Vols 1 and 2*, Charles Hadfield and Gordon Biddle, David and Charles, Newton Abbot, 1970

11 *The St Helens Railway*, J.M. Tolson, The Oakwood Press, 1982

12 *Waterways and Railways to Warrington*, Peter Norton, Railway and Canal Historical Society, 1974

13 *The Liverpool and Manchester Railway*, R.H.G. Thomas, B.T .Batsford Ltd, London, 1980

14 *Liverpool and Manchester Railway 1830-1980*, Frank Ferneyhough, Robert Hale, London, 1980

15 *Liverpool and Manchester Railway Operations 1831-1845*, Thomas A.Donaghy, David and Charles, Newton Abbot, 1972

16 *Crewe to Carlisle*, Brian Read, Ian Allan, 1964

17 *The Railways of the Manchester Ship Canal*, Don Thorpe, Oxford Publishing Company, Poole, 1984

CHAPTER TWO

THE CANALS AND THE MAIN LINE RAILWAYS

The Canals and the River Navigations

Water transport played a key role in the early industrial development of the region. The Mersey had always been navigable for coasting vessels as far as Warrington, although it was not until as late as 1876 [1] that the Upper Mersey Commissioners were appointed to improve the river.

Above Warrington the Mersey and the Irwell were canalised under an Act of 1721 [2]. Eight locks were constructed and the navigation to Manchester was opened in 1734 [3]. Many improvements were made over the years and in 1804 a new canal was opened from Latchford to Runcorn, avoiding a stretch of the Mersey which was impassable on neap tides [3].

An Act to improve the River Weaver was passed in 1721 [4]. Eleven locks were constructed and by 1732 boats were able to reach Winsford [3]. An additional lock and associated lock cut were built towards the end of the century to bypass the tidal part of the river above Frodsham Bridge and in 1807 powers were obtained [5] for the construction of a canal from the navigation above Frodsham Lock to Weston Point. This canal, together with a basin at Weston Point and a lock into the Mersey, were opened in 1810 [3]. As on the Mersey, many improvements were carried out over the years and by 1885 four large locks, capable of taking coasting craft, had replaced the original eleven and an extensive dock system had been developed at Weston Point.

The Sankey Brook Navigation which provided an outlet from collieries in the neighbourhood of St Helens was authorised in March 1755 [6]. Unlike the previous waterways, this was a true canal cut through land adjoining the Sankey Brook. The main line from the River Mersey at Sankey Quays was opened as far as Parr in 1757 [3] and the continuation from there to Gerard's Bridge was completed in 1759. The branch to Blackbrook Lower Basin was opened in about 1762 [3], being extended to Blackbrook Upper Basin some eight or ten years later. A branch to Boardman's Bridge was in use by 1772 [3] which was later extended to the Ravenhead Copper Works and to Burtonhead Colliery.

There were two extensions at the southern end of the canal, in both instances to avoid difficult sections of the River Mersey. The first, from Sankey Bridges to Fidler's Ferry was authorised in 1762 [7] and opened a few years later. In 1830 powers [8] were obtained to continue the line to Runcorn Gap, as Widnes was then known. The new length of canal together with a dock at Runcorn Gap were opened in July 1833 [3].

A branch was proposed in 1844, but later dropped, which was to run from Sankey Bridges through Bank Quay to join with the Mersey and Irwell Navigation at Warrington Bridge [9].

A second canal which would have competed with the Sankey Navigation was under active consideration in the 1770s. One of the proposed routes for this project, intended to link Liverpool and Leeds, ran to the south and east of St Helens, through the townships of Bold, Newton and Golborne before reaching Wigan. As a counter measure the Sankey Navigation put forward a plan to build its own line from Winwick to Ince and Pemberton. This was later abandoned as the Leeds and Liverpool Canal adopted a more northerly route between Wigan and Liverpool. [10]

There remains one further group of early canals, peripheral to the main story, but which needs to be mentioned as they influenced developments at Runcorn, one of the districts covered by our book.

The Duke of Bridgewater obtained parliamentary powers in 1762 [11] to extend his Worsley and Manchester Canal from Longford Bridge to Runcorn. The line was brought into use in stages, through traffic commencing on 21st March 1776 [3]. The Trent and Mersey Canal, which joined the Bridgewater at Preston Brook, was opened throughout in 1777, the two canals providing a through route between the North West of England and the Midlands. Consideration was given to extending the Bridgewater Canal to Liverpool, by crossing the Mersey at Runcorn on an aqueduct [3], but this scheme was soon dropped.

Following the death of the Duke of Bridgewater in 1803 his colliery and canal properties were managed by three trustees, who carried out improvements at Runcorn. A second line of locks was opened here in about 1827 [3] and work also began on the construction of a series of docks adjoining the River Mersey.

Francis, Earl of Ellesmere, who was sole beneficiary of the income from the Bridgewater Trust after the death of his father, the Duke of Sutherland, purchased a controlling interest in the Mersey and Irwell Navigation Company at the end of 1843. His shares were later acquired by the Trustees who assumed control of the Navigation Company as from 17th January 1846.

In 1853 the Earl of Ellesmere was authorised [12] to construct the Runcorn and Weston Canal to link the Francis Dock at Runcorn with the Weaver Navigation. It was purchased in an unfinished state by the Bridgewater Trustees in 1857 [13] and opened some two years later [3].

In June 1872 when the Bridgewater Canal, the Mersey and Irwell Navigation and the carrying business were sold to the chairmen of the Manchester, Sheffield and Lincolnshire and Midland Railways and transferred on 1st September to the Bridgewater Navigation Company, set up jointly by the two railways [3]. Before this there had been negotiations with a number of other railway companies including the North Staffordshire, which had already acquired the Trent and Mersey Canal.

The Liverpool and Manchester Railway and Connecting Lines

Serious competition to the monopoly held by the waterways, particularly in the transport of heavy goods, surfaced in the 1820s when a railway between Liverpool and Manchester was first mooted.

A Bill went before Parliament in 1825 based on a route which took the line to the north of St Helens, through Windle, Gerard's Bridge and Blackbrook [14]. Because of opposition from canal interests and from many of the landowners, the Bill was lost. A revised scheme, on the present more southerly route, through Huyton, Rainhill, St Helens Junction and Newton le Willows was submitted in the following year, and passed on 5th May 1826 [15]. The railway was opened throughout on 15th September 1830 [16].

The 1826 Act authorised two short colliery branches from the main line at the Ridings in Whiston; one was northwards to Whiston Potteries, the other southwards to Lower Houghton Heys. Neither of these was built and instead wayleaves were negotiated with the landowners for the construction of lines from Huyton Quarry which led to mines at Halsnead and Whiston. We leave the rather complicated history of what later became known as the Willis and Seel Branches until Part 2.

The Warrington and Newton Railway Company was authorised in 1829 [17] to build a line from a triangular junction with the Liverpool and Manchester at Newton le Willows, in a district later known as Earlestown, to a terminus in the Dallam district of Warrington. Also included were branches at Warrington to Coxhedge and to Liverpool Road [18]. The route was identical to that of a proposal of the previous year with the exception that the branch to Liverpool Road had then continued to the Mersey at Bank Quay [19].

The railway from Dallam to the south end of Newton was opened in time for the races in June 1831 [20]. Through trains to the Liverpool and Manchester line commenced over the west curve on 25th July 1831 [20], but the east curve was not brought into use until 4th July 1837 [20]. Traffic on the branch to Liverpool Road presumably started in June or July 1831, but the precise date does not seem to have been recorded. The branch to Coxhedge was never built.

Several extensions southwards from Warrington were proposed, but none gained Parliamentary approval. In 1829 plans [21] were put forward for a line which would have terminated alongside the Trent and Mersey Canal at Hassall Green. In the following year a connection was proposed with the projected Liverpool and Birmingham Railway at Preston Brook [22]. In 1831 there was a more modest scheme [23] for a branch to the Mersey and Irwell Navigation at Walton, from where there would have also been a short spur to the Chester Turnpike.

The Wigan Branch Railway Company was incorporated in 1830 [24] to construct a line from the Liverpool and Manchester Railway at Parkside to a terminal station in Wigan. It was opened for traffic on 3rd September 1832 [25]. The continuation northwards to Preston was authorised in 1831 [26], but in 1834, before this line was opened, the Preston and Wigan Railway amalgamated with the Wigan Branch Railway to form the North Union Railway [27].

An event of major significance occurred in 1833, when the Grand Junction Railway was incorporated [28] and authorised to build a line from Birmingham to an end on junction with the Liverpool Road Branch of the Warrington and Newton Railway near Bank Quay. The Grand Junction absorbed the Warrington and Newton Railway in 1835 [29] and the line from Birmingham to Warrington was opened throughout on 4th July 1837 [30]. A new station was built south of Liverpool Road bridge, leaving the original terminus of the Warrington and Newton at Dallam isolated on a branch line.

When the London and Birmingham Railway was opened in 1838 there was a continuous line of railway from London to the North West. Liverpool and Manchester could be reached over the Liverpool and Manchester Railway from Newton, while trains for Preston and beyond took the Liverpool and Manchester Railway from Newton to Parkside and then the North Union Railway. With the opening of the Lancaster and Carlisle Railway in 1846 and the Caledonian Railway from Carlisle to Glasgow in 1848, the Warrington and Newton and the North Union, which had started as purely local affairs, now formed part of the West Coast Main Line from London to Scotland.

The junction between the North Union and Liverpool and Manchester lines at Parkside faced towards Manchester and trains proceeding in the direction of Wigan and the north from Liverpool, Warrington and the south had to reverse there. As early as 1830 the Warrington and Newton had been granted powers [31] to construct a branch which terminated to the north of the Liverpool and Manchester line, beneath the latter company's Newton Viaduct. Plans for the continuation to join the Wigan line at Golborne Dale were prepared by the Wigan Branch Railway in 1831 [32] but were later dropped. As a result, no work was undertaken on the Warrington and Newton Railway's branch, although it appears that some land was purchased on the west side of what was to become the site of the Vulcan Foundry.

The difficulties at Parkside were alleviated by the construction of a west to north curve by the Liverpool and Manchester Railway, authorised in 1845 [33] and opened in 1847 [20]. Meanwhile the Grand Junction had proceeded with its own scheme and was granted powers in 1846 [34] to build a direct line from the Warrington and Newton near the junction with the Dallam Branch to the North Union at Parkside, together with a spur from Winwick to join the Liverpool and Manchester near Kenyon Junction [35,36]. This scheme was subsequently dropped and, as we shall see later, almost another twenty years were to elapse before West Coast Main Line trains were able to avoid the bottle necks at Earlestown and Parkside.

The independent existence of the Liverpool and Manchester Railway ended on 1st July 1845 when it was taken over by the Grand Junction [37]. The North Union Railway was leased jointly by the Grand Junction Railway and the Manchester and Leeds Railway as from 1st January 1846 [38]. Presumably the North Union Railway proposal of 1845 [39] for a line from Parkside to Prestbury on the Manchester and Birmingham Railway and an independent branch to Warrington was used as a bargaining counter in the negotiations.

Above - A Warrington to St Helens push and pull train stands in the branch platform at Earlestown. The station buildings are reputed to have been erected by the Liverpool and Manchester Railway company. *(J. A. Peden Collection)*

Below - Photographed on 17th June 1959 on the Liverpool and Manchester line 46132 approaches Rainhill on a coal train. The sidings serving Lea Green Colliery can be seen to the left of the main line and the colliery itself with its attendant spoil heap are in the background. *(J.B. Horne)*

On 16th July 1846 the Grand Junction amalgamated with the London and Birmingham and the Manchester and Birmingham to form the London and North Western Railway [40]. We return to the London and North Western later in the chapter but, before doing so, we need to consider other developments which were taking place.

The St Helens and Runcorn Gap Railway and the St Helens Canal and Railway

The St Helens and Runcorn Gap Railway was promoted as a purely local line to serve the industries of the district. Its history has been already been fully recorded [41] and only a brief summary of the main events is needed here.

The Company was incorporated in 1830 [42] and was authorised to construct the following railways as well as a dock at Widnes [43] :

Sutton Oak to Widnes Dock
Sutton Oak to the Ravenhead Plate Glass Works, with branches to Dobson's Wood, to Clare and Haddock's Colliery and to the Crown Glass Works
Sutton Oak to Broad Oak Colliery, with branches to Sankey Brook Colliery and Ashton's Green Colliery
Peasley Cross to Cowley Hill Colliery, continuing to Rushy Park Colliery
Bold Heath to Elton Head Colliery
Four spurs to the Liverpool and Manchester Railway

The main line included two rope worked inclined planes, one of which was equipped with a stationary engine. In the neighbourhood of St Helens, there were numerous swivel bridges where the railway crossed the various arms of the Sankey Navigation. Sections 25 and 26 of the Act required these to be kept open for canal traffic, except when they needed to be swung for trains to cross.

The north to east spur from the Liverpool and Manchester Railway and part of the Ravenhead line, probably only as far as Bournes and Robinson's Sutton Colliery, were opened for traffic on 2nd January 1832 [41]. A locomotive and wagons were borrowed from the Liverpool and Manchester as the St Helens Railway's own rolling stock had not yet been delivered. A station was built adjacent to the colliery, on the south side of Peasley Cross Lane, and a passenger service was introduced later that year.

The railway was formally opened on 21st February 1833 [41] when a coal train ran to Widnes from the Broad Oak Colliery of Bournes and Robinson. There had been at least one earlier train over the line on 28th November of the previous year [10,41]. The inclines were not fully operational until 4th March 1833 [41] and the dock at Widnes was not opened until July of the same year [41]. The branches to Sankey Brook and Ashton's Green Collieries were probably also opened in 1833. A short extension of the Ashton's Green Branch proposed in 1837 [44] was dropped from the 1838 Act [45].

Owing to financial difficulties, powers for the three remaining spurs to the Liverpool and Manchester line and for the cross country line from Bold Heath to Elton Head were allowed to lapse. Plans for a south to east spur at St Helens Junction were revived in 1851 [46] but the line was not built. The land was used for a new locomotive works and the rail connection to it.

The Ravenhead Branch was reported on 12th December 1834 to be ready for use [46], but stopped at a connection with Ravenhead Colliery, a mile or so short of the Parliamentary termination. The remaining portion of the line to serve the Ravenhead Plate Glass Works and David Bromilow and Company's Union Colliery was, as we discuss in Chapter 6, probably not completed until around 1851 or 1852. The proposed branch to Dobson's Wood was superseded by a line built by Bournes and Robinson and it seems that the branch into the Crown Glass Works was also built privately.

Construction of the line northwards from Peasley Cross was undertaken by the Union Plate Glass Company in 1836 on behalf of the railway company [46]. It was completed as far as Gerard's Bridge by 1837, although at the end of that year it was still not suitable for use by locomotives [46]. The authorised extension to Rushy Park Colliery was never built.

Parliamentary approval was given to the amalgamation of the St Helens and Runcorn Gap Railway and the Sankey Brook Navigation in 1845 to form the St Helens Canal and Railway Company [47]. The purchase of the canal does not seem to have been completed until 1850 [41].

By the early 1840s the dock at Widnes had become inadequate to deal with the increased output of coal and the capacity of the railway was severely limited by the cable operated inclines. In November 1845, plans [48] were put forward for a new dock at Garston and for a series of new railways :

Widnes to Garston
Widnes via Sankey Bridges to join the Grand Junction at Winwick
Sankey Bridges to Bridge Street, Warrington, to join the proposed Birkenhead, Lancashire and Cheshire Junction Railway
Winwick to Gerard's Bridge, following the course of the canal and intended as an alternative route from St Helens to Widnes avoiding the inclines
A branch from this near the Double Locks to Blackbrook Lower Basin
Gerard's Bridge to Four Lane Ends, Eccleston to join the authorised, but not yet constructed, Huyton and Rainford line of the Grand Junction Railway
A spur from the Eccleston line near Gerard's Bridge to join the authorised, but not yet constructed, St Helens and Rainford line of the Grand Junction Railway

There were also other proposals in 1845 for lines linking the Liverpool area with Warrington. Both the Grand Junction Railway and a newcomer, the Liverpool, Warrington and Stockport Railway, submitted plans for lines which left the Liverpool and Manchester at Huyton Quarry. The former was intended to pass through Ditton Village, Penketh and Great Sankey to join the Warrington and Newton line north of Bank Quay Station [49,50], while the latter was on a more northerly route through Cronton [51].

The outcome was that in 1846 the whole of the Grand Junction scheme was authorised by Parliament [52]. Despite a further Act in 1847 [53], which authorised a connecting spur to the St Helens and Runcorn Gap line, the powers were allowed to lapse.

The St Helens Railway only received approval for the construction of the new dock at Garston and the railway from there to Widnes [54]. The proposed line from Widnes to Warrington Bridge Street via Sankey Bridges was revived in the St Helens Railway Company's Bill of 1847 [55] and a north to east spur from the GJR station at Bank Quay was also included. Instead of the new railway from Gerard's Bridge to Sankey Bridges, it was intended to alter the inclines on the original St Helens to Widnes route to make them suitable for locomotive working and to double the track. These works, with the exception of the spur to the GJR at Warrington, were authorised by the St Helens Canal and Railway Company's 1847 Act [56].

Reconstruction of the Sutton Incline was completed in February 1849 followed by the Widnes Incline later that year [41]. On the railway from Widnes to Garston, the section to Ditton Mill was opened in June 1851, followed by the complete line, including a new station at Waterloo Road in Widnes, on 1st July 1852 [41]. Formal inauguration of Garston Dock took place on 21st June 1853 [41]. The line from Widnes to Warrington was opened as far as a temporary station near Litton Mill Level Crossing on 1st February 1853 and through to Bridge Street, Warrington, on 1st May 1854 [41].

The spur from the St Helens line to the Garston line at Widnes was originally on a very tight curve and was replaced on a new alignment in November 1856 [46]. Also at Widnes, a short branch was constructed, probably in the early 1850s, from the St Helens line to serve Muspratt and Sons' alkali works. Later known as the Gas Works Branch, it appears to have been built without specific Parliamentary powers.

Meanwhile, nearer to St Helens several developments had taken place. A new passenger and goods station was opened on a site near the corner of Raven Street (later Church Street) and Salisbury Street on 19th December 1849 [46]. This involved the construction of a short section of new railway, apparently without express Parliamentary powers, which crossed the canal on a swing bridge and joined the Ravenhead Branch not far from the original passenger station.

The Ashton's Green Branch was extended to Blackbrook under powers contained in the 1847 Act [55] and a single line was opened for traffic towards the end of 1850. The St Helens Railway Company Board gave approval to double the track from Sutton Oak to the junction with the Ashton's Green Branch in January 1858 [46] and on the rest of the line to Blackbrook in June 1861 [46]. This work was completed in 1862 [41].

A connection was provided with the Haydock Collieries railway system, Richard Evans and Company undertaking to despatch 20,000 tons of coal annually through Garston Dock [46]. The line, from the Ashton's Green Branch to Old Whint, was apparently built without Parliamentary powers. The opening date has not been discovered although it is known that construction was in progress in August 1851 [46].

The St Helens Canal and Railway Company's Act of 1853 [57] authorised branches to Rainford, to be dealt with later in the chapter, and to Eccleston. The latter left the Ravenhead Branch near the canal terminus. Beyond the Parliamentary termination 1½ chains west of the Home Farm Lane level crossing, it was continued, as described in Chapter 7, to Gillar's Green by agreement with the landowner. A trial trip over the whole length of the line took place on 2nd March 1859 [58].

The St Helens Canal and Railway was taken over by its larger neighbour, the London and North Western Railway, in 1860 when a 21 year lease was approved by Parliament. Although the Act [59] gave 1st July as the date when the lease was to commence, it appears that the LNWR did not take possession until 1st September [46].

LNWR trains were able to gain access to the St Helens Railway at Arpley and at St Helens Junction. In 1863 a third connection was proposed at Bank Quay, consisting of a west to north curve passing through the site of the glass works.[60] The scheme, however, was subsequently dropped.

The St Helens undertaking was purchased outright by the London and North Western as from 1st August 1864 under the St Helens Canal and Railway Transfer Act [61]. This Act also granted running powers to the Lancashire and Yorkshire Railway over all the former St Helens Company's lines north of Sutton Oak. Very importantly for the St Helens industrialists, it also fixed maximum tolls on traffic on both the canal and railway between St Helens, Widnes and Garston.

St Helens to Rainford and Huyton to St Helens

Leaving aside the first and unsuccessful Liverpool and Manchester project, it was not until the 1840s that firm proposals emerged to serve the districts north and west of St Helens. In 1844 the Liverpool and Manchester Railway submitted plans [62] for a line from Peasley Cross on the St Helens Railway to Rufford on the proposed Southport and Euxton Railway, passing through Gerard's Bridge, Rainford, Bickerstaffe and Blaguegate. Construction of the section between Peasley Cross and Rainford received Parliamentary approval in 1845, but the remaining portion was deleted from the Act [33]. Powers to lease the line were granted to the St Helens Railway in 1847 [55].

The Grand Junction Railway, which had absorbed the Liverpool and Manchester in the previous year, was granted powers in 1846 [34] for a direct link from the Liverpool and Manchester line at Huyton Quarry through Prescot and Gillar's Green to join the St Helens and Rainford line at Gerard's Bridge [63]. A competing scheme put forward in the same Parliamentary Session by the Liverpool and Bolton Direct Railway was subsequently dropped. This company's proposed line started at Garston and passed through Hunts Cross to Huyton where there was to be a triangular junction with the Liverpool and Manchester line. From here, the route lay through Thatto Heath, St Helens, Blackbrook and Ashton in Makerfield [64].

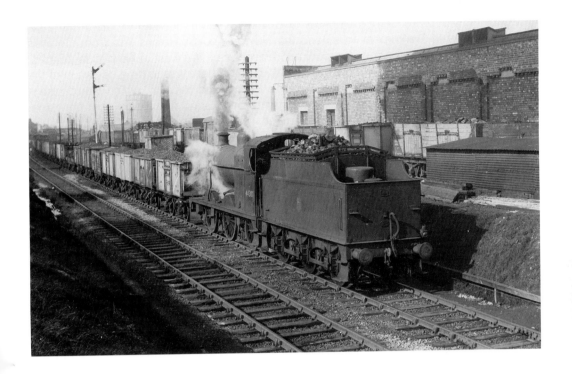

Three latter day views on the former St Helens Railway

Opposite Upper. Ravenhead Junction, looking south, on 20th August 1971. The tracks in the right foreground mark the start of the Ravenhead Branch; those on the left lead to Shaw Street Station, renamed Central Station by this date. Curving away to the right past the waste tips of the former Kurtz Alkali Works is the line to St Helens Junction and Widnes. The junction with the Pocket Nook Branch, by now out of use, was beyond the bridge over Warrington New Road. The gas works is to the left of the signal box, while on the opposite side of the railway, beyond the wooden fence, are sidings at the new Peasley Works of United Glass Ltd. (J.A. Sommerfield)

Opposite Lower. 46423 heads a local trip working over the complex junctions at Widnes on 10th November 1951. The train is drawing forward from the St Helens Railway line from Warrington across the branch to the Dock and on to the sidings by the canal. Muspratt's No. 1 Works is beyond the wooden footbridge. (C.H.A. Townley)

Above. A coal train hauled by ex LMSR locomotive 44300 passes the locomotive depot at Sutton Oak. The engine shed and workshops of the St Helens and Runcorn Gap Railway were about a quarter of a mile away at Sutton Oak Junction. They were later replaced by a new locomotive works at St Helens Junction and new engine sheds south of the Liverpool and Manchester line. The building in the photograph dates from the LNWR era, though much modified by British Railways. (B. Woodward)

Following the formation of the London and North Western Railway in July 1846, plans were submitted to Parliament to extend the Huyton and St Helens line from Gerard's Bridge to Collins Green on the Liverpool and Manchester line west of Newton le Willows, provision also being made for a branch to Blackbrook. There was to be a deviation of the St Helens and Rainford line between Gerard's Bridge and Hill Top, which would take it through Denton's Green where the junction with the Huyton line would now be made. Beyond Rainford, the line was to be extended to a junction with the East Lancashire Railway at Ormskirk. Finally a short branch was proposed from the Huyton and St Helens railway to Prescot Brook Colliery [65]. Of these proposals only the Prescot Brook Branch received approval [53].

The London and North Western Railway failed to build any of the lines which were authorised. The powers were allowed to lapse and it was left to the St Helens Railway to complete the link to Rainford. A scheme was put forward in 1851 for a St Helens to Southport railway. The intention was to build a line from St Helens to Skelmersdale, where a junction was to be made with the East Lancashire's Blaguegate branch; a second line would run from the East Lancashire at Ormskirk to Southport via Halsall [66].

The St Helens and Southport line was dropped, but two years later, in 1853, the St Helens Company was granted powers [57] for a branch to a point north of Rainford. Here there was a connection with the Lancashire and Yorkshire's Liverpool and Bury line and there was also an end-on junction with the East Lancashire Railway's extension of the Blaguegate branch which was authorised in the same year [67]. Under the Act, the East Lancashire Railway was granted running powers to St Helens.

The first coal train ran between Rainford Junction and St Helens on 5th December 1857 [68]. Passenger traffic commenced on 1st February 1858 [25], while the goods only connection to the East Lancashire line opened on 1st March [41].

Proposals for a direct line from Huyton Quarry to St Helens were not brought up again until after the London and North Western Railway had taken over the St Helens Railway. Powers were obtained in 1865 [69] and, after an extension of time granted in 1870 [70], goods traffic started on 18th December 1871 [41]. The rebuilt station at St Helens came into use on 17th July 1871 [41] and passenger services on the new line began on 1st January 1872 [41].

St Helens to Wigan - The Lancashire Union Railways and the South Lancashire Railway and Dock

St Helens and Wigan were not connected directly by rail until the 1860s, although there had been at least two earlier schemes which would have served the district around Ashton in Makerfield. A railway from Liverpool to Leeds and the Humber planned In 1830 would have passed through Rainford, Billinge, Downall Green and Ashton [71]. The Liverpool and Bolton Direct Railway of 1845, mentioned previously, would have run through Blackbrook and Ashton in Makerfield [64].

48895 working hard with a mixed goods up the gradient from St Helens towards Huyton on 19th April 1958. The corner of the United Glass Bottle Company's Ravenhead Works can be seen to the left, while the Greengate Brick Works stands above the cutting on the right The train is passing under the bridge featured in the Winkle File. (See Chapter 6).

(J.A. Peden)

It was not until 1864 that the Lancashire Union Railways Company was incorporated, promoted by the principal colliery owners in the Wigan area who were seeking direct access to Garston and other ports on the Mersey to ship their coal. The Act of 1864 [72] authorised a line starting from a junction with the former St Helens Railway's Broad Oak Branch at Parr through Haydock to Haigh and Adlington, with various spurs to existing railways in the neighbourhood of Wigan [73]. The intention was to make use of the London and North Western south of Parr to gain access to shipping facilities at Widnes, Garston and Runcorn.

Before work could start, a rival proposal was put forward by the South Lancashire Railway and Dock Company, which planned to construct a new dock on the Mersey Estuary at Otterspool and a railway from there to Wigan. The Deposited Plans of November 1864 [74] show that the railway was intended to pass through Childwall, Huyton, Prescot and Thatto Heath to St Helens, with spurs to the Cheshire Lines at Otterspool and to the LNWR at Huyton. North east of St Helens, the line was to pass through Blackbrook, Haydock and Ashton in Makerfield to reach the southern outskirts of Wigan on a route which closely paralleled that of the Lancashire Union, authorised in the previous year. From Old Whint there was to be a branch to join the St Helens and Rainford line at Moss Bank.

Numerous short branches were planned in the neighbourhood of St Helens, to Nutgrove Colliery, to Peasley Cross Colliery and to the former St Helens Company's Peasley Cross to Gerard's Bridge line. On the Moss Bank Branch connections were proposed at Blackbrook with the existing railways of the Haydock, Pewfall, Blackleyhurst and Laffak Collieries. There were to be branches off the main line serving the Haydock, Pewfall and Seneley Green Collieries.

Although the South Lancashire Railway and Dock scheme did not receive Parliamentary approval, the Lancashire Union decided on an alternative, more northerly route between Hindley and St Helens, passing through Tithe Barn Hillock and Carr Mill to join the former St Helens Railway's Rainford Branch at Gerard's Bridge. This was authorised in 1865 [75] and running powers granted to the Lancashire and Yorkshire Railway over the Lancashire Union to Gerard's Bridge, over the LNWR to Sutton Oak Junction and over other LNWR branches at St Helens.

The route authorised in 1864 was formally abandoned by the Lancashire Union Act of 1866 [76] and at the same time powers were granted for two new railways [77]. The first was a link line which left the 1865 route at Garswood and joined the London and North Western's Blackbrook Branch at Broad Oak Junction. For the last three furlongs, as in the 1864 scheme, it was intended to follow the course of the Broad Oak Branch which had probably been out of use since the colliery closed some seven years previously. The second was a short branch from this link line which terminated at the Sankey Canal near Havannah Colliery [77].

The main line of the Lancashire Union Railways was opened for goods traffic on 1st November 1869 [25]. Passenger trains should have started on 15th November, but this was deferred until 1st December to comply with the requirements of the Government inspector [78]. The link from Garswood to the Blackbrook Branch was abandoned in 1868 [79] before construction had started.

By 1869 work was under way on the now isolated Havannah Branch [80] and the three furlong length of the Broad Oak Branch east of the junction with the Blackbrook Branch was sold by the LNWR to the LUR in the same year [81,82]. As a result of negotiations with Richard Evans and Sons in 1870 and 1871, the line was stopped short at the entrance to the colliery [83,84,85]. The final 11½ chains from there to the parliamentary termination were formally abandoned by the Lancashire Union Act of 1871 [86]. An opening date August 1870 is recorded for the Havannah Branch in the Sidings Schedules.

The Lancashire Union Railways Company was taken over, as from 1st July 1883 [87], by the London and North Western Railway, which had supplied much of the capital and operated the line.

Liverpool to Runcorn and the South

Until 1869, there was no direct rail link from Liverpool to the Midlands and the South, all trains having to run over the Liverpool and Manchester line to Earlestown and then through Warrington. There had, however, been many previous projects.

As early as 1829 a proposal was put forward for a railway from the still unfinished Liverpool and Manchester line at Wavertree to a terminus alongside the Bridgewater Canal at Runcorn [88]. The Mersey was to be crossed, between West Bank at Widnes and Old Quay at Runcorn, on a skew bridge. Also included was a loop line from a point near West Bank to join the Liverpool and Manchester Railway at Huyton.

More ambitious but equally unsuccessful schemes followed. The Liverpool and Birmingham Railway project of 1830 [89] was for a line from a terminus in Ranelagh Street in Liverpool, to a junction with the proposed Manchester and Birmingham Railway at Chorlton, south of Crewe, passing through Ditton, Widnes and Preston Brook and crossing the Mersey at Cuerdley Moss. In 1837 [90,91], a line was proposed from the Liverpool and Manchester Railway at Huyton to the Grand Junction Railway at a point between Preston Brook and Moore, passing through Whiston Lane Ends and Barrows Green and crossing the Mersey at Fidler's Ferry.

In 1844 and 1845 plans [92,93] were drawn up for a short branch to Runcorn from the Grand Junction Railway near Preston Brook, which included connections to Runcorn Docks and to a basin on the Bridgewater Canal near Preston Brook. This scheme was superseded by one put forward by the Grand Junction Railway [94], which was authorised by Parliament in 1846 [34]. This line was to run from Aston on the Grand Junction's main line to Huyton on the Liverpool and Manchester Railway, crossing the Mersey at Runcorn. Also authorised was a branch from Runcorn to the Bridgewater Canal Dock, which the Earl of Ellesmere was empowered, under Section XLI of the Act, to take over if he elected to do so. No construction was undertaken and the powers lapsed.

The London and North Western Railway unsuccessfully submitted a Bill in the 1860 Parliamentary Session [46] for a line from Moore to Huyton which followed a similar route to that put forward in 1837, crossing the Mersey at Fidler's Ferry. The proposals also included a branch from Penketh to the West Coast Main Line north of Warrington, a connecting line at Warrington from Bank Quay to Bridge Street and a spur to the St Helens Railway at Fidler's Ferry [95].

The LNWR then submitted a revised scheme for a railway from Aston on the West Coast Main Line to Ditton on the St Helens Railway. There was to be a branch to the Bridgewater Dock at Runcorn and access to Liverpool was to be gained over the LNWR's Garston to Edge Hill railway. Parliamentary approval for the Aston and Ditton railway and for the dock branch was obtained in 1861 [96]. A connecting line from Runcorn to the Birkenhead Railway at Halton was authorised in 1869 [97].

The Aston and Ditton railway should have been completed before July 1866 and an extension of time was granted by Parliament in 1868 [98]. On 21st May 1868, to celebrate the completion of the high level bridge at Runcorn, 500 people were conveyed across it in wagons hauled by the contractor's locomotive ETHELFREDA. The line from Ditton Junction to Runcorn was opened for local traffic in June 1868 [41]. The portion from there to the West Coast Main Line at Birdswood Junction, later reconstructed as Weaver Junction, was opened for goods traffic on 1st February 1869 [25]. Passenger trains started to run on 1st April of the same year [25].

The Garston and Edge Hill line had already been opened on 15th February 1864 [46]. The Docks Branch at Runcorn is thought to have come into use at the same time as the railway from Ditton to Runcorn, although there appears to be no record of the precise date. The link from Norton Junction to Frodsham Junction on the Birkenhead Railway was opened on 1st May 1873 [25].

South and East of Warrington

The lines from Chester and Stockport, which served several of the industrual establishments at Warrington described in Part Three, figured prominently in the railway politics of the time as other companies sought to obtain running powers over them. In this way the Great Western Railway was able to work its own trains to Manchester and later the Great Northern and Manchester, Sheffield and Lincolnshire Companies were able to reach Liverpool.

The history is quite complicated and only an outline can be given here. The reader is referred to the books by Tolson [41], Norton [30] and Griffiths [99] for further information. A comprehensive, if somewhat biased, account of the Great Western Railway's negotiations with the LNWR to gain entry to Manchester can be found in the GWR history by Macdermott [100].

The story starts with a project which was put forward in 1844 [101] by the Birkenhead, Manchester and Chester Junction Railway. This was to run from the Birkenhead Railway at Hooton through Frodsham to the Grand Junction at Moore. Beyond Moore, the main line skirted round the south of Warrington through Lower Walton, Stockton Heath and Thelwall and then across country to Broadheath. Branches were proposed from Helsby to Chester and from Broadheath to Heaton Norris, Cheadle Hulme and Bowden. There was to be a separate terminus in Warrington, on the south side of the Mersey opposite Howley Quay, served by a short branch from a triangular junction near Stockton Heath.

The Birkenhead, Lancashire and Cheshire Junction Railway submitted a revised scheme in 1845 [102]. A different route was adopted at Warrington, passing through Arpley, keeping north of the river and the Woolston Cut and crossing the Mersey near Warburton. The company's Act of 1846 [103] authorised the construction of the lines from Hooton to Heaton Norris and from Helsby to Chester, together with spurs to the Manchester South Junction and Altrincham at Broadheath and the Grand Junction at Walton. The proposed branches from Warrington through Grappenhall and Knutsford to Macclesfield and from Frodsham to Northwich and Winsford were dropped from the Act, as well as a north to east curve at Warrington, from Arpley to the Grand Junction near Liverpool Road.

There were second thoughts about the course of the line through Warrington later in 1846 [104]. A new route was proposed which ran parallel to the Grand Junction from Walton as far as Bewsey Road bridge, where it turned east to join the authorised line at Paddington. The scheme was not, however, pursued.

The Birkenhead, Lancashire and Cheshire Junction Railway, which amalgamated with the Birkenhead and Chester Railway in 1847 [105], was only able to construct the portion of line from Chester to the Grand Junction at Walton. This was opened for traffic on 18th December 1850 [30] and the rest of the lines authorised in 1846 were formally abandoned in 1852 [106].

The Shrewsbury and Chester Railway entered the scene in 1851 when it was granted running powers [107], reconfirmed in 1854 [108], over the whole of the Birkenhead, Lancashire and Cheshire Junction Railway. In return the latter company was given running powers over the Shrewsbury and Chester.

The Shrewsbury and Chester had to resort to canal carriage from Warrington for its Manchester traffic owing to obstruction by the LNWR. To facilitate transhipment, the Shrewsbury and Chester was authorised in 1852 [109] to build branches from Norton to the Bridgewater Canal at Preston Brook and from Lower Walton to the Runcorn and Latchford Canal [110], over which the Birkenhead, Lancashire and Cheshire Junction Railway was to have running powers. The Preston Brook Branch is said to have opened in October 1853 [30]. Although land was bought for the branch to the Runcorn and Latchford Canal, no construction took place. The short branch to Preston Brook only had a brief life and the rails lifted by 1880 [30].

The scheme for a line eastwards from Warrington was brought to life again in 1851, when a new company, the Warrington and Altrincham Junction, was incorporated with powers to build a line from the St Helens Railway at Bridge Street, Warrington, to the Manchester South Junction and Altrincham railway at Timperley, together with a branch from Latchford to join the Birkenhead, Lancashire and Cheshire Junction railway at Lower Walton [111]. Between Latchford and Walton the route, closely followed that of the Birkenhead, Manchester and Chester Junction proposal of 1844, passing through Stockton Heath [112].

In 1853 the company was given powers to extend its line from Timperley to Stockport and to change its name to the Warrington and Stockport Railway [113]. A second Act [114] of the same year abandoned the Latchford to Lower Walton branch and substituted one from Arpley to the BL&CJR, together with a short spur to the Shrewsbury and Chester's authorised Walton Branch. Section 21 of the second Act also permitted the company to provide sidings and wharves on the south side of the River Mersey and on the Bridgewater Canal.

A single line was brought into operation between Broadheath and a temporary station at Wilderspool on 1st January 1853 and the railway was opened throughout from Timperley to the junction with the St Helens Railway at Arpley on 1st May 1854 [30]. No work was carried out on the extension to Stockport [115].

Arpley Station at Bridge Street in Warrington, photographed on 18th May 1952. The station, which opened on 1st May 1854, was operated jointly by the St Helens and Warrington and Stockport Railways These imposing buildings were used by the latter company as its headquarters. The station has now been demolished.   (C.H.A. Townley)

The branch to the Chester line was passed by the Board of Trade Inspector in November 1855 [30], but the opening seems to have been delayed due to difficulties raised by the LNWR, which had acquired a financial interest in the BL&CJR. The connection to the Shrewsbury and Chester at Walton was dropped and it seems unlikely that wharves were built either on the Mersey or the Bridgewater Canal.

The second Act of 1853 [114] granted a series of running powers to the Warrington and Stockport Railway and neighbouring companies:

> To the Warrington and Stockport Railway over the Birkenhead, Lancashire and Cheshire Junction and the Manchester South Junction and Altrincham Railways
> To the Birkenhead Lancashire and Cheshire Junction Railway over the Warrington and Stockport Railway
> To the Manchester South Junction and Altrincham over the Warrington and Stockport Railway

The scene was now set for the Great Western Railway to gain access to Manchester and, if not Liverpool, then the port of Birkenhead. The GWR and its associated companies had originaly adopted the 7 ft gauge for the network linking London, the West of England and South Wales, but the line from Oxford to Birmingham was laid as mixed gauge to accomodate both broad and standard gauge trains. The standard gauge Shrewsbury and Birmingham and Shrewsbury and Chester Railways were absorbed by the GWR in 1854 [116] in anticipation of the extension from Birmingham to Wolverhampton.

20 120 and 20 047 at the head of a coal train for Fiddler's Ferry Power Station on 27th May 1987. The train has reversed in the run round loop at Latchford and is passing Arpley Junction, where the Warrington and Stockport branch to Walton Junction diverged. *(J.A. Peden)*

With the acquisition of the Shrewsbury and Chester Railway the Great Western took over that company's running powers to Warrington [116]. In 1859 [117] the GWR and the LNWR were permitted to enter into joint working arrangements with the BL&CJR which at the same time adopted the shorter title of the Birkenhead Railway. At the same time the running powers of the Shrewsbury and Chester over the Birkenhead Railway were transferred to the GWR.

As from 1st January 1860 the Birkenhead Railway was vested jointly, but for separate and independent use, in the LNWR and GWR. The Act of 1861 [118] which confirmed the arrangements also transferred the running powers of the Birkenhead Railway over the Warrington and Stockport to the Great Western.

It is not clear how far the Birkenhead Railway, or the Great Western Railway as its successor, actually made use of the running powers over the Warrington and Stockport line. There was an agreement between the LNWR and the BL&CJR on 21st April 1850, followed by a supplemental agreement of 1st June 1851, under which the BL&CJR was permitted to handle all kinds of traffic over the LNWR between Lower Walton and Manchester provided it did not exercise its running powers over the MSJ&AR [119]. Certainly BL&CJR trains were routed through Earlestown and over the Liverpool and Manchester line by December 1857 [120].

The question of the route taken by GWR trains to Manchester came up again in 1858 when, under an agreement of 5th November with the LNWR [121], the Great Western was given until the end of 1865 to make a final choice. It opted to continue running its passenger and freight trains with its own locomotives via Earlestown, a practice which lasted until June 1943 [122].

The Warrington and Stockport Railway and the St Helens Railway's Warrington to Garston line also featured in a number of schemes by other companies to reach Liverpool.

There were several unsuccessful attempts by the North Staffordshire Railway to link the Potteries with South Lancashire. In 1845 a line was promoted from Kidsgrove to connect with the Grand Junction's authorised railway from Aston to Huyton and with the Birkenhead, Lancashire and Cheshire Junction's Walton Branch [46].

In 1851 plans were prepared for a line from Sandbach through Northwich to join the BL&CJR at Moore.[123] The latter scheme was revived in 1852 to continue beyond the junction at Moore to connect with the Warrington and Stockport Railway at Walton [124].Running powers were to be sought over the St Helens Railway and the Warrington and Stockport as well as authorisation to lease one or both companies [46].

By the late 1850s the Manchester, Sheffield and Lincolnshire Railway and Great Northern Railway were also looking for a share of the Liverpool traffic. A joint lease of the Warrington and Stockport, with running powers over the St Helens Railway, was proposed in 1858 but the Bill was thrown out by Parliament [46].

Instead the Warrington and Stockport was leased jointly to the LNWR and St Helens Railway Companies in 1859 for a term of 999 years [126] and running powers were granted to the St Helens Railway over the Birkenhead Railway. The Warrington and Stockport was absorbed by the LNWR in the following year and the purchase was confirmed by the LNW and St Helens Railways Arrangements Act of 1860 [59], under which the St Helens Railway was leased to the LNWR.

The London and North Western had made traffic arrangements with the Great Northern on 26th November 1858 and with the Manchester, Sheffield and Lincolnshire on 1st January 1859 [46], whereby trains of both companies were worked to and from Liverpool by LNWR locomotives. The Arrangements Act of 1860 [59] formally confirmed these agreements, which applied to trains routed over the Liverpool and Manchester line or via Altrincham, Timperley and Garston.

Powers for the MS&L and GN to work their traffic with their own locomotives were granted in 1861 [127]. These applied to the route from Timperley to Garston and also included the LNWR's recently authorised line from Garston to Edge Hill [128]. The MS&L and GN were given approval to purchase land at Wavertree in 1862, presumably for a goods depot [129]. As a quid pro quo, the LNWR acquired extensive running powers under the 1861 Act over the MS&L from Ardwick to Sheffield and over the GN from Peterborough northwards to York, Leeds, Wakefield, Doncaster, Sheffield, Hull, Grimsby, New Holland and Gainsborough.

Access to the centre of Liverpool from Garston was seen as important but, as this falls outside the area covered by the book, only a brief review will be provided. It is sufficient to note that on numerous occasions between 1847 and 1860 there were unsuccessful proposals for lines connecting the St Helens Railway at Garston with the centre of Liverpool [46]. Then in 1861, by the Act [127] which granted running powers over the LNWR, the MS&LR and the GNR were jointly authorised to construct a line from Garston to a terminus in Parliament Street. The proposed section north of Brunswick Dock was abandoned in 1862 [129] and revived in 1864 by the nominally independent Central Station Railway Company [130].

The line from Garston to Brunswick opened for traffic on 1st June 1864 [25] and that northwards to Central Station on 1st March 1874 [25]. Construction of the Cheshire Lines Railway enabled the MS&L and GNR to reach Brunswick Goods Yard and the Central Station without passing over other companies' tracks but, before we describe how this came about, we will complete the story of developments on the LNWR.

Improvements on the LNWR at St Helens

The period from 1860 to 1880 saw a substantial increase in the amount of goods and mineral traffic in the St Helens district and work was undertaken by the LNWR to provide additional facilities. A short west to north connecting line at Sutton Oak, permitting direct access from St Helens to the Blackbrook Branch, was sanctioned in 1865 [69]. It never had a regular passenger train service and its opening for goods traffic does not appear to have been recorded.

The Blackbrook Branch was extended to join the Lancashire Union line at Carr Mill Junction, enabling goods trains between Wigan, Widnes and Garston to avoid the congested St Helens Station area. Authorised in 1878 [131], it was opened on 23rd February 1880 [41]. An extra pair of tracks were added between Carr Mill Junction and Ince Moss Junction at Wigan which were brought into use on 16th October 1892 [132].

A new dive under line was built between Sutton Oak Junction and St Helens Junction so that passenger trains to and from St Helens could avoid conflicting movements with freight trains on the Widnes line. At the same time, the original Widnes line was widened and the levels altered from a point 250 yards south of the bridge over the L&M line to a point 200 yards north of Sutton Oak Junction. The work was authorised by LNWR (New Railways) Act of 1881 [133], but it has not proved possible to discover when the improvements were completed.

Finally a west curve was provided at Sutton Oak, north of the original St Helens Railway route, to give alternative access to the Widnes line for goods trains travelling from St Helens. As originally authorised in 1891 [134] , it was to run from the Pocket Nook Branch, at a point near Peasley Junction, to the Blackbrook Branch at Sutton Oak Junction [135]. Before construction had commenced, the scheme was altered in 1894 [136] and reduced to a short spur between the west to north curve of 1865 and the Blackbrook line [137]

Improvements on the LNWR at Widnes

As at St Helens, there was a need at Widnes to provide additional lines to alleviate congestion caused by increasing traffic. In 1865 the LNWR obtained powers [69] for a new railway which passed through the centre of Widnes on a high level so that through trains could avoid the level crossings over the docks branch and Waterloo Road. This new line from West Deviation Junction to Carterhouse Junction, together with a spur from the St Helens line were opened for goods traffic in 1869 [41]. Passenger trains started to use the route on 1st March 1870 [25], when a new station was opened to replace the earlier one at Waterloo Road.

Two additional tracks were provided from Speke to West Deviation Junction under the LNWR (New Railways etc) Act of 1878 [131]. The widened lines between Speke and Ditton were opened for traffic in 1884 [138] and between Ditton and West Deviation Junction on 2nd February 1885 [138]. East of Ditton Junction, both tracks were located on the south side of the Weaver Junction line and passed under this near West Deviation Junction to join the original St Helens Railway alignment.

Improvements on the LNWR at Newton le Willows and Warrington

The scheme for a direct line avoiding the sharp curves at Earlestown and Parkside was finally put in hand when the LNWR (New Lines Near Liverpool) Act of 1861 [96] authorised the construction of a railway from Winwick Junction to Golborne Junction, passing under the Liverpool and Manchester line. This direct line was opened for traffic on 1st August 1864 [25].

A second line from Warrington towards Manchester was proposed in 1879 [140]. This would have left the West Coast Main Line at Winwick Junction and then risen steeply, keeping to the north of the Liverpool and Manchester line as far as Kenyon Junction. The proposal was withdrawn before the LNWR Act of 1880 was passed by Parliament.

At Warrington, a new station at Bank Quay was opened on 16th November 1868, replacing the earlier Grand Junction station near Liverpool Road. Low level platforms were constructed to serve the former St Helens Railway line [46]. A pair of additional tracks were provided from Warrington to Winwick Junction under the LNWR (New Lines and Additional Powers) Act 1876 [141] and were opened in April 1881 [138].

Widening of the North Union line from Golborne Junction to Springs Branch Junction at Wigan was authorised in 1883 [87] and the new tracks were brought into use on 29th October 1888 [78]. At this date the North Union Railway was still leased jointly by the London and North Western and the Lancashire and Yorkshire Railways, but the portion from Parkside through Wigan to Euxton Junction, near Leyland, became the property of the LNWR in July 1889 [142].

South of Warrington there were major changes to the railway layout in the 1890s as result of the construction of the Manchester Ship Canal. These will be described later.

The Cheshire Lines Committee

With a foothold in Liverpool assured by the branch from Garston to Brunswick Dock, the Manchester, Sheffield and Lincolnshire Railway turned its attention to a line of its own to Liverpool, which would break the monopoly held by the LNWR in South Lancashire. In 1865, the Company was authorised, under its Extension to Liverpool Act [143], to construct two new lines. The first was from the Manchester, South Junction and Altrincham at Old Trafford to the Garston and Liverpool at Cressington. The second ran from Timperley on the Stockport, Timperley and Altrincham Junction to join the Liverpool line at Glazebrook. Running Powers were granted over the MSJ&AR, over the Liverpool Central Station Railway and over the LNWR between Ardwick and the MSJ&AR at London Road and between the MSJ&AR and Ordsall Lane.

In 1866 [144] the powers of the Extension to Liverpool Act were transferred to the Manchester, Sheffield and Lincolnshire, Great Northern and Midland Railways acting jointly under their Cheshire Lines Committee. A further MS&L Act [145] in the same year authorised the construction of a loop line through the centre of the town at Warrington and a spur to the LNWR at Allerton.

The Cheshire Lines Committee had been created in 1863 [146] so that the Great Northern could become joint owner with the MS&L of the Cheshire Midland, West Cheshire, the Stockport and Woodley and the Stockport, Timperley and Altrincham Junction Railways. They were joined by the Midland Railway in 1865 [147]. The Committee became a body corporate in 1867 [148] and in 1872 was granted powers [149] for the construction of a line from Cornbrook to a new Central Station in Manchester.

The railway from the Stockport, Timperley and Altrincham Railway at Skelton West Junction to Cressington Junction on the Garston and Brunswick line, via the loop at Warrington, was opened for goods traffic on 1st March 1873 [25] with passenger trains starting on 1st August of the same year [25]. It was followed by the line from the MSJ&AR at Cornbrook Junction to Glazebrook East Junction on 2nd September 1873 [25] and the extensions from Brunswick to Liverpool Central and from Cornbrook Junction to Manchester Central on 1st March 1874 [25] and 9th July 1877 [25] respectively. A spur to the MSJ&AR from Skelton East Junction, authorised in 1878 [150], was opened on 1st January 1879 [25].

The portion of the original route, authorised in 1866, which by-passed the town centre at Warrington, was not brought into use until 13th August 1883 for goods traffic and 7th September of the same year for passenger traffic [25]. What became known as the Warrington Straight Line ran from Padgate Junction to Sankey Junction and there had been two extensions of time for the construction, in 1878 [150] and in 1881 [151].

Various proposals were made for short industrial branches in Warrington. Plans were submitted to Parliament [152] in November 1871 for lines serving the Dallam and Whitecross Ironworks. Although neither line features in the Cheshire Lines Committee's Act of 1872 [149] both were subsequently built, apparently without express Parliamentary powers.

In November 1874, plans [153] were deposited for a branch to Rylands Brothers' wire works at School Brow. More extensive proposals were made in 1877 [154] for a branch which passed School Brow, went on to serve Howley Quay and then turned northwards to the gas works in Mersey Street. A second branch was included in the 1877 scheme which ran from the north side of the main line to a point near the Barracks, presumably to serve another wire works. Neither the 1874 nor the 1877 proposals received Parliamentary approval. No attempt seems to have been made to construct the lines shown on the plans, although both of Rylands Brothers' works were later served by short sidings, possibly built under Sections 56 and 59 of the MS&L Act of 1886 [155].

The Cheshire Lines, like the St Helens Railway previously, featured in a project to provide a direct link between the Potteries and Liverpool. Unsuccessful proposals had been made in 1863 [156] and again in 1864 [157] for a Knutsford and Warrington Railway. On the former occasion a junction was to be made with the Warrington and Stockport line at Latchford, while on the latter there was also a connection with the Warrington Straight Line near Dallam Lane. Both proposals included a branch to the Bridgewater Canal at Grappenhall.

In 1865 a revised scheme was put forward which included an extension from Knutsford to Macclesfield and a second connection with the Cheshire Lines Committee at Warrington, near the future Central Station [158]. The nominally independent Macclesfield, Knutsford and Warrington Railway was incorporated in 1866 [159] and running powers were granted to the Manchester, Sheffield and Lincolnshire Railway and the North Staffordshire Railway. The project fizzled out a few years later. An Act in 1871 [160] abandoned the portion between Warrington and Knutsford and granted an extension of time for the remainder. The company was vested in the Manchester and Lincolnshire in 1874 [161] after which nothing more is heard of the line

Another proposal of the early 1870s was for a line to St Helens which, however, failed to gain Parliamentary approval. The Deposited Plans [162], prepared in November 1872, show that this would have left the Liverpool Extension at a triangular junction near Sankey and would have run almost due north to St Helens. Here there was to have been a terminal station in Traverse St and a connection with the LNWR Pocket Nook Branch.

The Sheffield and Midland Joint Committee's Lines at Widnes and Runcorn

The Liverpool Extension of the Cheshire Lines Committee ran some two miles north of Widnes. A branch to serve the town was put forward in 1871 by the Widnes Railway Company, a nominally independent concern but promoted by Sir Edward Watkin and Mr William Fenton, respectively chairman and vice chairman of the Manchester, Sheffield and Lincolnshire Railway. An application was made in their names to the Board of Trade for a Certificate under legislation [163,164] which avoided the need for a separate Act.

The proposals were for a branch which left the CLC main line at Barrows Green and ran to a point immediately to the east of the LNWR Gas Works Branch and included a spur to the LNWR St Helens line near Appleton Station [165]. The Board of Trade introduced a Bill in Parliament on 10th June 1872 to confirm the Provisional Certificate it had issued, but was overruled because of objections from the LNWR and the Widnes Local Board [166]. Another application was made by the promoters in the following year in which the Appleton spur was to terminate short of the LNWR connection [167]. Objections by the Lancashire and Cheshire Land and Dock Company and by the LNWR were rejected. The Bill put forward by the Board of Trade on 24th February 1873 to confirm the new Provisional Certificate was this time passed by Parliament [168,169].

In 1874 the Widnes Railway was vested in the Manchester, Sheffield and Lincolnshire Railway, the only shareholder [161]. The Great Northern and Midland companies were then invited to become joint owners but only the Midland accepted the offer. In 1875 [170] the railway was transferred to the Sheffield and Midland Joint Committee, which had been set up in 1869 [171] to manage jointly owned lines on the Cheshire and Derbyshire border. It had become a corporate body in its own right under an MS&L Act of 1872 [172].

The 1875 Act [170] also authorised the construction of the Widnes Extension Railway, from the terminus of the Widnes Railway to Moor Lane, and a south to east curve at Barrows Green to replace the original connection which faced Liverpool [173].

The Widnes Railway from Barrows Green to its terminus beyond Tanhouse Lane was opened for goods traffic only on 3rd April 1877 [41], but the branch to Appleton does not appear to have been built. The south to east curve at Barrows Green opened on 17th April 1878 [41]. As a result, the south to west curve, forming the original junction facing towards Liverpool, became redundant. It was closed on 28th February 1880 [41], but part was used for wagon storage until the 1960s.

Beyond Moor Lane, railway developments were in other hands. Deposited Plans were prepared for the 1872 Parliamentary Session [174,175] for the Hale Bank and Widnes Canal, Dock and Railways. The promoters planned to build a sea wall along the north shore of the Mersey. A new canal, with an entrance lock at Halehead, was to run behind the sea wall to an enlarged dock system at West Bank. From here there was to be a second short canal giving access to the Sankey Navigation. Railways were to be provided linking the new docks with the LNWR at West Deviation Junction and with the Cheshire Lines Committee at Farnworth, where a triangular junction was proposed.

The prime mover appears to have been James Cross, formerly Chief Engineer of the St Helens Canal and Railway Company. By now he was the principal Trustee for the property of the late John Hutchinson, as well as having a personal stake in the Widnes and Ditton Land Company. He was thus responsible for the management of large areas of land which were ripe for industrial development and which required transport facilities.

The dock and canal project was evidently too ambitious but the railway scheme was resubmitted to Parliament in 1873 under the title of the Widnes West Junction Railway. Deposited Plans [176] again show a triangular junction to the west of Farnworth Station, with the line taking a southerly course as far as Ditton Road and then turning south west to an intended terminus near Ditton Brook Ironworks.

The Widnes West Junction Railway Bill did not proceed. Instead a series of lines, known collectively as the West Widnes Railway, were built without Parliamentary authority. One line started from the CLC near Hough Green and ran in a south easterly direction to Moor Lane, where a junction was formed with the Great Central and Midland's Widnes Extension railway. From Moor Lane a second line, later known as the Ditton Marsh Branch, turned south over Ditton Road before taking a circuitous course through the Hutchinson Estate to the Ditton Brook Ironworks. The embankments were formed from alkali waste, which later gave rise to complaints about nuisance from foul smells [177].

After some initial differences of opinion, construction of Cross's West Widnes Railway and the Joint Committee's Widnes Extension line went ahead together, using the same contractors and the same resident engineer [178 to 184]. As early as 1875 the MS&L and Midland Companies had agreed to purchase the West Widnes Railway [185]. and this was confirmed by Act of Parliament in 1878 [186].

The Widnes Extension and West Widnes Railways were reported complete on 13th June 1879 [187] and were opened to goods traffic on 1st July 1879 [41]. The original Widnes Railway, the Extension to Moor Lane and the section of the West Widnes Railway from Moor Lane to Hough Green formed a loop through the town. Passenger services using this route commenced on 1st August 1879 [41], Widnes Central Station being opened on the same day.

Some uncertainty surrounds a third line which ran from Moor Lane to the Broughton Copper Company's works at Ditton and then back in an easterly direction alongside Ditton Road. It was not included in the Midland Railway Act of 1878 which only refers to the transfer of the lines from Moor Lane to Hough Green and to Ditton Brook Ironworks. Known as the Landowners Branch, it was certainly the property of the Sheffield and Midland Joint Committee [188] but it is not known whether it was built prior to 1878 by the West Widnes Railway or subsequently by the Joint Committee without Parliamentary powers.

Before leaving the Sheffield and Midland Railways Joint Committee, we must mention a line which was planned at the southern extremity of the area covered by the present work. In 1873, contemporary with the Widnes activities, the Joint Committee obtained Parliamentary powers [189] to build a line to serve the industrial area of Runcorn.

This was to have run from the end of the LNWR Runcorn Dock Branch to the Cheshire Lines Committee's West Cheshire line at Helsby. Near the southern end there was to have been a spur to Thornton le Moors on the GWR and LNWR branch between Hooton and Helsby [190]. No construction was, however, undertaken and the project was abandoned in 1877 [191].

Finally we note that in 1904, as a consequence of the Manchester, Sheffield and Lincolnshire taking the name of the Great Central Railway, there was a change of title to the Great Central and Midland Joint Committee [192].

Branches to Wigan and St Helens

The Wigan Junction Railway was incorporated in 1874 [193] to build a line from Wigan to join the Liverpool Extension of the Cheshire Lines Committee at Glazebrook. A connecting line to the CLC at Padgate was authorised in 1875 [194].

Financial problems were experienced by the Wigan Junction. It turned for assistance to the Manchester, Sheffield and Lincolnshire which was authorised to subscribe capital under the Wigan Junction Act of 1878 [195]. The line from Strangeways Colliery, on the southern outskirts of Wigan, to Glazebrook was formally opened on 16th October 1879 for goods and mineral traffic [196].

The difficulties in completing the remainder of the line have been described in our earlier book *Industrial Railways of the Wigan Coalfield* [197]. Passenger traffic did not start until 1st April 1884 when the extension from Strangeways to Darlington Street at Wigan was opened [25]. A further extension to Wigan Central Station was brought into use on 1st August 1892 [25].

The branch to Padgate was not constructed and was formally abandoned by the MS&L (New Works) Act of 1881 [198]. Much later a short curve, from Dam Lane Junction to Glazebrook Moss Junction, permitting through running from Liverpool towards Wigan, was built by the Cheshire Lines Committee. Authorised by the CLC Act of 1900 [199], it was opened for traffic on 1st July of the same year [200].

The St Helens and Wigan Junction Railway was promoted largely by local interests in St Helens. It was incorporated in 1885 [201] and was authorised to construct a line from Lowton to St Helens [202]. In November of the same year proposals were submitted to Parliament to continue from St Helens to a junction with the Cheshire Lines and Southport Railway Extension at Fazackerley [203], thus providing access to Liverpool. Also included were a west to north curve at Lowton, a short branch to what later became the passenger station at St Helens and a deviation of the earlier route in the neighbourhood of Haydock. These were authorised by Parliament in 1886 [204] and, to reflect the new ambitions, the title of the company was changed to the Liverpool, St Helens and South Lancashire Railway in 1889 [205].

41

Like the Wigan Junction, the Liverpool, St Helens and South Lancashire had difficulty in raising funds and construction was only able to proceed with the financial assistance of the Manchester, Sheffield and Lincolnshire. This was authorised by the LSH&SL Act of 1889 [205] which also permitted an extension of time to complete the railway. Further extensions of time were granted in 1895 [206] and 1897 [207]. No work had been carried out on the line west of St Helens and this section was formally abandoned in the latter year [207].

The railway from St Helens to Lowton was opened for goods and coal traffic on 1st July 1895. Manchester, Sheffield and Lincolnshire locomotives worked between Lowton and Golborne, while over the remaining section of the line those owned by the contractor, S.W. Pilling, were used [200,208]. The MS&L assumed responsibility for freight train operation over the whole of the line on 21st October 1895 [200].

The Lowton to Ashton section was inspected by the Board of Trade in January 1899 and excursion trains were run to Haydock Park for the races in February [41,200,209]. Formal opening of the whole line for passenger traffic took place on 2nd January 1900 and regular public services started on the next day [200].

A scene little changed from pre-grouping days. A freight train from St Helens headed by an ex Great Central Railway 0-6-0, numbered 65173 in British Railways stock, on the single line section approaching Haydock on 24th July 1956. Note the special wagons near the front of the train loaded with plate glass from the Cowley Hill Works of Pilkington Brothers Ltd.

(B. Woodward)

Two short branches at St Helens were authorised in 1897 [207]. The first was to run from the main line immediately north of Standish Street bridge to the boundary of Pilkington Brothers' Plate Works. The second was from a point 75 yards west of the bridge over Parr Mill Road terminating near the United Alkali Company's Baxter Works. While the branch to Pilkington Brothers' works was in use by May 1900 [210], the other line was never built, despite extensions of time in 1900 [211], 1902 [212] and 1904 [213].

The Wigan Junction and Liverpool, St Helens and South Lancashire Railways were worked by the Manchester, Shefield and Lincolnshire and its successor, the Great Central Railway. They were both absorbed by the latter company on 1st June 1906 [214]

The Manchester Ship Canal

Dissatisfaction with the high costs at the port of Liverpool and the high rates charged by the railway companies led to the promotion of a ship canal which would bring ocean going vessels to Manchester.

A first Bill presented to Parliament in 1883 was unsuccessful. The canal was intended to join the Mersey at the Old Quay at Runcorn. The lowest lock was at Walton and the section from there to Runcorn was tidal [215]. Between Warburton and Walton, the canal took a course to the north of that eventually adopted and a dock was proposed at Warrington between the canal and the Mersey at Howley Lock.

A second Bill in 1884 was equally unsuccessful. Training walls were now proposed in the Mersey between Runcorn and Dungeon Bank, with a dredged channel between them. In the Warrington area the route had been moved to that finally chosen. A deviation of the river at Warrington was also proposed, with the dock now located on the old arm of the river [216].

A revised scheme was put forward in which the canal was extended from Runcorn along the south shore of the Mersey to Eastham, where locks gave access to the estuary. The Bill was eventually passed by Parliament, but only after significant concessions had been gained by the opponents. The Act [217] which created the Manchester Ship Canal Company received Royal Assent on 6th August 1885.

T.A. Walker was awarded the construction contract and the first sod was cut at Eastham on 11th November 1887 [218]. The canal was opened with great ceremony just over six years later, on 1st January 1894 [218] after numerous difficulties, both financial and technical, had been overcome.

The Bridgewater Navigation Company was bought out for £1,710,000 by the Manchester Ship Canal Company in July 1887 [3], under the terms of the 1885 Act. The Mersey and Irwell Navigation was for the most part obliterated by the new works. Only three small portions survived - the Woolston and Butchersfield cuts and the section of the Runcorn and Latchford Canal between Wilderspool and Latchford.

The River Mersey was diverted into a new channel between Walton and Warrington Bridge and this provided access, through a side lock at Walton, to Howley Quay and various industrial wharves between Bank Quay and Sankey Bridges. No work was carried out on the dock at Arpley Meadows, which would have occupied part of the old bed of the river, despite an extension of time for completion in 1893 [219]. A proposal [220] to construct a dam in the river below Monks, Hall and Company's works, to build a cut off channel and associated lock and to reconstruct the wharves in the vicinity of Bank Quay failed to obtain Parliamentary approval in 1904

Temporary railways were used extensively during the construction of the canal and some 200 locomotives were employed by the contractor. Following the completion of the works, the Ship Canal Company took steps to establish a permanent railway system, principally serving Manchester Docks and, later, Trafford Park industrial estate. Much of the Ship Canal Railway falls outside the area covered by the present book, but we deal with those parts of it which gave access to industrial establishments in Runcorn, Warrington and Irlam in the appropriate chapters. Those who wish to study the complete history of the railway system are referred to a publication by Don Thorpe [221].

Railway Developments Associated with the Manchester Ship Canal

Mention has been made in previous books in this series of the Lancashire Plateway scheme which was promoted by Liverpool shipping interests in an attempt to pre-empt the Manchester Ship Canal and to retain the monopoly of cotton import and exports. The wagons were to run on flangeless wheels. Steam locomotives were to be used on the Plateway proper, while it was intended to haul the wagons by horses on the ordinary roads within the port of Liverpool and from the termini to the mills. A Bill was presented to Parliament in 1882, but withdrawn. It was followed by a second Bill in 1883, but this failed to gain Parliamentary approval [222].

The Plateway would have been some 85 miles in total length, serving all the principal cotton manufacturing towns. Its two main lines would have passed through the area covered by the present book [223]. One, from the north of Liverpool, was intended to run through Knowsley, Gerard's Bridge and Blackbrook to Ashton in Makerfield, skirting the northern part of St Helens. At Ashton the line divided, one branch turning north to serve Wigan, Chorley, Accrington and Burnley, the other continuing by way of Leigh, Atherton and Bolton and eventually terminating at Rochdale. The second main line, from Liverpool to Manchester, Ashton and Oldham, would have passed through Childwall, Cronton and Farnworth. From here it would have continued on a course parallel to and on the north side of the Cheshire Lines railway, crossing the Mersey at Flixton.

Two more conventional railway schemes appeared in the 1890s which were intended to make use of the potential offered by the Manchester Ship Canal for the shipment of coal.

The Lancashire, Derbyshire and East Coast Railway was promoted by East Midlands colliery owners to provide two outlets for their coal, one through the Manchester Ship Canal Company's proposed dock at Warrington, the other through a dock on the east coast which the railway company intended to build near Mablethorpe. The proposed line was to run through Knutsford, Macclesfield, Buxton, Chesterfield and Lincoln [224,225]. The whole of the railway, including some minor deviations in the neighbourhood of the Warrington Dock [226], was authorised by Parliament in 1891 [227]. There was, however, considerable difficulty in raising the necessary capital and only the portion between Chesterfield and Lincoln was actually built. The section from Warrington to Chesterfield was formally abandoned in 1895 [228].

A more local affair was the Leigh and South Central Lancashire Railway [229]. Two main lines were proposed. One was intended to run from the Ince to Walkden through Leigh and Astley and there were to be twelve spurs to tap coal traffic from the public and private railways which it crossed. The other, intersecting with the first near Marsland Green, was intended to run from Tyldesley Colliery to a junction with the Manchester Ship Canal railway serving the Partington North coaling basin. There were to be curves to the CLC Manchester line east of Glazebrook, a spur to the CLC Timperley line and a short branch direct to the Ship Canal. A Bill was presented to Parliament in May 1895, but the Preamble was not proved and the project was dropped.

The most obvious changes brought about by the construction of the Ship Canal were the massive engineering works associated with the high level railway bridges. The bridges provided a clearance of 70ft to 75ft above the waterline and required lengthy approach embankments. Exceptionally, a tunnel had been proposed at Latchford on the Warrington and Stockport line in the 1883 scheme [215], but this was altered in the later submissions to Parliament.

These works, as well as a new junction at Acton Grange between the Birkenhead Railway and the West Coast Main Line, were authorised by the Manchester Ship Canal Act of 1885 [217]. The costs were borne by the canal company, which also had to pay lump sums to the railway companies to defray the extra expense in working trains over the steep gradients leading to the bridges. All the deviations were completed by 1893 and the dates when they were opened for traffic can be found in the Railway Chronology.

The old lines, replaced by the deviations, were formally abandoned by the Ship Canal Act of 1885 [217], although in the event the only tracks which were lifted were those of the CLC east of the canal at Flixton and those on the Warrington and Stockport line east of the canal at Statham. The CLC lines on both sides of the canal at Partington were incorporated into branches of the Ship Canal railway system as authorised in the 1885 Act. The original alignment of the CLC at Irlam was also taken over by the Manchester Ship Canal Company, apparently without Parliamentary authority.

On the LNWR, the old line at Latchford was retained by the railway company to give access to the Ship Canal railway, while at Walton the former Birkenhead Railway lines were also kept to provide a link with another section of the Ship Canal railway. The old tracks on the south side of the canal became sidings for the storage of wagons.

Railways and Canals 1900 to 1935

By 1900 the railway map of South Lancashire was virtually complete. The only new lines to be opened for traffic in the early years of the present century were, as we have already recorded, from Lowton St Mary's to St Helens and from Dam Lane Junction to Glazebrook Moss Junction. There was, however, one novel project. The Manchester and Liverpool Express Railway Company was incorporated in 1901 and authorised to construct an electrically operated suspended monorail between the two cities [230]. There was to be no intermediate station and it was intended to make the journey in half an hour.

The route ran from Liverpool through Dingle and Garston and then followed the Cheshire Lines Committee's railway as far as Glazebrook. Here the monorail turned north east across the edge of Chat Moss through Barton and Salford [231,232]. A further Act in 1902 [233] authorised a deviation at Pendleton, but the proprietors had difficulty in raising money for the scheme, which was subsequently abandoned.

Until the first world war, the supremacy of the railways was virtually unchallenged except where there was competition from the electric tramways. In the 1920s and 1930s, however, road transport took over an ever increasing amount of both goods and passenger traffic.

Under the Transport Act of 1921 [234] some rationalisation was achieved by the creation of four major companies from the very many that then existed. All the former London and North Western Railway lines in South Lancashire passed to the London, Midland and Scottish Railway. The London and North Eastern Railway took over the Great Central lines from Glazebrook to Wigan and Lowton St Mary's to St Helens.

The Cheshire Lines Committee and the Great Central and Midland Joint Committee retained their identities. The LNER, which acquired the Great Northern Railway as well as the Great Central, had a two thirds share in the CLC, while the LMSR, which had acquired the Midland Railway, had only a one third share. In the Great Central and Midland Committee, the two companies were equal partners.

In the period up to the second world war, there were no railway closures in the area covered by the present book, although the St Helens Canal became a casualty to competing methods of transport. The extreme end of the Ravenhead Branch, from the Tavern Swing Bridge to the terminal basin, had already been abandoned by Section 17 of the LNWR Act of 1898 [235], while the Burtonhead Branch appears to have become disused before 1891 when the survey was made for the revision of the first edition of the 25 inch map.

By the end of the first world war, traffic north of Newton Common Lock was almost non existent, the last recorded flats working through in 1919 [3]. Part of the Ravenhead Branch passing through the centre of St Helens was abandoned in 1920 [236] and the remainder of the canal north of Newton Common in 1931 [237]. The railway dock at Widnes also closed in 1933 [238].

Railways 1935 to 1996

Only one new line was opened during the period up to the end of the second world war and that was in connection with the Ordnance Factory at Risley which was built in the late 1930s as part of a hurried re-armament programme. To supplement the main rail access from the Cheshire Lines Committee, a second link with the rail network was provided in 1942 or 1943 by means of short branch from Newchurch on the Glazebrook to Wigan line [239,240]. The branch was probably the property of the Government but was operated by the LNER and carried a workmen's service as well as goods traffic.

The railways were nationalised as from 1st January 1948 [241] bringing all the lines in South Lancashire under a single ownership for the first time under the auspices of the British Transport Commission.

With increasing competition from public road transport and the private car, many of the passenger services became wholly uneconomical and were withdrawn in the 1950s and 1960s. Local freight facilities suffered a similar fate in subsequent years, although some wagon load traffic lingered on until the late 1980s. The closures which took place are too numerous to describe in detail here but further information will be found in the Railway Chronology which follows this chapter.

By contrast, the West Coast Main Line and the railway from Weaver Junction to Liverpool were electrified. At the time of writing both continue to carry a heavy traffic of all types. On other routes that escaped closure diesel locomotives and diesel multiple units replaced steam traction. Many passenger trains are now subsidised by the local authorities and, with a few exceptions, provide a better service than at any time previously. Freight is generally limited to special categories of traffic, such as oil and imported coal, which can be carried in train load quantities.

A few short sections of new line were built after nationalisation either to serve new factories or to enable other parts of the system to be taken out of use.

At Irlam a short branch was constructed under the BTC Act of 1954 [242] which ran from the sidings at Glazebrook along the south side of the former CLC Manchester line. It gave direct access to the steelworks, which was at that time being redeveloped, and avoided transfer of traffic over the Manchester Ship Canal Railway. The line was opened in the mid 1950s, although we have been unable to trace the precise date.

At Widnes a connection was put in soon after nationalisation between the former Great Central and Midland and LNWR lines where they ran close together east of Ditton Junction. This enabled all shunting locomotives at Widnes to be supplied from the former LNWR engine shed. The connection, as shown on contemporary plans [243,244], consisted of little more than a crossover from the Ditton Marsh Branch to the independent single line between Ditton Junction and Mathiesons Works. Again the date of completion seems to have gone unrecorded, although it was probably brought into use before the former GC&M engine shed at Tanhouse Lane closed on 16th April 1954 [41].

The new plant built by the United Sulphuric Acid Company at Widnes was provided with a short branch from the former Great Central and Midland Joint line at Tanhouse Lane. This was built under the British Transport Commission Act of 1953 [245] and, according to the Sidings Schedules, the first test train ran on 15th November 1954.

Impending closure of the former Great Central and Midland line through Widnes meant that traffic to the USAC works had to be re-routed. To enable trains from the direction of Sutton Oak to reach the factory, a new chord was constructed from the former LNWR line near Widnes No. 1 Signal Box to join the 1954 branch at Tanhouse Lane. The chord seems to have been built without specific Parliamentary powers and was brought into use on 16th March 1961 [246].

There were yet further changes in the Tanhouse Lane area in 1981 so as to permit the closure of the railway between Widnes No. 7 and Widnes No. 1 Signal Boxes, by now the only surviving portion of the original St Helens and Runcorn Gap Railway south of Sutton Oak. A cement terminal, built on the site of the closed USAC works, was initially served by the 1961 chord. A new link line was now constructed between Carterhouse Junction, on the former LNWR Widnes to Warrington line, and Tanhouse Lane. Originally mooted, according to the Sidings Schedules, in 1953, the line was again apparently built without Parliamentary powers and was opened for traffic on 18th April 1982 [247].

Anhydrite, mined at Long Meg in Cumbria, was transported by rail to the USAC works at Widnes. Here 92019 is seen at the head of an empty wagon train leaving Tanhouse Lane over the 1961 chord to Widnes No.7 at the start of its return journey. (Eddie Bellass)

At Golborne a chord was built from the West Coast Main Line to the former Great Central St Helens line to enable the section of the latter between Lowton St Mary's and Edge Green Sidings to be closed. Authorised by the British Railways Act of 1967 [248], the chord was brought into use on 22nd April 1968 [249].

The most recent development has been at St Helens, where the remaining portion of the Ravenhead Branch, serving Pilkington Brothers' oil terminal, was in the way of a new road scheme. A spur was constructed from the Huyton to St Helens line to a new terminal on a site adjacent to the earlier one and was commissioned on 25th October 1992 [250].

Parliamentary powers for two other schemes have been obtained in recent years, but with the reorganisation of the railway industry it seems unlikely that either will be implemented. The British Railways Act of 1990 [251] authorised the construction of a chord at Warrington which would enable coal trains to Fiddler's Ferry Power Station to travel from Walton Old Junction to the Widnes line without the need to reverse at Arpley. The 1993 Act [252] contained provisions to reinstate the part of the line between St Helens and St Helens Junction which had been lifted. This was in connection with a proposal to restart a passenger service over the line.

Canals 1935 to 1996

The St Helens Canal was nationalised in 1948 and was later transferred from the British Transport Commission to the British Waterways Board. The southern portion was used by flats working to the Sankey Sugar Company's wharf at Earlestown until 1959 [46] when the firm changed to road transport. The remaining section of the canal, between Newton Common Lock and Widnes, was formally abandoned by the British Waterways Act of 1963 [253], although the basin at Widnes is still used as moorings for pleasure craft.

The Weaver Navigation was also nationalised. Until the 1980s it was still used commercially by coasting craft which travelled as far the ICI works at Winnington. It is now given over almost entirely to pleasure boating.

The Bridgewater Canal, like the Manchester Ship Canal Company which owned it, escaped nationalisation. Commercial traffic had practically ceased south of Old Trafford by the end of the 1960s. The canal still remains open for pleasure boats, except for the two flights of locks at Runcorn, which were formally abandoned by the Manchester Ship Canal Act of 1966 [254] and demolished to make way for redevelopment. This Act also authorised the abandonment of the Runcorn and Weston Canal, Francis Dock, the Graving Dock, the Coal Basin and the Old Basin. The Arnold Dock had apparently been filled in earlier. The remaining docks were modernised and took on a new lease of life.

The Manchester Ship Canal was quite busy until the 1970s but it was unable to accommodate the newer and very much larger ships which were then being introduced. Traffic tailed off and today very few vessels proceed beyond the oil terminals at Eastham and Ellesmere Port. The dock side facilities at Manchester have largely been demolished to make way for redevelopment.

Taken on 4th May 1958 from the Sankey Viaduct on the Liverpool and Manchester line, this view shows barges unloading at the Sankey Sugar Company's wharf on the St Helens Canal. All traffic on the canal ceased in the following year. *(Peter Norton)*

References to Chapter 2

1   Upper Mersey Navigation Act, 39 & 40 Vic cap civ; 13th July 1876
2   7 Geo 1 cap XV; 17th June 1721
3   *The Canals of North West England, Vols 1 and 2,* Charles Hadfield and Gordon Bidder, David and Charles, Newton Abbot, 1970
4   7 Geo 1 cap X; 23rd March 1721
5   47 Geo 3 Session 2 cap 82; 8th August 1807
6   28 Geo 2 cap VIII; 20th March 1755
7   2 Geo 3 cap LVI
8   11 Geo 4 cap I; 29th May 1830
9   LRO PDR 373
10 *A Merseyside Town in the Industrial Revolution,* T.C. Barker and J.R. Harris, Revised Edition, Frank Cass & Co Ltd, London, 1959
11 2 Geo 3 cap XI
12 16 Vic cap xxxvii; 14th June 1853
13 20 & 21 Vic cap 4; 25th August 1857
14 LRO PDR 132
15 7 Geo 4 cap xlix; 5th May 1826
16 *Liverpool and Manchester Railway Operations 1831-1845,* Thomas A. Donaghy, David and Charles, Newton Abbot, 1980
17 10 Geo 4 cap xxxvii; 14th May 1829
18 LRO PDR 174
19 LRO PDR 165
20 *Crewe to Carlisle,* Brian Reed, Ian Allan, 1969
21 CRO QDP 88
22 CRO QDP 97
23 LRO PDR 214
24 11 Geo 4 cap lvi; 29th May 1830

25 *Chronology of the Railways of Lancashire and Cheshire*, M.D. Greville, Revised Edition, Railway and Canal Historical Society, 1981

26 1 Wm 4 cap lvi; 22nd April 1831

27 4 Wm 4 cap xxv; 29th May 1834

28 3 & 4 Wm 4 cap xxxiv; 6th May 1833

29 5 & 6 Wm 4 cap viii; 12th June 1835

30 *Waterways and Railways to Warrington* Peter Norton, Railway and Canal Historical Society, 1974

31 11 Geo 4 cap lvii; 29th May 1830

32 LRO PDR 215

33 8 & 9 Vic cap cxxiii; 21st July 1845

34 9 & 10 Vic cap cclxi; 27th July 1846

35 LRO PDR 425

36 LRO PDR 426

37 8 & 9 Vic cap clxvi; 31st July 1845

38 9 & 10 Vic cap ccxxxi; 27th July 1846

39 CRO QDP 214A

40 9 & 10 Vic cap cciv; 16th July 1846

41 *The St Helens Railway*, J.M. Tolson, The Oakwood Press, 1982

42 11 Geo IV cap lxi; 29th May 1830

43 LRO PDR 188

44 LRO PDR 208

45 1 & 2 Vic cap xxi; 11th June 1838

46 Information supplied to the authors by John Tolson

47 8 & 9 Vic cap cxvii; 21st July 1845

48 LRO PDR 465

49 LRO PDR 430

50 LRO PDR 431

51 LRO PDR 477

52 9 & 10 Vic cap cxciii; 16th July 1846

53 LNWR (Widnes and Prescot Brook Colliery Branches) Act, 10 & 11 Vic cap ccxiv; 22nd July 1847

54 9 & 10 Vic cap clxxxiii; 16th July 1846

55 LRO PDR 533

56 10 & 11 Vic cap cclxxi; 22nd July 1847

57 16 & 17 Vic cap cxxxiv; 4th August 1853

58 *St Helens Intelligencer* 5.3.1859

59 23 & 24 Vic cap lxxix; 14th June 1860

60 LRO PDR 769

61 27 & 28 Vic cap ccxcvi; 29th July 1864

62 LRO PDR 407

63 LRO PDR 424

64 LRO PDR 481

65 LRO PDR 511

66 LRO PDR 572

67 16 & 17 Vic cap clxiii; 4th August 1853

68 *WO* 11.12.1857

69 LNWR (Additional Powers England) Act 1865, 28 & 29 Vic cap cccxxxiii; 5th July 1865

70 LNWR (Additional Powers) Act 1870, 33 & 34 Vic cap cxii; 4th July 1870

71 LRO PDR 192

72 27 & 28 Vic cap cclxxiii; 25th July 1864

73 LRO PDR 768

74 LRO PDR 800

75 28 & 29 Vic cap cxciii; 29th June 1865

76 LUR Act 1866, 29 & 30 Vic cap ccxxxiii; 16th July 1866

77 LRO PDR 819

78 *The Lancashire Union Railways*, John Marshall, *Railway Magazine*, April, May, June 1970

79 LUR Act 1868, 31 & 32 Vic cap cxv; 13th July 1868

80 WRO DDX/EI 76/74

81 Note on Line Plan of St Helens Railway, 2 chains to 1 inch, LNWR, Rugby 1871 at BRPB, Manchester Office

82 WRO DDX/EI 76/46

83 WRO DDX/EI 76/52

84 WRO DDX/EI 76/61

85 WRO DDX/EI 76/96

86 34 Vic cap x; 25th May 1871

87 LNWR (New Rlys) Act 1883, 46 & 47 Vic cap cx; 16th July 1883

88 LRO PDR 181

89 LRO PDR 189

90 LRO PDR 286

91 LRO PDR 312

92 CRO QDP 187

93 CRO QDP 218

94 LRO PDR 430

95 LRO PDR 691

96 LNWR (New Lines near Liverpool) Act 1861, 24 & 25 Vic cap cxxviii; 11th July 1861

97 LNWR (New Rlys and Addl Pwrs) Act 1869, 32 & 33 Vic cap cxv; 12th July 1869

98 LNWR (Additional Powers) Act 1868, 31 & 32 Vic cap cxviii; 13th July 1868

99 *The Cheshire Lines Railway*, R. Prys Griffiths, Oakwood Press, Godstone, 1947

100 *History of the Great Western Railway* E.T.MacDermott, Great Western Railway Co, London, in two volumes, 1927 and 1931

101 CRO QDP 183

102 CRO QDP 246

103 9 & 10 Vic cap xci; 26th June 1846

104 CRO QDP 269

105 Birkenhead, Lancashire and Cheshire Junction and Chester and Birkenhead Railways Amalgamation Act, 10 & 11 Vic cap ccxxii; 22nd July 1847

106 Birkenhead, Lancashire and Cheshire Junction Consolidation Act, 15 & 16 Vic cap clxvii; 1st July 1852

107 Shrewsbury and Chester Railway (Birkenhead Station) Act, 14 & 15 Vic cap cxxxi; 7th Aug 1851

108 Shrewsbury and Chester Railway Act 1854, 17 & 18 Vic cap cxx; 3rd July 1854

109 Shrewsbury and Chester Railway (Norton and Walton Branches) Act, 15 & 16 Vic cap cxlvi; 30th June 1852

110 CRO QDP 301

111 14 & 15 Vic cap lxxi; 3rd July 1851

112 CRO QDP 297

113 Warrington and Stockport Rly Act, 16 & 17 Vic cap cxxii; 4th Aug 1853

114 Warrington and Altrincham Junction Railway Act, 16 & 17 Vic cap ccxviii; 20th Aug 1853

115 Preamble to W&S Rly Leasing Act, 22 & 23 Vic cap cxxxviii; 13th Aug 1859

116 Great Western, Birmingham and Chester Rys Act 1854, 17 & 18 Vic cap ccxxii; 7th August 1854

117 Birkenhead Railway Act 1859, 22 & 23 Vic cap lxxiv; 1st Aug 1859

118 Birkenhead Railway (Vesting) Act, 24 & 25 Vic cap cxxxiv; 11th July 1861

119 Schedule to W & S Rly Leasing Act 22 & 23 Vic cap cxxxviii; 13th Aug 185

120 LNWR Northern Division Working Timetable December 1857 at NRM York

121 Schedule to Birkenhead Railway (Vesting) Act, 24 & 25 Vic cap cxxxiv; 11th July 1861

122 *Journal of the Stephenson Locomotive Society*, Feb 1975, quoting from article in *Mancunian* of Aug 1974

123 CRO QDP 300

124 CRO QDP 341

125 CRO QDP 340

126 Warrington and Stockport Railway Leasing Act, 22 & 23 Vic cap cxxxviii; 13th Aug 1859

127 24 & 25 Vic cap xxxv; 17th May 1861

128 22 & 23 Vic cap ii; 1st July 1859

129 25 & 26 Vic cap cxxiv; 7th July 1862

130 27 & 28 Vic cap ccxc; 29th July 1864

131 LNWR (New Rlys etc) Act 1878, 41 & 42 Vic cap clxxxii; 22nd July 1878

132 *LMerc* 17.10.1892

133 LNWR (New Railways) Act 1881, 44 & 45 Vic cap cxli; 18th July 1881

134 54 & 55 Vic cap cxxxvii; 21st July 1891

135 LRO PDR 1414

136 57 & 58 Vic cap xcii; 20th July 1894

137 LRO PDR 1476

138 *Railway Reminiscences*, G.P.Neele, McCorquodale, London, 1904

139 LNWR Act 1880, 43 & 44 Vic cap cxlv; 6th August 1880

140 LRO PDR 1142

141 LNWR (New Lines and Addl Pwrs) Act 1876, 39 & 40 Vic cap clxxx; 24th July 1876

142   52 & 53 Vic cap xcviii; 26th July 1889

143   MS&LR (Extension to Liverpool) Act, 1865, 28 & 29 Vic cap ccclxxviii; 6th July 1865

144   MS&LR (Liverpool Extension) Act 1866, 29 & 30 Vic cap cxci; 16th July 1866

145   MS&LR (New Lines) Act 1866, 29 & 30 Vic cap cxcii; 16th July 1866

146   GNR (Cheshire Lines) Act 1863, 26 & 27 Vic cap cxlvii; 13th July 1863

147   Cheshire Lines Transfer Act 1865, 28 & 29 Vic cap cccxxvii; 5th July 1865

148   Cheshire Lines Act 1867, 30 & 31 Vic cap ccvii; 15th August 1867

149   CLC Act 1872, 35 & 36 Vic cap lvii; 27th June 1872

150   MS&LR Act 1878, 41 & 42 Vic cap xxx; 16th April 1878

151   CLC Act 1881, 44 & 45 Vic cap cxxxi; 18th July 1881

152   LRO PDR 934

153   LRO PDR 992

154   LRO PDR 1071

155   MS&LR (Additional Powers) Act 1886, 50 Vic cap xlix; 25th Sept 1886

156   CRO QDP 424

157   CRO QDP 430

158   Macclesfield, Knutsford and Warrington Rly Act 1866 29 & 30 Vic cap clix; 28th June 1866

159   CRO QDP 445

160   Macclesfield and Knutsford Rly Act 1871, 34 Vic cap lii; 16th June 1871

161   MS&LR Act 1874, 37 & 38 Vic cap cxxxii; 16th July 1874

162   LRO PDR 947

163   The Railways Construction Facilities Act 1864, 27 & 28 Vic cap 121; 29th July 1864

164   The Railways (Powers and Construction) Act 1870, 33 & 34 Vic cap 19; 20th June 1870

165   LRO PDR 920

166   Parly Papers 1872, Vol LI

167   LRO PDR 955

168   Parly Papers 1873, Vol LVII

169   The Railway Provisional Certificate Confirmation Act 1873, 36 & 37 Vic cap lxxxiv; 7th July 1873

170   S&M Companies Committee Act 1875, 38 & 39 Vic cap ciii; 29th June 1875

171   MS&LR and MR (Joint Lines) Act 1869, 32 & 33 Vic cap xxv; 24th June 1869

172   MS&LR (Additional Powers) Act 1872, Section, 29 35 & 36 Vic cap clxxviii; 6th August 1872

173   LRO PDR 988

174   LRO PDR 949

175   CRO QDP 515

176   LRO PDR 943

177   *Widnes Weekly News* 6.9.1884

178   S&M Joint CommitteeMinutes17.5.1876

179   Ibid 21.6.1876

180   Ibid 16.5.1877

181   Ibid 20.6.1877

182   Ibid 18.7.1877

183   Ibid 17.9.1877

184   Ibid 17.10.1877

185   MS&LR Minutes 2.1.1875

186   Midland Railway (Additional Powers) Act 1878, 41 Vic xcvi; 17th June 1878

187   S&M Joint Committee Minutes 13.6.1879

188   Plan of the Sheffield Midland Joint Lines at Widnes, 1 inch to 2 chains, no date, at BRPB, Manchester Office

189   S&M Companies Committee Act 1873, 36 Vic cap liv 26th May 1873

190   CRO QDP 516

191   S&M Cttee's Abandonment Act 1877, 40 & 41 Vic cap xlii; 28th June 1877

192   GC&M Act 1904, 4 Ed 7 cap lxxxiv; 22nd July 1904

193   37 & 38 Vic cap cxvii; 16th July 1874

194   38 & 39 Vic cap clxxxix; 2nd August 1875

195   41 Vic cap xcvii; 17th June 1878

196   *WO* 17.10.1879

197   *Industrial Railways of the Wigan Coalfield Part One*, C.H.A.Townley, F.D.Smith, J.A.Peden, Runpast Publishing, Cheltenham, 1991

198 MS&LR (New Works) Act 1881, 44 & 45 Vic cap cxxxvi; 18th July 1881
199 CLC Act 1900, 63 Vic cap vi; 25th May 1900
200 *Great Central*, G.Dow, Ian Allan, London, in three vols, 1959, 1962, 1965
201 48 & 49 Vic cap cxxi; 22nd July 1885
202 LRO PDR 1274
203 LRO PDR 1295
204 50 Vic cap xxxiii; 25th September 1886
205 StH&WJR Act 1889, 52 & 53 Vic cap xci; 26th July 1889
206 MS&LR Act 1895, 58 & 59 Vic cap cxlviii; 6th July 1895
207 LStH&SLR Act 1897, 60 & 61 Vic cap cxi; 15th July 1897
208 *WO* 25.5.1895
209 *WO* 28.1.1899
210 Pilkington Brothers Ltd Plate Board Minutes 24th May 1900, at IM&S
211 GCR Act 1900, 63 & 64 Vic cap xlx; 25th June 1900
212 GCR Act 1902, 2 Edw 7 cap cxxxv; 22nd July 1902
213 GCR Act 1904, 4 Edw 7 cap xcv; 22nd July 1904
214 GCR Act 1905, 5 Ed 7 cap clxxviii; 4th July 1905
215 LRO PDC 53
216 LRO PDC 55
217 48 & 49 Vic cap clxxxviii; 6th August 1885
218 *History of the Manchester Ship Canal*, Sir Bosdin Leech, Sherratt and Hughes, Manchester and London, 1907
219 56 Vic cap iii; 28th March 1893
220 CRO QDP 819
221 *The Railways of the Manchester Ship Canal*, Don Thorpe, Oxford Publishing Co, Poole, 1984
222 *An Account of the Proposed Lancashire Plateway Company*, Alfred Holt, Liverpool, 1883, with an Appendix dated 1889

223 LRO PDR 1215
224 LRO PDR 1411
225 CRO QDP 668
226 CRO QDP 669
227 54 & 55 Vic cap clxxxix; 5th Aug 1891
228 58&59 Vic cap cxli; 6th July 1895
229 LRO PDR 1491
230 1 Edw 7 cap cclxv; 17th Aug 1901
231 LRO PDR 1716
232 LRO PDR 1756
233 2 Edw 7 cap xxiv; 23rd June 1902
234 11 & 12 Geo 5 cap 55; 19th July 1921
235 61 & 62 Vic cap ccxxiv; 12th Aug 1898
236 Ministry of Transport Order, 20th Oct 1920
237 Ministry of Transport Order, 21st May 1931
238 LMSR Act 1933, 23 & 24 Geo 5 cap xlix; 8th July 1933
239 *The Mancunian* (Journal of the Manchester Locomotive Society), No. 120, May 1984
240 Information supplied by Mr R. Clough
241 Transport Act 1947, 10 & 11 Geo 6 cap 49; 6th Aug 1947
242 2 & 3 Eliz 2 cap lv; 30th July 1954
243 Line Plan of Aston, Runcorn and Ditton Rly, 1:1250, BR, Euston, 1963, at BRPB Manchester Office
244 LMSR Sdg Diag 309; May 1964
245 1 & 2 Eliz 2 cap xliii; 31st July 1953
246 BLN 360
247 BLN 448
248 1967 cap xxxi; 27th July 1967
249 Information supplied by Mr Richard Maund
250 BLN 694
251 1990 cap xxv; 17th July 1990
252 1993 cap iv; 29th Mar 1993
253 1963 cap xii; 10th July 1963
254 1966 cap xxvii; 9th Aug 1966

RAILWAY CHRONOLOGY

LONDON AND NORTH WESTERN RAILWAY

Became London, Midland and Scottish Railway	1. 1. 1923
Became British Railways	1. 1. 1948

Liverpol and Manchester Railway

Absorbed by Grand Junction Railway	8. 8. 1845.
Became LNWR	16. 7. 1846.

Opened :

Liverpool (Crown St) to Manchester (Liverpool Rd)	15. 9. 1830	(Ref 1)
West Curve at Parkside	1847	(Ref 2)
Willis Branch	See Note 1	
Seel Branch	See Note 1	

Closed :

Seel Branch	See Note 2
Willis Branch	See Note 3

Still in use :

Liverpool to Manchester and west curve at Parkside

Notes		
	1	These lines were built under wayleave agreements with the landowners and were opened around 1832 or 1833. For more details see Part 2.
	2	The wayleave agreement in respect of the Seel Branch was not renewed in 1911, but the branch continued to operate under the auspices of Tushingham's Metallic Brick Co until about 1930.
	3	Traffic ceased following the closure of Cronton Colliery on 2. 3. 1984. The branch had been out of use for a period between 1971 and 1974, when road transport was used by the colliery.

Warrington and Newton Railway

Absorbed by Grand Junction Railway	12. 6. 1835
Became LNWR	16. 7. 1846.

Opened :

Warrington (Dallam) to Newton [Note 1]	1 . 6. 1831	(Ref 1)
West curve at Newton	25 . 7. 1831	(Ref 2)
East curve at Newton	4 . 7. 1837	(Ref 2)
South Junction at Newton to Haydock Crossing	See Note 2	
Branch to Liverpool Road, Warrington	See Note 3	

Double line converted to quadruple track:

Warrington to Winwick Junction	4. 1881	(Ref 3)

Closed:

Dallam Branch closed to passengers	See Note 4	
End of Dallam Branch (Allied Brewery Sdg to Foundry St Coal yard over Tanners Lane Level Crossing)	9. 8. 1965	(Refs 4,5)
Rest of Dallam Branch	By 10. 1980	(Ref 6)
Earlestown No. 1 to Earlestown No. 3 [Note 5]	2. 1. 1967	(Ref 7)

Still in use :

Warrington to Earlestown, including four tracks from Warrington to Winwick Jct

Notes	1	This area around the junction was later renamed Earlestown.
	2	This short line was included on the Deposited Plans for the Warrington and Newton. It is not known whether it was built by the Warrington and Newton or by one of its successors. Parallel tracks between the same points were built by the owners of Haydock Colliery, probably in 1831.
	3	Date not discovered, presumably mid 1831.
	4	Probably on opening of Grand Junction station at Warrington in July 1837.
	5	This presumably refers to the ex-LNWR line. There were parallel tracks between these two points owned by the National Coal Board (see Note 2 and Part 2). The date is that of the official closure; traffic ceased in 1966.

Wigan Branch Railway

Became North Union Railway	22. 5. 1834
Leased to Grand Junction and Mcr & Leeds Rlys	1. 1. 1846
Became LNWR and L&YR joint property	7. 8. 1888
Became sole property of LNWR	26. 7. 1889

Opened:

Parkside to Wigan for passengers and goods, including east curve at Parkside	3. 9. 1832	(Ref 1)

Double line converted to quadruple track :

Golborne Jct to Springs Branch Jct   29.10. 1888   (Ref 8)

Still in use:

Throughout, including third and fourth lines from Golborne Jct to Wigan

Grand Junction Railway

Became LNWR   16. 7. 1846

Opened :

Birmingham to end on junction with Liverpool Road Branch
    of Warrington and Newton Rly   4. 7. 1837   (Ref 1)

Closed :

Walton Old Jct to north side of Ship Canal and south side
    of Ship Canal to Moore [Note 1]   8. 7. 1893   (Ref 1)

Still in use :

Throughout except for portions of line abandoned as a result of construction of
    Manchester Ship Canal

Note   1   Replaced by Ship Canal Deviation opened for goods traffic on 17.2.1893
               (Ref 9) and for pasengers on 9.7.1893 (Ref 1). The old alignment north of
               the Ship Canal was abandoned. That south of the Ship Canal was retained
               for wagon storage.

St Helens and Runcorn Gap Railway

Became St Helens Canal and Railway	21. 7. 1845
Leased to LNWR	1. 7. 1860
Absorbed by LNWR [Note 1]	1. 8. 1864

Opened:

St Helens and Widnes

St Helens (1st Stn) to St Helens Jct for passengers	2. 1. 1832	(Ref 10)
Sutton Oak to Widnes Dock [Note 2]	21. 2. 1833	(Ref 10)
Deviations at Sutton and Widnes inclines	1849	(Ref 10)
Branch from St Helens line to Muspratts Works at Widnes	See Note 3	

St Helens Branches

Broad Oak Colliery to Sutton Oak [Note 2]	21. 2. 1833 (Ref 10)
Ashton's Green Branch	See Note 4
St Helens (1st Stn) to connection with Ravenhead Colliery	See Note 5
Peasley Cross to Gerard's Bridge	1837
Branch to St Helens 2nd station at Raven Street	19. 12. 1849 (Ref 11)
Fleet Lane to Blackbrook	Late 1850 (Ref 10)
Haydock Jct to junction with Haydock Colly Rly	Late 1851, early 1852 (Ref 10)
Ravenhead Colliery to Ravenhead Plate Glass Works	See Note 5
Eccleston Jct to Eccleston (Home Farm Lane)	See Note 6

Garston and Warrington

Widnes to Ditton Mill and curve at Widnes Dock	6. 1851 (Ref 10)
Ditton Mill to Garston	1. 2. 1853 (Ref 10)
New station at Waterloo Rd, Widnes	1. 7. 1852 (Ref 10)
Widnes to Whitecross (Nr Litton Mill)	1. 2. 1853 (Ref 10)
Whitecross to Bridge Street (Arpley)	1. 5. 1854 (Ref 10)
New Curve at Widnes from St Helens line to Garston line	11. 1856 (Ref 10)

St Helens and Rainford

Ravenhead Jct to Rainford Jct - for coal traffic	5. 12. 1857 (Ref 12)
- for passengers, together with 3rd St Helens station at Shaw Street	1. 2. 1858 (Ref 10)
Randle Jct to end on junction with East Lancashire Railway at Rainford	1. 3. 1858 (Ref 10)

Single lines converted to double track :

Sutton Oak Jct to Broad Oak Jct (Fleet Lane)	1858 or 1859 (Ref 10)
Broad Oak Jct (Fleet Lane) to Blackbrook	Spring 1862 (Ref 10)
Sutton Oak Jct to Widnes	1849 (Ref 10)
Peasley Jct to Pocket Nook Jct (in part)	11. 1869 (Ref 10)
Gerard's Bridge Jct to Rainford Jct	1890 (Ref 3)

Double lines converted to quadruple track:

200 yds north of Sutton Oak Jct to Clock Face Sidings	See Note 7
Ditton Jct to Speke	1884 (Ref 3)
Ditton Jct to Widnes	2. 2. 1885 (Ref 3)

Converted from quadruple to double track :

Sutton Oak Jct to Clock Face Sidings	1969 (Ref 13)

Converted from double to single track :

Sutton Oak Jct to Farnworth and Bold [Note 8]	14. 12. 1969 (Ref 10)
Farnworth and Bold to Widnes No. 1	4. 11. 1973 (Ref 15)
St Helens to Leathers Ground Frame	See Note 9

Closed:

Broad Oak Jct (Fleet Lane) to Broad Oak Colliery	See Notes10 and 11
Pocket Nook to Gerard's Bridge (original alignment)	See Note 12
Haydock Jct to Old Fold [Note 13]	6 4. 1964 (Ref 7)
Fleet Lane Level Crossing to Carr Mill Jct	6. 4. 1964 (Ref 7)
Sutton Oak Jct to Fleet Lane Crossing [Note 14]	6.10. 1969 (Ref 10)
Eccleston Branch, Marsh's Xing to Triplex Wks [Note 15]	10.10. 1967 (Ref 10)
Pilkington Bros Oil Terminal (Bibby's Sdg) to End of Ravenhead Branch (Menzies Sdg)	See Note 16
Ravenhead Jct to Pilkington Bros Oil Terminal [Note 17]	22. 6. 1992 (Ref 16)
St Helens to St Helens Jct for passengers	14. 6. 1965 (Ref 10)
Peasley Jct to Pocket Nook Jct	4. 5. 1970 (Ref 17)
Leathers GF to St Helens Jct via high level lines at Sutton Oak Jct	27. 1. 1989 (Ref 7)
Gerard's Bridge Jct to Rainford Jct for passrs [Note 18]	wef 18. 6. 1951 (Ref 7)
Randle Jct to Bushey Lane Jct	See Note 19
Rainford Jct to Old Mill Lane Sdg for goods	6. 7. 1964 (Ref 10)
Old Mill Lane Sdgs to Pilkingtons Sdg	30. 1. 1967 (Ref 10)
Sutton Oak Jct to Widnes for passrs [Note 20]	wef 18. 6. 1951 (Ref 18)
Lugsdale Branch (Lugsdale Depot closed) [Note 21]	1. 4. 1966 (Ref 11)
Clock Face Colliery Sdgs (Sutton Manor Colliery) to Farnworth and Bold closed to all traffic	1.11. 1981 (Ref 10)
Farnworth and Bold to Widnes No. 7 taken out of use [Note 22]	18. 4. 1982 (Ref 10)
Sutton Oak Jct to Clock Face Colliery Sdgs (Sutton Manor Colliery) [Note 23]	10.10. 1987 (Ref 7)
Warrington to Ditton Jct for passengers [Note 24]	10. 9. 1962 (Ref 10)
Widnes West Deviation Jct to Ditton Jct (Original St Helens Rly tracks)	14. 2. 1966 (Ref 10)
Widnes No. 4 to Canal Bridge taken out of use	4.11. 1968 (Ref 11)
Carterhouse Jct to Widnes West Deviation Jct (original St Helens Railway alignment via Waterloo Road Level Crossing) [Note 25]	2.12. 1968 (Ref 10)
Widnes No. 7 to Widnes No. 1 [Note 26]	18. 4. 1982 (Ref 10)

Still in use :

For passenger and freight

St Helens to Gerard's Bridge Jct

For freight only

Gerard's Bridge Junction to Pilkingtons Siding (Oil Terminal)
St Helens to Heys Chemical Co's Works (former Leathers Ground Frame)
Ditton Junction to Warrington (Arpley) via 1885 goods lines and deviation built by LNWR

Notes   1   Reference 1 gives 19. 7. 1864.
        2   This was the formal opening date. The first coal train ran from Broad Oak Colliery to Widnes on 28.11.1832 as the result of a wager (Ref 10).
        3   Later known as the Gas Works Branch or the Lugsdale Branch. Probably opened in 1851 or 1852.
        4   Probably 1833 or 1834.
        5   The first section of the branch was ready for use in December 1832 (Ref 10). The remaining mile to the Ravenhead Plate Glass Works was not opened until 1851 or 1852 (See Chapter 6).
        6   This line continued to Gillars Green under an agreement with the landowner. There was a trial trip over the whole line on 2. 3. 1859 (Ref 19). There was probably little if any traffic beyond Boundary Road until Gillars Green Colliery opened around 1873. For further information see Chapter 7.
        7   Probably about 1885.
        8   Reference 14 gives early 1970.
        9   Not known, probably about 1990.
     10   The name Broad Oak Junction was applied to different places at different dates. Sutton Oak Junction was originally known as Broad Oak Junction. After the line was extended to Blackbrook, the name Broad Oak Junction appears to have been used to describe the location later known as Fleet Lane. Latterly the signal box between Peasley and Sutton Oak, where the spur to Marsh's Siding diverged was named Broad Oak Junction.
     11   No traffic after closure of Broad Oak Colliery in 1858 or early in 1859. First 3 furlongs of track bed sold to Lancashire Union Railways in 1869 and used for Havannah Branch. For reopening and final closure see below.
     12   Replaced north of Pocket Nook Junction by new line to Rainford.
     13   LNWR Sidings Diagram No. 189 shows that only the first 571 yards of the Branch were the property of the railway company. The rest of the line to Old Fold was the property of Richard Evans and Co Ltd and later of the National Coal Board.
     14   According to Reference 11 Sutton Oak Jct to Fleet Lane singled. Sutton Oak Jct. to Marsh's Sdgs became siding after July 1966 and later taken out of use.
     15   First 100 yards retained for access to Pilkington Bros crate yard.
     16   By early 1979 reduced to sidings status and Marsh's Crossing Signal Box and Ground Frames at Menzies Sdg and Ravenhead Sdg closed (Ref 20). Last Traffic at some date between 1984 and 1988.
     17   Replaced by new terminal and branch - See British Railways section.
     18   Used for excursion trains after that date.
     19   Not known, probably about 1964.
     20   Available for passenger train diversions until Widnes No. 7 to Sutton Oak Jct reduced in status to goods line December 1967 (Ref 10). Despite this, there were diversions between Ditton Jct, Widnes No. 7 and St Helens on 2nd December 1973 (Ref 15).

21   Portion from bridge under LNWR deviation line to bridge under GC&M line transferred to ICI Ltd 29.12.1945 (Ref 21).

22   Line cut as through route 1.11.1981, last traffic some days before that (Ref 22).

23   Sutton Manor to Sutton Oak closed officially 2.10.1987. Out of use since 15.8.1987 (Ref 23).

24   Widnes Station closed to regular passenger traffic at this date, but used by excursion trains until 1965. Warrington to Ditton Junction line used by York and Liverpool mail trains until rerouted on 4. 1. 1965 (Ref 9). Carterhouse Jct to West Deviation Jct was built by LNWR (see below).

25   Portion at east end retained to serve Albright and Wilson's works and from 1972 a roadstone terminal. Reference 7 gives 3.1969 as date of closure of section from Widnes No. 4 to West Deviation Jct.

26   Widnes No. 7 to Widnes No. 2 built by LNWR after takeover of St Helens Railway. See below.

Lancashire Union Railways

Absorbed by LNWR   1.10. 1883   (Ref 8)

Opened:

Gerards Bridge Jct to Ince Moss Jct for goods	1.11. 1869	(Ref 1)
Gerards Bridge Jct to Ince Moss Jct for passengers	1.12. 1869	(Ref 1)
Broad Oak Jct (Fleet Lane) to Havannah Colliery [Note 1]	8. 1870	(Ref 24)

Double line converted to four tracks:

Carr Mill Jct to Ince Moss Jct	16.10. 1892	(Ref 8)

Converted from four tracks to double track :

Carr Mill Jct to Garswood Hall	4 . 5. 1958	(Ref 8)
Garswood Hall to Ince Moss Jct	25. 8. 1958	(Ref 8)

Closed :

Fleet Lane Level Crossing to Havannah Colliery [Note 2]	3. 6. 1951	(Ref 18)

Still in use
  Gerard's Bridge Junction to Ince Moss Junction and thence to Wigan

Notes   1   The first 3 furlongs purchased from LNWR in 1869 and had originally been part of the Broad Oak Colliery Branch.

          2   Connection to Havannah Branch spiked out of use by August 1947. Work ordered to recover branch 19.3.1951 (Ref 23). Portion of branch beyond the connection with Richard Evans and Co's (later National Coal Board) line to Old Fold may have been taken out of use following the closure of Havannah Collieries in 1936.

Warrington and Altrincham Junction Railway

Became Warrington and Stockport Railway   1. 9. 1853
Absorbed jointly by LNWR and St Helens Canal and Rly   13. 8. 1859
Became LNWR property (see Chap 2)   1860

Opened:

Wilderspool to Broadheath	1.11. 1853	(Ref 25)
Throughout from Arpley (Junction with St Helens Railway) to		
Timperley Jct	1 . 5. 1854	(Ref 25)
Arpley Jct to Walton Jct	See Note 1	

Closed:

Thelwall to south side of Ship Canal [Note 2]	8. 7 .1893	(Ref 1)
Latchford to north side of Ship Canal [Note 2]	8. 7. 1893	(Ref 1)
Warrington to Timperley Jct for passengers [Note 3]	10. 9. 1962	(Ref 10)
Warrington to Broadheath Jct for goods [Note 4]	8. 7. 1985	(Ref 26)
From connection to Greenall's Brewery siding to exchange sidings with Manchester Ship Canal Railway at Latchford [Note 5]	1. 4. 1968	(Ref 7)
Arpley to connection to Greenall's Brewery siding	See Note 6	

Still in use for freight only :

Walton Old Junction to Arpley Headshunt

Notes   1   Arpley Jct to Walton Jct inspected 8.11.1855, but not opened immediately (Ref 25). Probably opened late 1855 or early 1856. Walton Junction later renamed Walton Old Junction.

            2   Replaced by Ship Canal Deviation opened for goods traffic on 17.2.1893 (Ref 9) and for pasengers on 9.7.1893 (Ref 1). Old alignment from Latchford to west side of Ship Canal later used for access to private sidings and Manchester Ship Canal Railway.

            3   Includes Ship Canal Deviation built after absorption by LNWR. Timperley Jct to Broadheath Jct closed to all traffic on this date and subsequently lifted. Broadheath Jct to Warrington used by York and Liverpool mail trains until rerouted on 4. 1. 1965 (Ref 10). Broadheath Jct to Walton Old Jct was used by summer season expresses until 19.9.1971 (Ref 27). It was also used for Sunday diversions, as in March 1980.

            4   Includes Ship Canal Deviation built after absorption by LNWR. Arpley Jct to point short of Latchford Station retained as head shunt for reversal of trains between Walton Old Jct and Widnes line.

            5   Portion of original alignment from Latchford to Thelwall.

            6   Remaining portion of original alignment from Latchford to Thelwall. Date of closure not known.

Lines built in the St Helens area after absorption of St Helens Railway by LNWR

Opened:

Huyton Quarry to St Helens - for goods	18.12. 1871	(Ref 10)
- for passengers	1. 1. 1872	(Ref 10)
Blackbrook Colliery to Carr Mill Jct	23. 2. 1880	(Ref 10)
Sutton Oak Jct to St Helens Jct (Dive under passr lines)	See Note 1	
Broad Oak Jct (Peasley) to Marsh's Siding [Note 2]	See Note 3	
Broad Oak Jct (Peasley) to Sutton Oak Jct goods		
curve [Note 2]	See Note 4	

Closed:

Broad Oak Jct (Peasley) to Sutton Oak Jct (goods curve)	See Note 5	
Broad Oak Jct (Peasley) to Marsh's Siding	6.10. 1969	(Ref 10)
St Helens Jct to Sutton Oak dive-under lines		
- closed for passenger traffic	14. 6. 1965	(Ref 10)
- taken out of use	2. 3. 1969	(Ref 10)

Still in use :

Huyton Quarry to St Helens

Notes 1   Not known, probably about 1883 or 1884.

       2   The name Broad Oak Junction was applied to different places at different dates. The Broad Oak Junction referred to here was located between Peasley and Sutton Oak, where the spur to Marsh's Siding diverged.

       3   Probably before 1870.

       4   This curve ran on the north side of the original St Helens Railway line and was probably opened about 1900.

       5   Connection at Sutton Oak Jct taken out by 1926, when the 25 inch Ordnance Survey map was revised.

Lines built at Widnes and Runcorn after absorption of St Helens Railway by LNWR

Opened

Carterhouse Jct to West Deviation Jct (Widnes No. 8) and		
connection from St Helens line (Widnes No. 2 to Widnes No. 7)		
- for goods	1.12. 1865	(Ref 10)
- for passengers and new station at Widnes	1. 3. 1866	(Ref 10)
West Deviation Jct to Ditton Jct (goods lines)	2. 2. 1885	(Ref 3)
Ditton Jct to Runcorn for goods traffic	6. 1868	(Ref 11)
Runcorn to Birdswood Jct for goods traffic [Note 1]	1. 2. 1869	(Ref 1)
Ditton Junction to Birdswood Jct for passr traffic [Note 1]	1. 4. 1869	(Ref 1)
Runcorn Docks Branch (goods only)	See Note 2	
Halton Junction to Frodsham Junction	1. 5. 1873	(Ref 1)

Closed:

Carterhouse Junction to West Deviation Jct for passenger
   traffic   [Note 3]   10. 9. 1962 (Ref 10)
Connecting line Widnes No. 2 to Widnes No. 7
  - for pasenger traffic   [Note 4]   18. 6. 1951 (Ref 10)
  - for goods traffic   18. 4. 1982 (Ref 10)
Halton Junction to Frodsham Junction [Note 5]   5. 5. 1975 (Refs 28,29)

Still in use :

For passenger and freight

Weaver Junction to Ditton Jct and thence to Speke and Liverpool

For freight only

Ditton Junction to Warrington (Arpley) via 1885 goods lines and deviation
Runcorn Dock Branch

Notes   1   Birdswood Junction remodelled as Weaver Junction.
        2   Possibly at same date as Ditton Junction to Runcorn section.
        3   Widnes Station closed to regular passenger traffic at this date, but used by
            excursion trains until 1965. Warrington to Ditton Junction used by York
            and Liverpool mail trains until rerouted on 4th January 1965 (Ref 10).
            Only section from Carterhouse Jct to West Deviation Jct built by LNWR.
        4   Available for passenger train diversions until Widnes No. 7 to Sutton Oak
            Jct reduced in status to goods line Dec 1967 (Ref 10). But there were also
            passenger diversions on 2.12.1973 using the line between Speke Jct and
            St Helens via Widnes No. 7, Widnes No. 2 and Sutton Oak Jct (Ref 15).
        5   Out of regular use except for one Summer Saturday train.

Lines at Warrington and Newton le Willows built after formation of LNWR

Opened:

Winwick Junction to Golborne Junction   1. 8. 1864 (Ref 1)
Manchester Ship Canal Deviation - Moore to Warrington
   (Bank Quay) via Acton Grange Jct
    - for goods trains   27. 2. 1893 (Ref 9)
    - for passenger trains   9. 7. 1893 (Ref 1)
Manchester Ship Canal Deviation - Latchford to Thelwall
    - for goods trains   27. 2. 1893 (Ref 9)
    - for passenger trains   9. 7. 1893 (Ref 1)

Closed:

Manchester Ship Canal Deviation - Latchford to Thelwall
    - for passenger trains   [Note 1]   10. 9. 1962 (Ref 10)
    - for goods trains   8. 7. 1985 (Ref 26)

Note   1   Used by York and Liverpool mail trains until rerouted on 4th January 1965 (Ref 10) and by summer season expresses until 19.9.1971 (Ref 27). Also used for Sunday diversions, as in March 1980.

LONDON AND NORTH WESTERN AND GREAT WESTERN JOINT LINES

Became LMSR and GWR joint property	1. 1. 1923
Became British Railways	1. 1. 1948

Birkenhead, Lancashire and Cheshire Junction Rly

Amalgamated with Chester and Birkenhead Railway	22. 7. 1847	(Ref 1)
Name changed to Birkenhead Railway	1. 8 .1859	(Ref 1)
Became LNWR and GWR joint property	1. 1 .1860	(See Chap 1)

Opened:

Chester to Walton Junction [Note 1]	18. 2. 1850	(Ref 1)

Closed:

Daresbury to south side of Ship Canal and north side of Ship Canal to Walton Old Jct [Note 2]	8. 7 .1894	(Ref 1)

Still in use :

Throughout via Ship Canal Deviation lines, except for portion between Walton New Jct and Acton Grange Viaduct.

Notes   1   Later renamed Walton Old Junction.
           2   Replaced by Ship Canal Deviation opened for goods traffic on 17.2.1893 (Ref 9) and for pasengers on 9.7.1893 (Ref 1). Old alignment from Walton Old Jct to north side of Ship Canal later used for access to Manchester Ship Canal Railway. South side of Ship Canal to Daresbury retained as siding until about 1970.

Lines built after absorption by LNWR and GWR

Opened :

Manchester Ship Canal Deviation (Daresbury - Acton Grange Jct - Walton Old Jct) - for goods trains	27. 2. 1893	(Ref 9)
- for passenger trains	9. 7. 1893	(Ref 1)
Manchester Ship Canal Deviation (Acton Grange Jct - Walton New Jct)	16. 7. 1894	(Ref 1)

Closed :

Walton New Junction to Acton Grange Viaduct	1968 (Ref 25)

GREAT WESTERN RAILWAY

Shrewsbury and Chester Railway

Absorbed by Great Western Railway	1. 9. 1854	(Ref 30)
Opened:		
Norton to Bridgewater Canal at Preston Brook	10. 1853	(Ref 25)
Closed:		
Norton to Preston Brook	By 1880	(Ref 25)

GREAT CENTRAL, GREAT NORTHERN AND MIDLAND JOINT LINES (CHESHIRE LINES COMMITTEE)

Became LNER and LMSR Joint Property	1. 1. 1923	
Became British Railways	1. 1. 1948	

Opened:

Skelton Junction to Cressington via Warrington Central		
- for goods traffic	1. 3. 1873	(Ref 1)
- for passenger traffic	1. 8 .1873	(Ref 1)
Cornbrook Jct to Glazebrook East Jct	2. 9 .1873	(Ref 1)
Warrington Straight Line (Padgate Jct to Sankey Jct)		
- for goods traffic	13. 8. 1883	(Ref 1)
- for passenger traffic	7. 9. 1883	(Ref 1)
Dallam Forge Branch at Warrington	See Note 1	
Whitecross Branch at Warrington	See Note 1	
Ship Canal Deviation (Irlam to Flixton)		
- for goods traffic	9. 1. 1893	(Ref 1)
- for passenger traffic	6. 3. 1893	(Ref 1)
Ship Canal Deviation (Glazebrook to Partington)		
- for goods traffic	27. 2. 1893	(Ref 1)
- for passenger traffic	29. 5. 1893	(Ref 1)
Glazebrook (Dam Lane Jct) to Glazebrook Moss Jct	1. 7. 1900	(Ref 31)

Closed:

Irlam to west side of Ship Canal and east side of Ship Canal to Flixton [Note 2]	25. 3. 1893	
Glazebrook to west side of Ship Canal and east side of Ship Canal to Partington [Note 3]	28. 5. 1893	
Glazebrook East Jct to Skelton Jct for passenger traffic	20.11. 1964	(Ref 7)
Glazebrook East Jct to Partington Jct [Note 4]	3. 8. 1982	(Refs 32to34)

Partington Jct to Skelton Jct	See Note 5	
Dam Lane Jct to Glazebrook Moss Jct [Note 6]	11. 5. 1965	(Ref 7)
Padgate Jct to Sankey Jct (Warrington Straight Line)	22. 7. 1968	(Ref 7)
Warrington (Bewsey) to Dallam Forge out of use by	1. 1970	(Ref 7)
Warrington (Bewsey) to Whitecross Wire Works	6. 1970	(Ref 7)

Double track converted to single track

Skelton Jct to Partington Jct	6. 1964	(Refs 35,36)

Still in use:

Manchester Central to Allerton Jct and thence to Liverpool Lime Street

Notes		
	1	Not known, probably in the mid 1870s.
	2	Replaced by Ship Canal Deviation. Line at Irlam transferred to Manchester Ship Canal Railways. Line at Flixton abandoned.
	3	Replaced by Ship Canal Deviation. Lines on both sides transferred to Manchester Ship Canal Railways.
	4	Freight trains ceased earlier. Last use was by a ballast train on 29.7.1982. Officially taken out of use on date quoted above. (Refs 32,33,34).
	5	Not in use in 1997 and probably no regular traffic for a year or two before that.
	6	Last passenger services were workmen's trains between Wigan and Risley CLC station which finished as from 2. 1.1961 (Ref 37).

GREAT CENTRAL AND MIDLAND JOINT COMMITTEE'S LINES

Became LNER and LMSR joint property	1. 1. 1923	
Became British Railways	1. 1. 1948	

Opened:

Widnes West Junction to Tanhouse Lane for goods [Note 1]	3. 4. 1877	(Ref 10)
Curve to Widnes East Junction [Note 2]	17. 4. 1878	(Ref 10)
Tanhouse Lane to Hough Green Jct for goods [Notes 3, 4]	1. 7. 1879	(Ref 10)
Throughout from Widnes East Junction to Hough Green		
for passenger traffic	1. 8. 1879	(Ref 10)
Ditton Marsh Bch (Moor Lane Jct to Ditton Iron Wks)[Note 4]	1. 7. 1879	(Ref 10)
Landowners Branch (Moor Lane Jct to Broughton Copper		
Works, Ditton,and Broughton Copper Works to Liver Alkali		
Works, Widnes)	See Note 5	

Closed:

Curve to Widnes West Jct	28. 2. 1880	(Ref 10)
Hough Green Jct to Widnes East Jct	5.10. 1964	(Ref 7)
Landowners Branch and line to Liver Alkali Wks	1. 6. 1953	(Ref 10)
Ditton Marsh Branch	1964	(Ref 10)

Notes 1 Authorised by Widnes Railway Act. The Widnes Railway was absorbed by the Manchester, Sheffield and Lincolnshire Railway on 16.7.1874 and transferred to the Sheffield and Midland Joint Committee on 29.6.1875. The Sheffield and Midland Joint Committee was renamed the Great Central and Midland Joint Committee on 22.7.1904 (See Chapter 2).

2 Authorised by Sheffield and Midland Joint Committee Act.

3 Tanhouse Lane to Moor Lane authorised by Sheffield and Midland Joint Committee Act.

4 Construction of the line from Hough Green Jct to Moor Lane and the Ditton Marsh Branch was started by the West Widnes Railway. This railway was taken over by the Sheffield and Midland Joint Committee on 17.6.1878 (See Chapter 2).

5 The date of opening is not known but was probably in the 1880s.

GREAT CENTRAL RAILWAY

Became LNER	1. 1. 1923
Became British Railways	1. 1. 1948

Wigan Junction Railway

Worked by MS&LR and later by GCR	
Absorbed by GCR	1. 1. 1906

Opened:

Glazebrook to Strangeways Colliery for coal traffic	16.10. 1879	(Ref 31)
Glazebrook to Strangeways Colliery for goods traffic	17.10. 1879	(Ref 31)
Glazebrook to Wigan (Darlington St) for passenger traffic	1. 4. 1884	(Ref 1)
Wigan (Darlington St) to Wigan (Central) for passr traffic	3.10. 1892	(Ref 1)

Closed:

Glazebrook West Jct to Wigan (Central) for passr traffic	2.11. 1964	(Ref 7)
Lowton St Mary's to Hindley South for goods traffic	4. 1. 1965	(Ref 7)
Glazebrook West Jct to Lowton St Mary's for goods trafic	26. 4. 1968	(Ref 7)

St Helens and Wigan Junction Railway

Became Liverpool, St Helens and South Lancashire Rly	26. 7. 1889
Worked by MS&LR and later GCR	
Absorbed by GCR	1. 1. 1906

Opened

Throughout for goods traffic [Note 1]	1. 7. 1895	(Ref 31)
Throughout for passenger traffic [Note 2]	3. 1. 1900	(Ref 31)

Closed:

Throughout for passenger traffic [Note 3]	3. 3. 1952 (Ref 38)
Ashton in Makerfield to St Helens Central for goods traffic [Note 4]	4. 1. 1965 (Ref 38)
Lowton St Mary's to Edge Green for goods traffic [Note 5]	22. 4 .1968 (Ref 40)
Edge Green to Ashton in Makerfield for goods traffic	3. 1987 (Ref 40)

Still in use :

Edge Green, junction with chord line from Golborne LNWR, to connection with Kelbit Ltd's sidings and headshunt.

Notes

1   Worked by contractor's locomotives between Golborne and St Helens until 21.10.1895 (Ref 31).

2   Special trains from Lowton to Haydock Park Race Course in February 1899 (Ref 31).

3   Special trains to Haydock Park Race Course Station ran via Lowton St Mary's up to and including 1963. Special trains for the Races also ran, for one year only, in 1975, to Ashton in Makerfield via the new chord line. Dates of operation were 22.5.1975, 7.6.1975, 7.1975, 9.8.1975 and 4.10.1975 (Ref 39).

4   Ashton in Makerfield to Haydock Oil Depot reopened July 1968. Closed again between Ashton in Makerfield and Haydock in February 1983 (Ref 40).

5   New chord line opened from Golborne to Edge Green on this date (Ref 40). See under British Railways.

LONDON AND NORTH EASTERN RAILWAY

Became British Railways	1. 1. 1948

Opened:

Newchurch to Risley Royal Ordnance Factory (workmen's service)	See Note 1

Closed:

Newchurch to Risley Royal Ordnance Factory (workmen's service) [Note 2]	as from 3. 12. 1945

Notes

1   This line was probably Government property but was operated by the London and North Eastern Railway. The line seems to have opened in 1942 or possibly early 1943 when the workmen's service from St Helens and Wigan started (Ref 37).

2   The workmen's trains from St Helens ceased to use the line as from 3.12.1945 when they were diverted to Risley CLC station via Dam Lane Jct at Glazebrook (Ref 37). It appears that the line was mothballed for a few years after that.

BRITISH RAILWAYS

Lines built by British Railways (Goods traffic only)

Opened:

Connection from Ditton Marsh Branch to ex LNWR line near Ditton	See Note 1	
Chord line Golborne LNW to Edge Green GC [Note 2]	22. 4. 1968	(Ref 40)
Glazebrook East Junction to Irlam Steelworks	See Note 3	
Tanhouse Lane to U S A C Works, Widnes [Note 4]	15.11. 1954	(Ref 41)
Widnes No. 1 to Tanhouse Lane	16. 3. 1961	(Ref 11)
Carterhouse Jct to Tanhouse Lane	18. 4. 1982	(Ref 11)
Spur from Huyton and St Helens line to Pilkington Bros Ltd Oil Terminal at Bibby's Yard	15.10. 1992	(Ref 42)

Closed

Connection from Ditton Marsh Branch to ex LNWR line near Ditton		See Note 5	
Widnes No. 1 to Tanhouse Lane	as from	18. 4. 1982	(Ref 11)
Glazebrook East Jct to Irlam Steelworks		See Note 6	

Still in use for freight only :

Golborne chord
Carterhouse Jct - Tanhouse Lane - Cement Terminal (on site of USAC Works)
Spur to Pilkington Bros Oil Terminal

Notes		
	1	Probably about 1953 or 1954.
	2	Used by special passenger trains to Ashton in Makerfield, in connection with Haydock Park Races, during 1975 (Ref 38).
	3	Opening date not recorded, probably about 1957.
	4	Date is that of first test train.
	5	Probably in 1964, when Ditton Marsh Branch closed.
	6	Probably in 1979, when Irlam Steelworks closed.

References to Chronology

1 *Chronological List of the Railways of Lancashire and Cheshire*, M.D.Greville, Revised Edition, Railway and Canal Historical Society, 1981

2 *Crewe to Carlisle*, Brian Reed, Ian Allan, 1969

3 *Railway Reminiscences*, G.P.Neele, McCorquodale, London, 1904

4 Note on Plan of Railways at Warrington, No 2, 1:1250, BR, Euston, 1970, at BRPB, Manchester Office

5 *A Guide to Closed Railway Lines in Britain*, N.J.Hill and A.O.McDougall, Branch Line Society, Feb 1977

6 *BLN* 409

7 *Register of Closed Railways - 1948 to 1991*, Geoffrey Hurst, Milepost Publications, Worksop, 1992

8 *The Lancashire Union Railways*, John Marshall, *Railway Magazine*, April, May, June 1970

9 *Railways of the Manchester Ship Canal*, Don Thorpe, Oxford Publishing Co Ltd, Poole, 1984

10 *The St Helens Railway*, J.M.Tolson, The Oakwood Press, 1982

11 Information supplied by Mr J.M.Tolson

12 *WO* 11.12.1857

13 *BLN* 163

14 *BLN* 157

15 *BLN* 238

16 *BLN* 698

17 Note on Line Plan of St Helens Railway, Widnes to 8 MP, 2 chains to 1 inch, LMSR, Euston, 1925, at BRPB, Manchester Office

18 *LNWR Chronology 1900 - 1960*, C.R.Clinker, David and Charles, Dawlish, 1961

19 *St Helens Intelligencer* 5.3.1859

20 *BLN* 370

21 Note on Line Plan of Sheffield and Midland Joint Railway, 2 chains to 1 inch, no date, no publisher, at BRPB Manchester Office.

22 *BLN* 430

23 *BLN* 573

24 Sidings Schedules 18 and 18A

25 *Waterways and Railways to Warrington*, Peter Norton, Railway and Canal Historical Society, 1974

26 *BLN* 523

27 *BLN* 273

28 *BLN* 266

29 *BLN* 272

30 *History of the Great Western Railway*, E.T.Macdermott, Great Western Rly Co, London, in two vols, 1927 and 1931

31 *Great Central*, G.Dow, Ian Allan, London, in three volumes, 1959, 1962, 1965

32 *BLN* 431

33 *BLN* 441

34 *BLN* 454

35 *BLN* 493

36 *BLN* 496

37 *Mancunian*, Journal of the Manchester Locomotive Society, No 122, Sept 1984

38 Ibid No 124, Jan 1985

39 Information supplied by Mr Bob Miller

40 Information supplied by Mr Richard Maund

41 Sidings Schedule 42

42 *BLN* 694

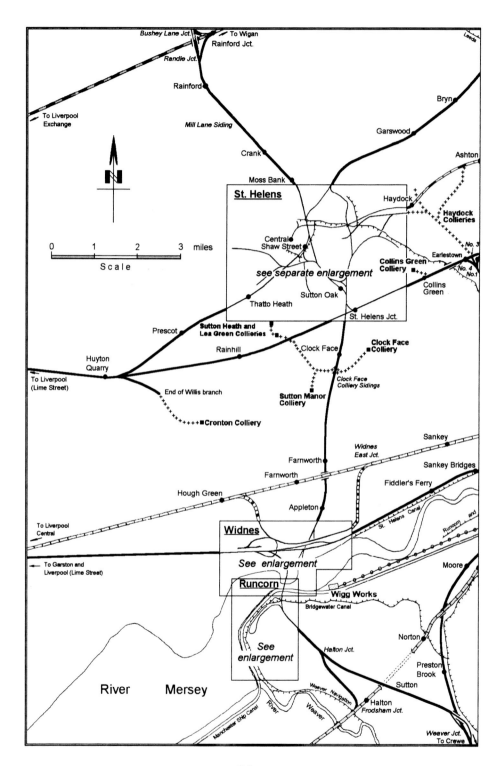

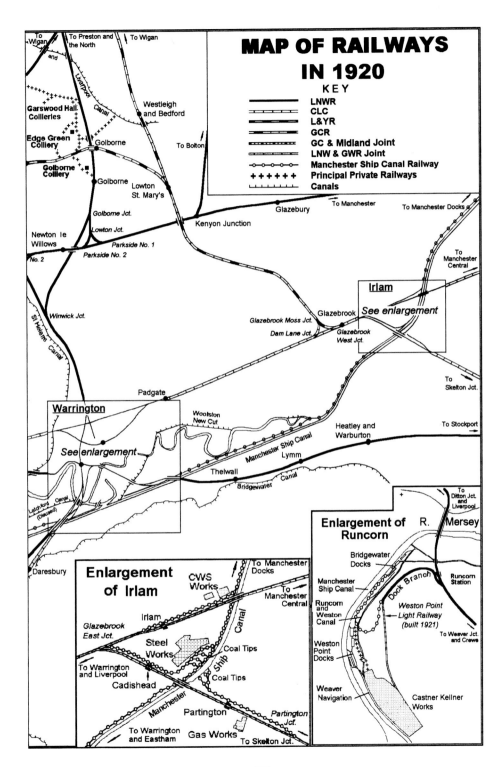

MAP OF RAILWAYS IN 1920

KEY

─────	LNWR
─+─+─+─	CLC
━━━━━	L&YR
═════	GCR
══╪══╪══	GC & Midland Joint
─═─═─═─	LNW & GWR Joint
─o─o─o─	Manchester Ship Canal Railway
+ + + + + +	Principal Private Railways
┴┴┴┴┴┴	Canals

To Wigan
and

To Preston and the North

To Wigan

Liverpool Canal

Garswood Hall Collieries

Edge Green Colliery

Golborne

Westleigh and Bedford

To Bolton

Golborne Colliery

Golborne

Lowton St. Mary's

Golborne Jct.

Lowton Jct.

Newton le Willows

Parkside No. 1

Parkside No. 2

No. 2

Glazebury

Kenyon Junction

To Manchester

To Manchester Docks

To Manchester Central

Winwick Jct.

St Helens Canal

Irlam
See enlargement

Glazebrook

Glazebrook Moss Jct.

Dam Lane Jct.

Glazebrook West Jct.

To Skelton Jct.

Padgate

Woolston New Cut

Heatley and Warburton

To Stockport

Warrington

See enlargement

Manchester Ship Canal

Lymm

Thelwall

Bridgewater Canal

Latchford Canal (Disused)

Daresbury

Enlargement of Irlam

CWS Works

To Manchester Docks

To Manchester Central

Glazebrook East Jct.

Irlam

Canal

Steel Works

Coal Tips

To Warrington and Liverpool

Ship

Coal Tips

Cadishead

Manchester

Partington

Partington Jct.

To Warrington and Eastham

Gas Works

To Skelton Jct.

Enlargement of Runcorn

R. Mersey

To Ditton Jct. and Liverpool

Bridgewater Docks

Manchester Ship Canal

Dock Branch

Runcorn Station

Runcorn and Weston Canal

Weston Point Light Railway (built 1921)

To Weaver Jct. and Crewe

Weston Point Docks

Weaver Navigation

Castner Kellner Works

73

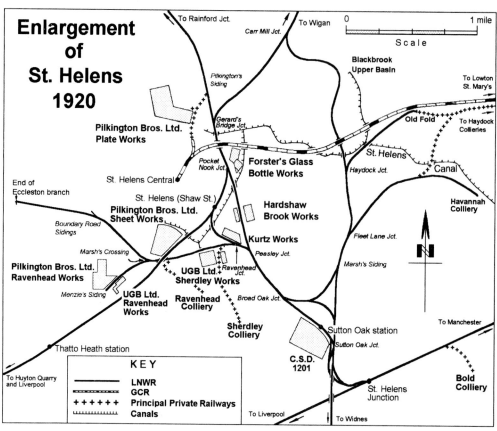

Enlargement
of
St. Helens
1920

To Rainford Jct.

Carr Mill Jct.

To Wigan

Scale
0 — 1 mile

Blackbrook
Upper Basin

To Lowton
St. Mary's

Pilkington's
Siding

Gerard's
Bridge Jct.

Old Fold

To Haydock
Collieries

**Pilkington Bros. Ltd.
Plate Works**

Pocket
Nook Jct.

**Forster's Glass
Bottle Works**

St. Helens

Canal

St. Helens Central

Haydock Jct.

End of
Eccleston branch

St. Helens (Shaw St.)

**Hardshaw
Brook Works**

Havannah
Colliery

**Pilkington Bros. Ltd.
Sheet Works**

Boundary Road
Sidings

Kurtz Works

Fleet Lane Jct.

Marsh's Crossing

Peasley Jct.

Marsh's Siding

N

**Pilkington Bros. Ltd.
Ravenhead Works**

**UGB Ltd.
Sherdley Works**

Ravenhead
Jct.

Menzie's Siding

**UGB Ltd.
Ravenhead
Works**

**Ravenhead
Colliery**

Broad Oak Jct.

To Manchester

**Sherdley
Colliery**

Sutton Oak station

Sutton Oak Jct.

Thatto Heath station

**C.S.D.
1201**

**Bold
Colliery**

To Huyton Quarry
and Liverpool

K E Y

——— **LNWR**
-·-·-·- **GCR**
++++++ **Principal Private Railways**
⊔⊔⊔⊔⊔ **Canals**

St. Helens
Junction

To Liverpool

To Widnes

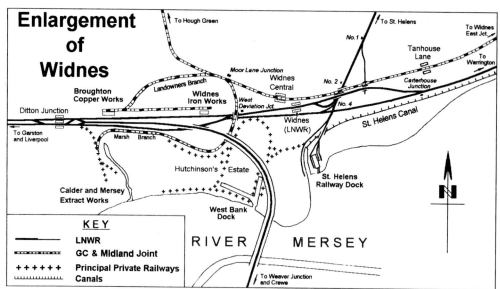

Enlargement
of
Widnes

To Hough Green

To St. Helens

To Widnes
East Jct.

No. 1

Tanhouse
Lane

To
Warrington

Moor Lane Junction

Widnes
Central

No. 2

Carterhouse
Junction

**Broughton
Copper Works**

Landowners Branch

**Widnes
Iron Works**

West
Deviation Jct.

No. 4

Ditton Junction

Widnes
(LNWR)

St. Helens Canal

To Garston
and Liverpool

Marsh Branch

Hutchinson's + Estate

**St. Helens
Railway Dock**

N

**Calder and Mersey
Extract Works**

West Bank
Dock

R I V E R   M E R S E Y

K E Y

——— **LNWR**
-·-·-·- **GC & Midland Joint**
++++++ **Principal Private Railways**
⊔⊔⊔⊔⊔ **Canals**

To Weaver Junction
and Crewe

74

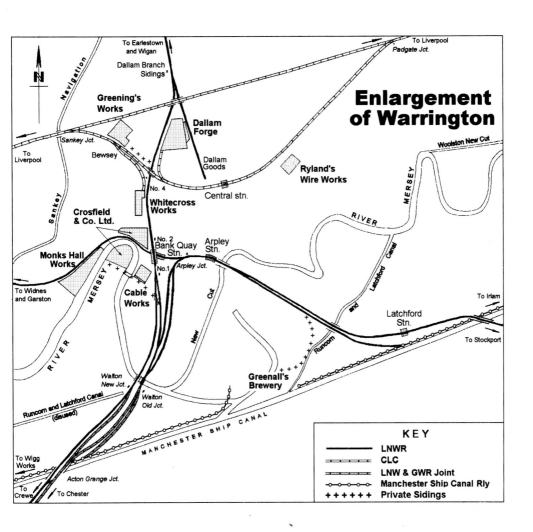

Ravenhead and and Peasley 1996

© Crown Copyright 87627M

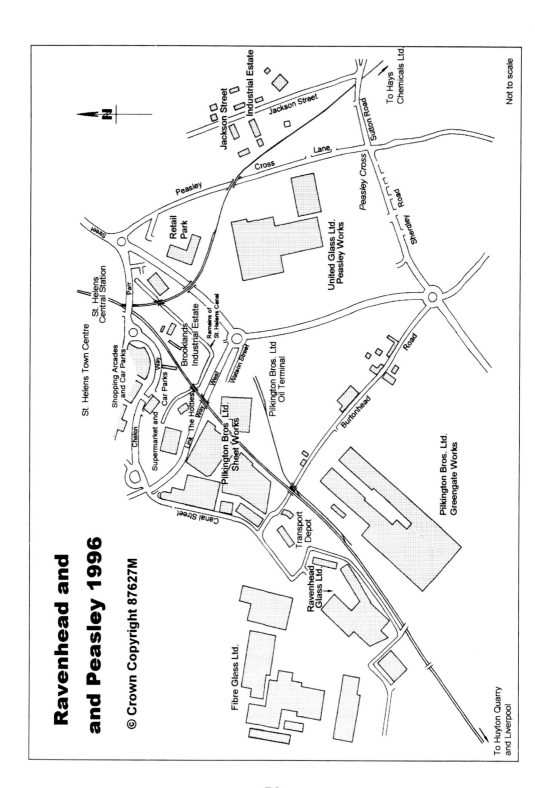

Not to scale

CHAPTER THREE

AROUND RAVENHEAD JUNCTION

Coal mines to the south of St Helens town centre had been opened up in the 1760s by Jonathan Case, who took a lease of the Burtonhead Estate [1] and neighbouring properties. The Ravenhead Branch of the Sankey Navigation and the short Burtonhead arm which led off it provided the means of transporting the coal to Liverpool and elsewhere.

Following Case's bankruptcy in 1778, some of the colliery property was purchased by Thomas Mackay, while the Burtonhead Estate was acquired by Thomas West [1]. By the 1820s, when we pick up the story, other firms had moved in to take over the mines.

The St Helens and Runcorn Gap Railway appeared on the scene in the 1830s. The railway company's Act of 1830 [2] provided for the construction of a line from Sutton Oak to the Ravenhead Plate Glass Works and also several subsidiary branches, including one to Dobsons Wood [3]. A site chosen for the St Helens Station was adjacent to Peasley Cross Lane, later renamed Warrington Old Road, near where the Dobsons Wood line was intended to diverge from the Ravenhead Branch.

The line from the St Helens Station to the Liverpool and Manchester Railway at St Helens Junction was opened for freight traffic on 2nd January 1832 [4] and a portion of the Ravenhead Branch, as far as Ravenhead Colliery, followed in December 1834 [4]. The complicated story of the extension to the Plate Glass Works is dealt with in a later chapter. No work seems to have been carried out by the railway company on the line to Dobsons Wood and it was left to one of the colliery companies to construct a branch of its own to serve this area.

The original railway station at Peasley Cross Lane was replaced by more commodious premises at Raven Street in 1849 [4] which were approached by tracks diverging from the Ravenhead Branch at what later became known as Ravenhead Junction. The final development was the construction of a line from Ravenhead Junction through the third St Helens Station at Shaw Street, which opened in February 1858 [4], at the same date as the passenger train service through to Rainford

Coal mining continued throughout the nineteenth century and well into the twentieth, the last remaining pit closing during the Second World War. Meanwhile in the third quarter of the nineteenth century glassworks and chemical works were established alongside the Ravenhead Branch railway. Glass manufacture is still carried on at the modern works operated by United Glass Containers Ltd, but the remaining sites have been redeveloped and are now unrecognisable.

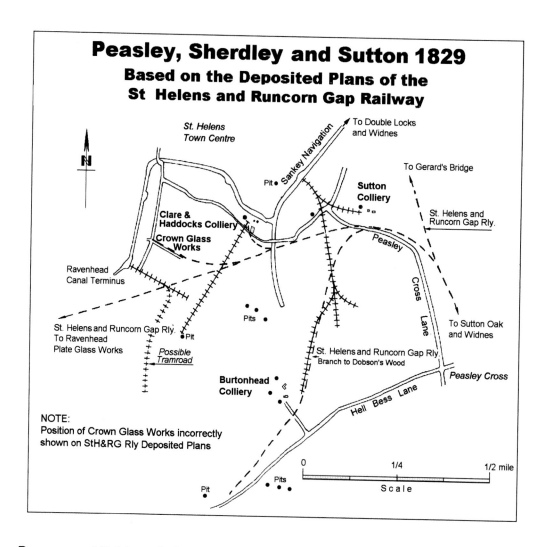

Peasley, Sherdley and Sutton 1829
Based on the Deposited Plans of the
St Helens and Runcorn Gap Railway

St. Helens Town Centre

To Double Locks and Widnes

Sankey Navigation

To Gerard's Bridge

Pit

Sutton Colliery

St. Helens and Runcorn Gap Rly.

Clare & Haddocks Colliery

Crown Glass Works

Peasley

Ravenhead Canal Terminus

Cross Lane

To Sutton Oak and Widnes

St. Helens and Runcorn Gap Rly. To Ravenhead Plate Glass Works

Pit

Pits

Possible Tramroad

St. Helens and Runcorn Gap Rly. Branch to Dobson's Wood

Peasley Cross

Burtonhead Colliery

Hell Bess Lane

NOTE:
Position of Crown Glass Works incorrectly shown on StH&RG Rly Deposited Plans

0   1/4   1/2 mile

Scale

Pits

Pit

Bournes and Robinson's Sutton, Peasley Cross and Sherdley Collieries

The first pits of the Sutton Colliery were sunk by John Bourne in 1812. These appear to have been on the north side of Peasley Cross Lane, on a site later occupied by part of the Kurtz Alkali Works. They were connected by a tramroad to a wharf on the canal where coal could be loaded on to barges [3].

In 1825 the proprietors were recorded as John Bourne and Company [5], in which the brothers John, James and Peter Bourne were partners [6]. In 1824 they had formed a partnership with Robert Robinson, under the title of Bournes and Robinson, to sink a colliery at Elton Head, near Rainhill.

Contemporary directories suggest that until the early 1830s [5,7] Sutton Colliery remained under the control of John Bourne and Company while Robert Robinson was sole proprietor of the Broad Oak Colliery at Parr [7], which we deal with in Part Two. Both collieries were later taken over by the Bournes and Robinson partnership, which also owned a salt works at Winsford, in Cheshire.

By 1829, when the Deposited Plans for the St Helens and Runcorn Gap Railway [3] were prepared, further pits had been sunk at Sutton, to the south of the original site. These, too, were linked to the canal by an extension of the tramroad system.

The branch which the St Helens and Runcorn Gap Railway proposed to build to Dobsons Wood, terminating in the vicinity of Hell Bess Farm, near one of Bournes and Robinson's more southerly pits, would have largely replaced the tramroad. As mentioned earlier, the railway company failed to build this line and it was left to Bournes and Robinson to reconstruct their tramroads as standard gauge railways.

The first edition of the 6 inch map, surveyed in 1846 and 1847, shows the colliery railway running from the Larkhill Pit, south of Hell Bess Lane, and from a Sutton Colliery, near Burtonhead, to the canal wharf. A short branch served pits near Peasley House and another ran from a point near the canal wharf to provide rail access to the Kurtz Alkali Works, then a very small affair. There was a level crossing over the St Helens and Runcorn Gap Railway's Ravenhead Branch and near here a connecting curve which joined the main line at the passenger station. The original Sutton Colliery pits, north of Peasley Cross Lane, do not appear to have been linked to the standard gauge system and the impression is that, by this date, they had gone out of production.

Bournes and Robinson's Ansdale Wood Colliery at Elton Head was already on the point of closure, production ceasing in the late 1840s or early 1850s. When Broad Oak Colliery finished around 1859 the partnership's mining activities were centred on the Sutton area.

Peasley House Colliery first appears in the Mines Lists for 1856 and seems to have been a redevelopment of earlier workings. Its name was changed to Peasley Cross Colliery in 1872, presumably indicating further developments. Sherdley Colliery was sunk on a new site to the south of the Peasley Cross to Lea Green road and first appears in the Mines List for 1873. Surplus plant, apparently used in the construction work at both Peasley Cross and Sherdley, was auctioned on 5th August 1872 [8,9].

By 1881, when the survey was made for the first edition of the 25 inch map, the canal wharf had been abandoned and the level crossing over the Ravenhead Branch had been taken out. The firm's railway system now ran from the exchange sidings with the LNWR to Sherdley Colliery, with a short branch serving Peasley Cross Colliery. The locomotive shed was situated in the fork between the Sherdley and Peasley Cross lines.

Part of the earlier line to Larkhill Pit was retained to serve a brickworks, which the map describes as disused. The remainder of the track had been lifted. The brickworks was presumably the one owned by Pilkington Brothers [10], ordered to be demolished as useless in May 1880 [11], which is known to have had rail access.

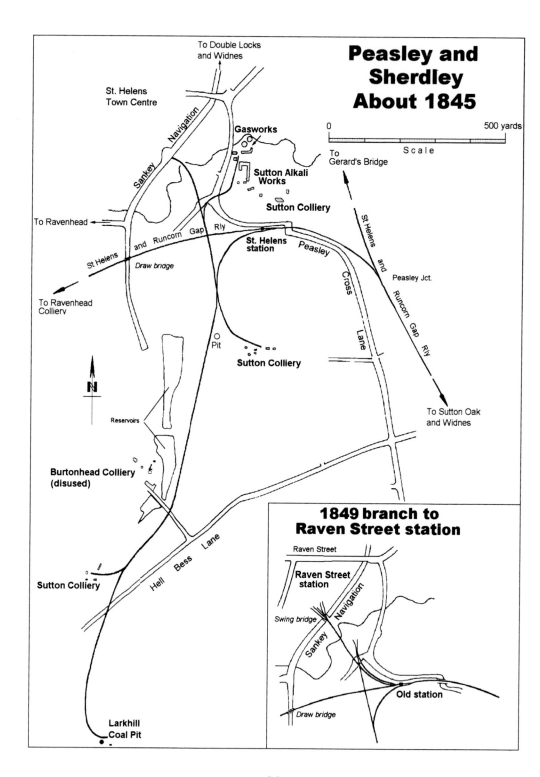

Peasley and Sherdley About 1845

To Double Locks and Widnes

St. Helens Town Centre

Gasworks

Sutton Alkali Works

Sutton Colliery

0   500 yards

Scale

To Gerard's Bridge

To Ravenhead

Sankey Navigation

St Helens and Runcorn Gap Rly

Draw bridge

St Helens

To Ravenhead Colliery

St. Helens station

Peasley Cross Lane

St Helens and Runcorn Gap Rly

Peasley Jct.

Pit

Sutton Colliery

N

Reservoirs

To Sutton Oak and Widnes

Burtonhead Colliery (disused)

1849 branch to Raven Street station

Raven Street

Raven Street station

Sankey Navigation

Swing bridge

Old station

Draw bridge

Sutton Colliery

Hell Bess Lane

Larkhill Coal Pit

Over the years there were numerous changes in the Bournes and Robinson partnership. Robert Robinson retired in April 1857 [12]. Thereafter the firm was entirely in the hands of members of the Bourne family, although the title Bournes and Robinson was retained. In June 1859, when John Thomas Bourne retired [13], the partners, still described as coal and salt proprietors, were recorded as Cornelius Bourne, John Bury Bourne, Thomas Rymer Bourne, James Bourne, Thomas Bourne and Peter Bourne. The salt works must have been sold soon afterwards, as the firm is only described as a colliery proprietor when Thomas Rymer Bourne retired in March 1865 [14].

Between 1876 and 1883 no less than five members of the Bourne family died [15,16,17] and the decision was taken to dispose of the Peasley Cross and Sherdley Collieries. They were sold to the Whitecross Company Ltd, an old established firm which operated steel and wire works at Warrington, the transfer taking place on 1st February 1887 according to the Sidings Schedules.

Before continuing the story of the collieries under their new ownership, mention must be made of the locomotives used by Bournes and Robinson. The firm was quick to take advantage of the opportunities offered by the opening of the Liverpool and Manchester Railway, which passed close to the Ansdale Wood Colliery at Elton Head.

James Bourne, who was also a director of the Liverpool and Manchester Railway, purchased a locomotive from Edward Bury in 1832 [18]. Named COLLIER, it was presumably a typical Bury product with a haystack firebox, bar frames and inside cylinders. The locomotive was passed as fit to run over the Liverpool and Manchester Railway in October 1832 [18] but, because of its 5ft 6in driving wheels, its speed was restricted to 12 mph. As well as hauling coal trains from Elton Head to Liverpool and other destinations on the L&M line, it is more than likely that COLLIER worked to the firm's Sutton and Broad Oak Collieries over the St Helens Railway, although there is no record of this.

In 1834, the Liverpool and Manchester Board received a request from the Leeds and Selby Railway for the loan of a locomotive to open the line on 22nd September [18]. The request was declined and it was suggested that the Leeds and Selby could either buy a Liverpool and Manchester locomotive or alternatively it might be possible to hire COLLIER from Bournes and Robinson. In that case, the Liverpool and Manchester would work Bournes and Robinson's coal trains until COLLIER was returned.

There is no evidence that the Leeds and Selby actually hired COLLIER. If indeed the locomotive ever went to Yorkshire it must only have been for a short period, as it was in Láncashire on 6th November 1834, when it was hauling a coal train which was involved in an accident on the L&M [18].

The next we hear of COLLIER is in April 1836. John Jones of the Viaduct Foundry, Newton le Willows at that time held the contract to operate the locomotives on the St Helens Railway [4]. He had promised to build two new locomotives for the railway company but the Directors discovered that he intended to sell both of them to other customers.

Peasley and Sherdley
About 1880

LNWR to Shaw Street
and Rainford

To Double Locks
and Widnes

St. Helens Canal

LNWR to
Pocket Nook

To Ravenhead

Ravenhead Jct

Lyon Brothers
Glass Works

Warrington
Old Road

LNWR to Ravenhead
and Eccleston

Peasley Jct.

McKechnie's Copper Works

Private line to
Messrs. Bibby's Copper Works

LNWR to
Sutton Oak
and Widnes

Peasley Cross Lane

Peasley Cross
Colliery

Sutton Lodge
Chemical Works

Cannington, Shaw & Co.
Sherdley Glass Works

N

Ell Bess Lane

Marshalls Cross Road

Brickworks
(disused)

Sherdley
Colliery

0   500 yards

S c a l e

82

Evidently one of these customers was Bournes and Robinson and a compromise was reached under which the firm had one of the new locomotives. The St Helens Railway had the other together with COLLIER [4], which Jones must have taken in part payment from Bournes and Robinson.

There is then a gap in our knowledge of Bournes and Robinson's locomotives. It is not known when the firm ceased to work its own trains over the Liverpool and Manchester line although it was possibly some time in the mid 1840s. Perhaps it is significant that two locomotives built by Jones and Potts were advertised for sale in 1844 [19] and that enquiries were directed to either Robert Daglish, of the St Helens Foundry, or to Robin Robinson, of Sutton. There is some circumstantial evidence, which we discuss in Chapter 9, to suggest that these may have been owned by Bournes and Robinson.

By 1870 the firm had at least two standard gauge locomotives in use at Sutton, but no information has survived about them. All we know is that, in March 1869, Pilkington Brothers were seeking to borrow Bournes and Robinson's spare locomotive as the firm's own was in need of repair [20].

In August 1872 it is recorded [21] that Bournes and Robinson bought a second hand locomotive from the London and North Western Railway for £1050, presumably to cater for the extra traffic expected when Sherdley Colliery came into production. It was a relatively new six-coupled machine, with the water tank below the bunker, which had been built by Sharp Stewart and Company of Manchester in 1863 for the Ludlow and Clee Hill Railway and had been taken over by the LNWR in 1867.

Towards the end of 1873 Bournes and Robinson hired the spare locomotive SHERDLEY to Pilkington Brothers but apart from the name no other information has survived. It evidently suffered some damage and Pilkington Brothers had to pay for the cost of repairs by Edward Borrows [22,23].

In addition to the standard gauge locomotives, it is known that Bournes and Robinson purchased a four-coupled narrow gauge locomotive from Alexander Chaplin and Company of Glasgow in 1868 [24]. This was one of the manufacturer's standard products, with a vertical boiler and with vertical cylinders driving on to the coupled wheels. As the gauge quoted in Chaplin's records is 2ft 2in, it was presumably used for hauling pit tubs, but it is not clear what its duties were. The first edition of the 25 inch map, surveyed in 1881, shows nothing in the way of a narrow gauge railway system except on the waste tips at Peasley Cross Colliery.

Peasley Cross and Sherdley Collieries 1887 to 1903

Under the Whitecross Company, Peasley Cross and Sherdley Collieries continued to operate with apparently little change, although the former was probably coming to the end of its productive life. It is shown as discontinued in the Mines Lists for a period in the 1890s.

It appears that the ex Ludlow and Clee Hill locomotive was taken over from Bournes and Robinson, because it was later at Glengarnock Steel Works in Ayrshire, where old employees said that it had come from England around 1898 [25].

The Industrial Railway Society lists also suggest that the narrow gauge Chaplin locomotive passed into the hands of the Whitecross Company. However, we cannot confirm this.

In 1888 the Hunslet Engine Company of Leeds supplied a four-coupled saddle tank named CHAMPION. It was despatched to St Helens on 8th February.

The manufacturer's records show that the Manning Wardle locomotive named NORTON was later with the Whitecross Company at St Helens. This had originally been supplied in 1888 to T.A. Walker for the Manchester Ship Canal contract and was presumably acquired in the 1890s after the work had been completed.

It is also known that Peckett and Sons of Bristol supplied a new four-coupled saddle tank to the Whitecross Company in 1901. This appears to have been used at St Helens, rather than the firm's Warrington works, although we have no independent confirmation.

In 1903 the Whitecross Company decided to dispose of its mining interests. Sherdley Colliery and its connecting railway were sold to Sutton Heath and Lea Green Colliery Co Ltd, a firm which we deal with in greater detail in Part Two, while Peasley Cross was taken over by the Peasley Cross Colliery Co Ltd. Surplus plant at Peasley Cross Colliery was advertised for sale by the Whitecross Company in July and August 1903 [26,27]. It included a complete underground haulage system, 800 tubs, about 800 tons of double headed and flanged rails and three 4-coupled locomotives with 10 inch, 13 inch and 14 inch cylinders.

The 10 inch locomotive is something of a mystery. The Manning Wardle had 12 inch by 18 inch cylinders and was transferred to the firm's Warrington works, where it survived until the 1930s. May be the dimensions quoted in the advertisement were incorrect, may be there was another locomotive which has gone unrecorded.

The 13 inch locomotive was presumably CHAMPION, which was purchased by Peasley Cross Colliery Co Ltd. The 14 inch locomotive may have been the 1901 Peckett, which appeared at Latham Brothers' Rose Bridge Colliery at Wigan shortly afterwards.

Peasley Cross and Sherdley Collieries 1903 to 1944

Peasley Cross Colliery appears to have been something of a white elephant. The Mines Lists suggest that it was not worked after 1906 and the plant was auctioned on 3rd March 1908, by order of the receiver for the debenture holders [28]. A locomotive with 12 inch by 20 inch cylinders built by the Hunslet Engine Company was included in the sale. This may well have been an error, as CHAMPION, with 13 inch by 18 inch cylinders, was still with the firm in February 1905, when spare parts were supplied. On the other hand there may have been a second locomotive.

Opposite - Two of the Sherdley Colliery locomotives, probably photographed during the Whitecross Company's period of ownership. The upper picture is of SIR CHARLES, originally built for the Ludlow and Clee Hill Railway. The lower photograph is of the Hunslet, CHAMPION, delivered to Sherdley Colliery in 1888.

(Wigan Museum Service)

PRESTON photographed at Lea Green Colliery sidings   *(P.G. Hindley collection)*

In contrast to the failure of the Peasley Cross venture, Sherdley Colliery continued in operation until towards the end of the Second World War under the ownership of Sutton Heath and Lea Green Collieries Ltd. In 1938 the Mines Lists show that over 700 men were employed, but production was run down after that. By 1944 mining had ceased, although one shaft was subsequently used for pumping purposes by the National Coal Board.

No complete list of locomotives employed here after 1903 has survived and the story is complicated by the fact that there were several exchanges between the various collieries owned by the Sutton Heath and Lea Green company.

A six-coupled saddle tank, named BARKER, is known to have been delivered to Sherdley Colliery by Hudswell, Clarke and Company in 1910. In 1938 BARKER was noted at Lea Green while PRESTON and LOMAX were at Sherdley. PRESTON was a four-coupled well tank, built by Edward Borrows and Sons in 1904, while LOMAX was a six-coupled saddle tank built by the Hunslet Engine Company in 1902. FANNY was also at Sherdley for a time according to old employees. This was a six-coupled saddle tank, built by the Vulcan Foundry in 1876 for stock and sold to James Radley, for use at the Sutton Heath and Lea Green Collieries, in 1877.

When the colliery closed, the two locomotives allocated there were LOMAX and PRESTON. LOMAX was returned to Lea Green Colliery. PRESTON was said to have been sold to Vickers Armstrong Ltd, although this cannot be confirmed.

McKechnie's Copper Works

Duncan McKechnie, who had previously been a partner in the Old Quay Works at Runcorn, established a new plant on a site to the north of Peasley Cross Colliery in 1870 [29]. Pyrites was processed to produce copper and also sulphuric acid, a raw material for the Leblanc alkali process. McKechnie apparently received financial support from Mason and Barry, a firm which owned pyrites mines in Portugal [1]. A siding connection was laid in with the adjacent LNWR Ravenhead Branch, probably at the time that the works was erected.

The works was taken over by the United Alkali Company Ltd on its formation in November 1890 [30]. The revised first edition of the 25 inch map, surveyed in 1891, shows that there had been very large extensions during the previous decade to the manufacturing facilities and to the internal railway system. A connection had also been put in to the nearby sidings belonging to Sherdley Colliery so that coal could be delivered directly to the works without passing over LNWR metals.

In 1891, the Liverpool and Hull Red Oxide Co Ltd built a factory for the production of pigments on a site to the south east of the McKechnie works [31]. The premises were served by a number of short sidings which connected with the copper works railway system.

The McKechnie works, which was little altered during the twentieth century, was closed down by the United Alkali Company in 1927 [30]. The site was purchased by St Helens Corporation in 1930 and the buildings were subsequently demolished. It was redeveloped in the 1960s when United Glass Ltd erected the new Peasley Glass Works, a small portion having been used earlier for minor extensions to the Sherdley Works.

The Liverpool and Hull Red Oxide Company's works survived until June 1961, when production was transferred to the firm's other factories at Stalybridge and Hull. The 3½ acre site was then sold to United Glass Ltd [32]. Successive large scale maps show that, after the closure of the McKechnie works, one of the sidings running through the site was retained to provide rail access from the main line to the red oxide works.

We have no knowledge of any locomotive used at the McKechnie works until the early 1880s. The Industrial Railway Society's Pocket Book for Lancashire [33] lists two four-coupled well tanks, named ALICE and AGNES. Both were built locally by Edward Borrows, the former possibly in 1882 and the latter in 1883. They appear to have been ordered to coincide with the extensions being made to the factory at that period. Before this it is possible that the shunting was carried out by locomotives from Bournes and Robinson's colliery, but we cannot confirm this. Alternatively horses may have been used, as the extent of the railway system was relatively small.

The next information we have comes from an inventory of United Alkali Company plant on 30th June 1919 [34], when two locomotives named AGNES and KATE, both with 12in cylinders, were recorded. KATE may have been a new name for the engine previously known as ALICE, although there is nothing to confirm this. There were 1,900 yards of sidings in the works. The rolling stock consisted of 48 bogies and trucks, eight 8-ton dumb buffer wagons for internal use and 12 wagons for main line traffic. It is assumed that AGNES and KATE survived until the works closed and were cut up when the plant was dismantled.

There is no record of any locomotive owned by the Red Oxide Company. Up to 1927 we believe that any shunting which was necessary was performed by the copper works locomotive. We think it likely that wagons were moved by a road tractor after the copper works closed down.

Sherdley Glass Bottle Works and Sutton Lodge Chemical Works

The Sherdley Glass Bottle works, west of the sidings serving Bournes and Robinson's collieries, was built in the late 1870s by Cannington, Shaw and Company [1] and the first furnaces came into operation in 1877 [35]. A siding connection to the LNWR, at a point along the branch 146 yards from Ravenhead Junction, was probably installed when the factory opened.

The firm had been founded in 1866, when the brothers John and Edward Cannington joined John Shaw at his Ravenhead Bottle Works [35]. This works, not to be confused with a later establishment of the same name owned by Nuttall and Company, was closed in 1878 [35] and taken over by Pilkington Brothers on 1st January 1879 [35,36].

AGNES photographed at Edward Borrows' Providence Foundry before delivery to McKechnie's Alkali Works. (St Helens Library, Borrows Collection)

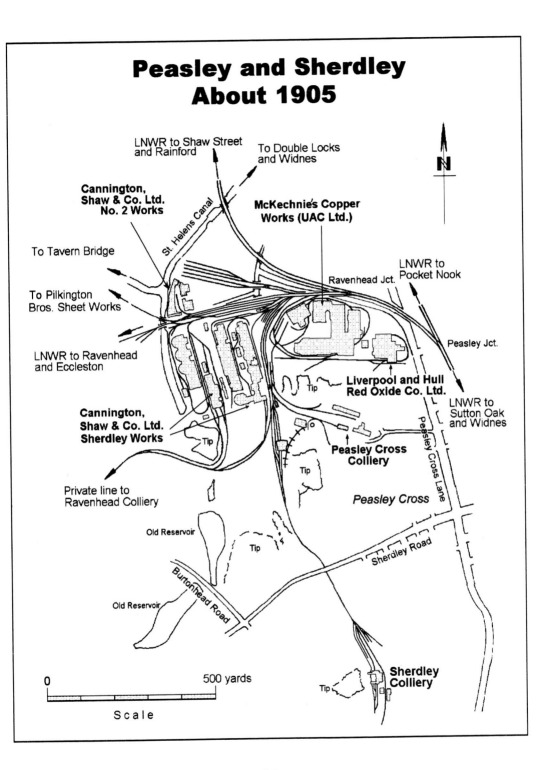

Peasley and Sherdley
About 1905

LNWR to Shaw Street
and Rainford

To Double Locks
and Widnes

N

**Cannington,
Shaw & Co. Ltd.
No. 2 Works**

**McKechnie's Copper
Works (UAC Ltd.)**

St. Helens Canal

To Tavern Bridge

LNWR to
Pocket Nook

Ravenhead Jct.

To Pilkington
Bros. Sheet Works

Peasley Jct.

LNWR to Ravenhead
and Eccleston

**Liverpool and Hull
Red Oxide Co. Ltd.**

Tip

LNWR to
Sutton Oak
and Widnes

**Cannington,
Shaw & Co. Ltd.
Sherdley Works**

Tip

Peasley Cross Lane

**Peasley Cross
Colliery**

Tip

Private line to
Ravenhead Colliery

Peasley Cross

Old Reservoir

Tip

Sherdley Road

Burtonhead Road

Old Reservoir

0

500 yards

Tip

**Sherdley
Colliery**

S c a l e

Cannington, Shaw and Co Ltd was formed in 1892 [1] and in the same year [35] the firm acquired the premises of Lyons Brothers on the opposite side of the Ravenhead Branch, which we describe in Chapter 4. Lyons Brothers' factory was subsequently known as the Cannington Shaw No. 2 Works to distinguish it from the Sherdley plant. It was closed in 1911 [35] and the site was taken over by Pilkington Brothers Ltd [37].

The Cannington and Shaw partners set up the Sutton Lodge Chemical Company to erect an alkali works adjacent to and on the west side of the Sherdley Glass Works [1,35]. Construction commenced about 1875, because in April of that year the LNWR was negotiating with Pilkington Brothers for the sale of land on which to build new sidings to serve the works [38]. This was agreed in September 1875, subject to the LNWR giving rail access to Pilkington's brickworks [39].

Connections with the LNWR were provided at each end of the works, at 189 yards and 444 yards from Ravenhead Junction, under an agreement with the Sutton Lodge Chemical Company, dated 19th June 1876 [40]. Tracks parallel to the LNWR linked the internal railway system at Sutton Lodge with that at Sherdley Glass Works. The first edition of the 25 inch map, surveyed in 1881, shows that there was also a line which ran between the Sutton Lodge Works and Bibby's Copper Works, crossing the Burtonhead arm of the canal by means of a draw bridge. This had been taken up by 1891 when the survey was made for a revision of the map.

Sutton Lodge Chemical Works passed to the United Alkali Co Ltd in 1890 and closed down in 1896 [30]. The premises were repurchased by Cannington, Shaw and Co Ltd. and the site used for a new glass works which opened in 1900 [35]. Although sometimes referred to as the Sutton Lodge Glass Works, the new factory was essentially an extension of the Sherdley Works where Nos 11,12,13,and 14 shops were located [35].

The old and new sites were physically separated by a right of way leading to Sherdley Road. As a consequence the rail connection between the two parts of the works was by means of the pair of sidings adjacent to the Ravenhead Branch which had been originally laid in to serve the Sutton Lodge Chemical Works. By 1905, when the survey was made for the second edition of the 25 inch map, a new railway had been laid across land to the south which gave direct rail access to both parts of the Sherdley Glass Works from Ravenhead Colliery. This enabled coal to be supplied to the works without paying tolls to the LNWR and supplemented the earlier connection from the Sherdley Colliery sidings which probably dated from the Bournes and Robinson era.

The earliest locomotive which we have on record is a four-coupled saddle tank, supplied to the Sutton Lodge Chemical Company by Hudswell, Clarke and Rodgers of Leeds in 1877, probably to coincide with the opening of the works. It was named SUTTON LODGE and was not a new locomotive.

It had a complicated history which is fully described in the Industrial Railway Society Handbook for North Wales [41]. Originally built by Kitson and Company of Leeds in 1871 for the contractor of the Koslov to Rostov Railway in Russia, it was one of two locomotives on a ship which sank off the coast of Sweden. Both were salvaged and were purchased by Hudswell, Clarke and Rodgers. One was sold in 1873 to George Watkinson and Sons for use at that firm's Buckley Colliery in North Wales. It was then repurchased by Hudswell, Clarke and Rodgers and overhauled before a further sale to the Sutton Lodge Chemical Company took place. It was presumably taken over by the United Alkali Company in 1890. but its subsequent history is not accounted for.

The first locomotive known to have been delivered to the Glass Works was a four-coupled saddle tank which came in 1883 from Hudswell, Clarke and Company and was named SHERDLEY. We do not know if the glass works had a previous locomotive or if shunting was performed prior to 1883 by SUTTON LODGE.

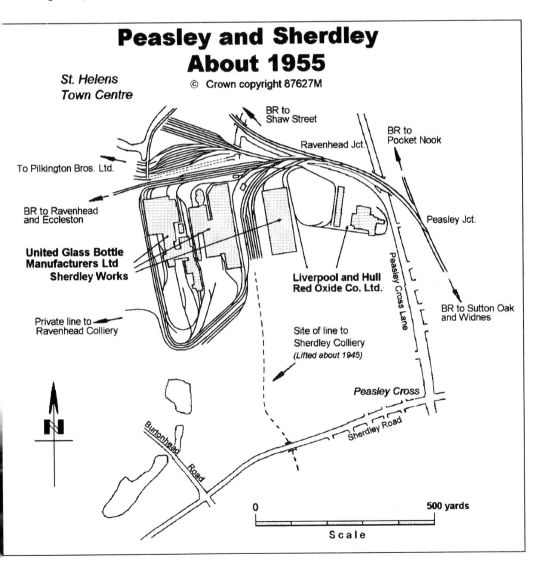

Peasley and Sherdley
About 1955

St. Helens
Town Centre

© Crown copyright 87627M

BR to Shaw Street

Ravenhead Jct.

BR to Pocket Nook

To Pilkington Bros. Ltd.

BR to Ravenhead and Eccleston

United Glass Bottle Manufacturers Ltd Sherdley Works

Peasley Jct.

Peasley Cross Lane

Liverpool and Hull Red Oxide Co. Ltd.

BR to Sutton Oak and Widnes

Private line to Ravenhead Colliery

Site of line to Sherdley Colliery
(Lifted about 1945)

Peasley Cross

Sherdley Road

N

Burtonhead Road

0   500 yards

Scale

91

SHERDLEY was followed about ten years later by another four-coupled saddle tank which had been built in 1886 by Manning Wardle and Company of Leeds for the Barry contract of T.A. Walker, where it was named ST FAGANS. After being at the glass works for only a few years, it was sold around 1900 to the St Helens dealer J.J. Poole who resold it to Thomas Mitchell and Sons of Bolton in February 1901.

The Manning, Wardle was replaced by another four-coupled saddle tank, similar to SHERDLEY, which came in 1900 from Hudswell Clarke and Company. This new locomotive was named SUTTON LODGE, presumably to celebrate the opening of the extensions to the works.

Cannington, Shaw and Co Ltd merged with Nuttall and Co Ltd to form United Glass Bottle Manufacturers Ltd, which was registered on 31st March 1913 [42]. Nuttall's Ravenhead Works and its locomotives and railways feature in a later chapter.

Both works continued in production with very little change, except for some additional shops which were bult at Sherdley, probably in the 1920s. In the 1930s two second hand locomotives were purchased to supplement SHERDLEY and SUTTON LODGE. A four-coupled saddle tank, built by Kerr, Stuart and Company of Stoke on Trent in 1920, came from F.V. Clarkson, machinery merchants, of Wigan, in 1934. It had previously been the property of the Mersey Docks and Harbour Board and was named JUBILEE at Sherdley. The other locomotive came from R.S. Hayes Ltd, machinery merchants, of Bridgend in South Wales. It had been built in 1899 by Peckett and Sons of Bristol and had previously seen service at the Redding Colliery near Falkirk in Scotland. It received the name PEASLEY in the UGB stock.

During the period immediately after the Second World War, major alterations were made at the Sherdley Works and new buildings were erected on the adjacent McKechnie site. The 25 inch map, published in 1958 and revised a few years earlier, shows that there had been considerable alterations and extensions to the internal railway system.

The locomotives at the Sherdley and Ravenhead Works, hitherto kept separate, were brought together in a common pool and were given numbers as well as names. No. 4 THE QUEEN, a four- coupled well tank, built by Edward Borrows and Sons in 1906, was transferred from the firm's Ravenhead Works around 1950 and major repairs were undertaken. It had returned to Ravenhead by August 1952 but was back at Sherdley by June 1953. By May 1955 it was back at Ravenhead, where it remained until it was broken up in March 1958.

Opposite, upper - The United Glass Bottle Manufacturers' Hudswell Clarke saddle tank SUTTON LODGE at Sherdley Glass Works on 19th April 1958. (J.A. Peden)

Opposite, lower - NORTHERN and CORONATION in the sidings at Sherdley Glass Works, looking towards Ravenhead Junction. The NWGB's gasholder, on the opposite side of the Ravenhead Branch, forms a prominent feature of the landscape.

(J.B. Horne)

To cater for the increase in traffic at Sherdley, additional locomotives were purchased. No. 6 CORONATION came new from the Hunslet Engine Company in 1952 and was followed by two second hand locomotives. PRINCESS, which should have been No. 7 in the list, was built by Andrew Barclay Sons and Company of Kilmarnock in 1898. It was transferred from U G B's Charlton Works in London, probably before the end of 1956. No. 8 NORTHERN, built by the same firm in 1944, came second hand from Boots Pure Drug Co Ltd of Nottingham, arriving at Sherdley on 3rd January 1957 [43]. PRINCESS does not seem to have been much of a success. It was reported in August 1957 as being out of service and was subsequently broken up.

Several of the Sherdley locomotives were sent to the Ravenhead Works at this period. SUTTON LODGE was seen working there in June 1953 but came back and was broken up at Sherdley in 1960. No. 5 PEASLEY was at Ravenhead in June 1953. It did not return to Sherdley and was scrapped at Ravenhead in 1959. SHERDLEY was also transferred to Ravenhead and was noted there in May 1955. It was broken up at Ravenhead in March 1958.

SUTTON LODGE lasted until 1960, leaving CORONATION, JUBILEE and NORTHERN to handle the traffic at Sherdley until the arrival of the first diesel locomotive in 1961. This was a four-wheeled machine with mechanical drive, built by F.W. Hibberd and Co Ltd of Park Royal in 1947, which was acquired from Canning Town Glass Works Ltd. A second similar locomotive was purchased new from Hibberd and given the name SHERDLEY.

With the diesels taking over the work, NORTHERN was taken out of service and scrapped in July 1964. JUBILEE was cut up in August 1967 and CORONATION in June 1968.

Peasley Glass Works

United Glass Ltd was registered on 1st March 1959 as a holding company, and was later taken over by the Distillers Co Ltd and Owens Illinois Inc, of the United States [42]. The Sherdley Glass Works subsequently came under the control of a subsidiary company - United Glass (England) Ltd [44].

A decision was taken to expand production facilities at St Helens and in the 1960s plans were drawn up for a modern bottle making plant to replace the out-dated works at Sherdley, Ravenhead and Charlton, in South London. Redevelopment of the older, eastern part of the Sherdley Glass Works was followed by the construction of an entirely new factory on the sites formerly occupied by the McKechnie copper works and the Red Oxide Works.

Two modern furnaces at the new Peasley Glass Works were started up in 1966 and 1967 and the factory was formally opened in 1967 [35]. Some production continued at the former Sherdley Works until March 1981, when the last of the furnaces there was shut down [45]. Meanwhile control of the complex had passed from United Glass (England) Ltd to United Glass Containers Ltd, as the result of a further reorganisation of United Glass Ltd in 1969 [46].

PRINCESS, the 1898 Barclay which came from UGB's Charlton Works in South East London, photographed at Sherdley on 19th April 1958.   *(J.A. Peden)*

The Peasley Works had an extensive internal railway system which linked up with that of the Sherdley Works. Motive power in the first few years was provided by the two Hibberd diesel locomotives mentioned above. It is doubtful whether the last remaining steam locomotive, CORONATION, saw much, if any, service at the new works, as it was broken up in June 1968.

A third diesel locomotive arrived in 1967 from United Glass (England) Ltd's Charlton Works, which had been closed down at the end of 1965 [47]. Named PEASLEY after its arrival at St Helens, it had been built in 1956 by the Vulcan Foundry to the order of the Drewry Car Company.

Another Hibberd four-wheeled diesel mechanical locomotive, built in 1961, was purchased second hand from the Tees and Hartlepool Port Authority, Grangetown, around October 1972. The name SHERDLEY was transferred from the 1963 locomotive, which was subsequently scrapped. The unnamed Hibberd diesel, which had come from Canning Town in 1961, was sold to Lowton Metals Ltd, Haydock, in 1974.

Finally, two diesel electric locomotives, built by the Yorkshire Engine Company in 1957 and 1958, were acquired from Fibreglass Ltd early in 1984 after rail traffic ceased at that firm's Ravenhead Works. They became No. 1 PEASLEY and No. 2 PEASLEY in United Glass ownership. The Drewry of 1956 and the ex Tees and Hartlepool Port Authority Hibberd of 1961, were then broken up.

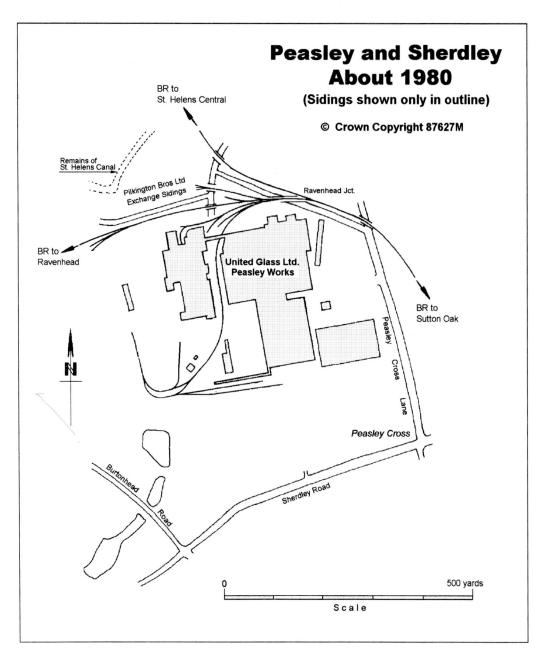

Peasley and Sherdley About 1980

(Sidings shown only in outline)

© Crown Copyright 87627M

BR to
St. Helens Central

Remains of
St. Helens Canal

Pilkington Bros Ltd
Exchange Sidings

Ravenhead Jct.

BR to
Ravenhead

**United Glass Ltd.
Peasley Works**

BR to
Sutton Oak

Peasley Cross Lane

Peasley Cross

Burtonhead Road

Sherdley Road

N

0   500 yards

Scale

By this date, the only significant rail movement consisted of sand, which came in block trains from Oakamoor in Staffordshire. This too ceased in 1988, as British Rail found the traffic uneconomical. The last sand train left Oakamoor on Tuesday 30th August 1988 [48]. No. 1 PEASLEY was recorded as the last working locomotive [49].

United Glass put its internal rail system into mothballs in the hope that British Rail could be prevailed upon to restart the service [49], but this proved not to be so. No. 1 PEASLEY went to Booth Roe Metals Ltd of Rotherham for scrap at the end of 1991. No. 2 PEASLEY was sold to Balfour Beatty Ltd for use on the construction of North Pole Carriage Maintenance Depot in West London for the Channel Tunnel trains.

LOCOMOTIVE SUMMARY

Sutton, Peasley Cross and Sherdley Collieries

Sutton Colliery
    John Bourne and Co 1812 to early 1830s
    Bournes and Robinson from early 1830s
    Colliery closed by 1881

Peasley Colliery
    Sunk about 1856 as Peasley House Colliery
    Bournes and Robinson until 1887
    Whitecross Co Ltd 1887 to 1903
    Peasley Cross Colliery Co Ltd from 1903
    Colliery closed 1906

Sherdley Colliery
    Sunk about 1873
    Bournes and Robinson until 1887
    Whitecross Co Ltd 1887 to 1903
    Sutton Heath and Lea Green Collieries Ltd from 1903
    Colliery closed about 1943

Locomotives used by Bournes and Robinson

COLLIER	0-4-0Tender	EB	1832	5' 6"

New
Sold 1836 to John Jones in part payment for new loco and resold to St Helens Rly

	0-4-0Tender	Jones	1836 (?)	
	or 0-4-2Tender			

New
Scrapped or sold
May have been one of the two locos advertised for sale in 1844 (see text)

SHERDLEY
    Hired to Pilkington Brothers, end 1873, and repaired by Edward Borrows
    Scrapped or sold

SIR CHARLES   0-6-0BT OC SS   1477 1863   16"x22" 3'10"
    Ex LNWR 1189 in June 1872, originally Ludlow and Clee Hill Rly
    Probably taken over by Whitecross Co Ltd in 1887

2' 2" gauge

                        0-4-0TGVB   Chaplin 988 1868
    New to Bournes and Robinson
    Possibly taken over by Whitecross Co Ltd

Locomotives used by Whitecross Co Ltd

SIR CHARLES   0-6-0BT OC SS   1477 1863   16"x22" 3'10"
    Believed to have been taken over from Bournes and Robinson

    At Glengarnock Steelworks by about 1898
CHAMPION   0-4-0ST OC HE   428 1888   13"x18" 3'1"
    New to Sherdley Colliery, February 1888

    To Peasley Cross Colliery Co Ltd in 1903
                        0-4-0ST OC MW   1061 1888   12"x18" 3'0"
    Class H
    New to T.A. Walker, Irlam, as NORTON,
    At Whitecross Co Ltd, Sherdley Colliery, probably by mid 1890s
    Transferred to Whitecross Co Ltd, Warrington Works

                        0-4-0ST OC P   895 1901   14"x20" 3'2"
    Class W4
    Believed to have been at Sherdley Colliery

    To Thos and Wm Latham, Rose Bridge Colliery, Wigan
Three locomotives for sale, July and August 1903, with 10", 13" and 14" cylinders

Locomotive used by Peasley Cross Colliery Co Ltd

CHAMPION   0-4-0ST OC HE   428 1888   13"x18" 3'1"
    Ex Whitecross Co Ltd
    At Griffiths and Son, Glenburn Colly, Skelmersdale, by 1911

Locomotives used by Sutton Heath and Lea Green Collieries Ltd

PRESTON   0-4-0WT OC EBS   46 1904
    Possibly new to Sherdley Colliery
    At Sherdley Colliery in March 1938 and April 1943
    Believed to have been sold about 1944 to Vickers Armstrong Ltd, Walker on Tyne

BARKER	0-6-0ST IC	HC	909	1910	15"x20"	3'3½"

New to Sherdley Colliery, March 1907
Later transferred to other Sutton Heath and Lea Green Co's collieries

FANNY	0-6-0ST IC	VF	796	1876	12"x18"	3'6"

At Sherdley for a time from another of Sutton Heath and Lea Green Co's collieries

LOMAX	0-6-0ST OC	HE	799	1902

Transferred to Sherdley from another of Sutton Heath and Lea Green Co's collieries
Noted at Sherdley in March 1938, July 1939 and April 1943
To Sutton Heath Colliery by 1944

McKechnie's Alkali Works

Duncan McKechnie 1870 to November 1890
United Alkali Co Ltd from November 1890
Works closed 1927

ALICE	0-4-0WT OC	EBS	11	1882(?)

Believed new to Duncan McKechnie
Scrapped or sold

AGNES	0-4-0WT OC	EBS	16	1883	12"

Believed new to Duncan McKechnie
Scrapped or sold

An inventory of June 1919 list two 12" locomotives - AGNES and KATE

Sutton Lodge Chemical Works

Sutton Lodge Chemical Co mid 1870s to November 1890
United Alkali Co Ltd from November 1890
Works closed 1896 and site taken over by Cannington, Shaw and Co Ltd

SUTTON LODGE	0-4-0ST OC	HCR	198	1877	12"x18"	3'0"

Built by Kitson and Co, Leeds in 1871, maker's no. 1773
For previous history see text
Reconditioned by Hudswell, Clarke and Rodgers in 1877 and delivered to Sutton
    Lodge Chemical Works April 1877
Scrapped or sold

Sherdley Glass Bottle Works

Cannington, Shaw and Company mid 1870s to 1892
Cannington, Shaw and Co Ltd 1892 to 1911
United Glass Bottle Manufacturers Ltd 1911 to 1959
United Glass (England) Ltd (Subsidiary of United Glass Ltd) 1959 to 1969
United Glass Containers Ltd (Subsidiary of United Glass Ltd) from 1969
Part of works operated in conjunction with Peasley Glass Works from 1966 to 1981

SHERDLEY	0-4-0ST OC	HC		251	1883	13"x20"	3'3"

New
No. 1 from about 1952
Scrapped at Sherdley March 1958

	0-4-0ST OC	MW		952	1886	12"x18"	3'0"

Class H
New to T.A. Walker, St Fagans, ST FAGANS
Sold to Joseph Poole, machinery merchant, St Helens and resold February 1901

SUTTON LODGE	0-4-0ST OC	HC		564	1900	13"x20"	3'3"

New
Temporarily at Ravenhead Works, noted there in June 1953
Scrapped at Sherdley Works in 1960

JUBILEE	0-4-0ST OC	KS		4149	1920	15"x20"	3'6"

Ex Mersey Docks and Harbour Board No. 30, via F.V. Clarkson, dealer, Wigan, in 1934
No. 3 from about 1952
Scrapped at Sherdley Works, August 1967

PEASLEY	0-4-0ST OC	P		763	1899	14"x20"	3'2½"

Class W4, new to Stewart and Menzies, Coatbridge
Ex R.S. Hayes Ltd, dealers, Bridgend
Transferred to Ravenhead Works late 1952 or early 1953
No. 5 from about 1952
Scrapped about 1958 at Ravenhead Works

QUEEN	0-4-0WT OC	EBS		50	1907	12"x20"	3'2½"

No. 4 from about 1952
Temporarily transferred from Ravenhead Works to Sherdley Works from about 1950 to 1952 and again in 1953

No. 6 CORONATION	0-4-0ST OC	HE		3773	1952	

New
Scrapped at Sherdley Works by Tompa Metals, June 1968

PRINCESS	0-4-0ST OC	AB	836 1898	12"x20" 3'2"

Rebuilt AB 9472 1924
Ex United Glass Ltd, Charlton Works, London, January 1956
Scrapped at Sherdley Works about 1958

No. 8 NORTHERN	0-4-0-ST OC	AB	2166 1944	14"x22" 3'5"

Ex Boots Pure Drug Co Ltd, Beeston, arriving at Sherdley Works 3.1.1957
Scrapped at Sherdley Works July 1964

SHERDLEY	4wDM	FH	4007 1963

New
Scrapped about October 1972

	4wDM	FH	3147 1947

Ex Canning Town Glass Works Ltd, early 1961
To Lowton Metals Ltd, Haydock, 1974

Peasley Glass Bottle Works

United Glass (England) Ltd (Subsidiary of United Glass Ltd) to 1969
United Glass Containers Ltd (Subsidiary of United Glass Ltd) from 1969

Some of the diesel locomotives listed under Sherdley Works shunted at the new Peasley
Works which was on an adjoining site

378/626 PEASLEY	0-4-0DM	DC	2582 1956	153HP 3'3"
		VF	D296 1956	

Ex United Glass Ltd, Charlton Works, London, 1967
Scrapped April 1984

378/625 SHERDLEY	4wDM	FH	3964 1961

Ex Tees and Hartlepool Port Authority, Grangetown, about October 1972
Scrapped July 1983

No. 1 PEASLEY	0-4-0DE	YE	2653 1957	200 HP

Ex Fibreglass Ltd about March 1984
To Booth Roe Metals Ltd, Clarence Metal Works, Armour St, Rotherham for scrap
between 12.10.1991 and 15.11.1991

No. 2 PEASLEY	0-4-0DE	YE	2730 1958	200 HP

Ex Fibreglass Ltd about March 1984
To Balfour Beatty Ltd 21.8.1991 for use on construction of North Pole Carriage
Maintenance Depot for Channel Tunnel trains

References to Chapter 3

1   *A Merseyside Town in the Industrial Revolution   St Helens 1750 - 1900*, T.C. Barker and J R. Harris, Frank Cass & Co Ltd, London, 1959

2   11 Geo 4 cap lxi; 29th May 1830

3   LRO PDR 188

4   *The St Helens Railway*, J.R. Tolson, The Oakwood Press, 1982

5   *History, Directory and Gazetteer of the County Palatine of Lancaster*, E Baines, Liverpool, 1824-25

6   *The Story of Rainhill*, Robert and Florence Dickinson, publ Rainhill Civic Society, 1968, reprint 1979

7   *Pigot & Co's National Commercial Directory*, J. Pigot and Co, London and Manchester, 1834

8   *MG* 6.7.1872

9   *BC* 6.7.1872

10 Pilkington Bros General Board Mins 24.9.1875 at IM&S

11 Ibid 13.5.1880

12 *LG* 8.3.1859

13 *LG* 28.2.1860

14 *LG* 21.4.1865

15 *LG* 17.10.1876

16 *LG* 29.8.1882

17 *WO* 23.11.1883

18 *The Liverpool and Manchester Railway*, R.H.G. Thomas, B.T. Batsford Ltd, London, 1980

19 *Herepath* 20.7.1844

20 Pilkington Bros General Board Mins 25.3.1869 at IM&S

21 *British Locomotive Catalogue 1825 - 1923, Vol 2A LNWR*; ed David Baxter, Moorland Publishng Co, Ashbourne, 1978

22 Pilkington Bros General Board Mins 8.12.1873 at IM&S

23 Ibid 7.1.1874

24 LeiRO 28D69/95

25 Information supplied to the authors by Mr Frank Jones

26 *CG* 31.7.1903

27 *CG* 14.8.1903

28 *CG* 28.2.1908

29 *A Directory of the Chemical Works of St Helens   1820-1889*, J.D. Turton, C. Kay and P. Meara, Halton Historical Publications, No. 15

30 CRO DIC UA 12/20

31 *StHNews* 7.2.1891

32 *StHNews* 21.6.1961

33 *The Industrial Locomotives of Lancashire*, Birmingham Locomotive Club, 1952

34 CRO DIC/UA 10/7

35 *Sherdley Peasley Glass Works 1877 - 1977*, United Glass Ltd pamphlet, xerox at StHLH A 37.8 (P))

36 Pilkington Bros General Board Mins 10.1.1879, at IM&S

37 Ibid 14.11.1911

38 Ibid 29.4.1875

39 Ibid 14.8.1875

40 LNWR Sdg Diag 172; 12.1916

41 *Industrial Locomotives of North Wales*, Compiled by V.J. Bradley, Industrial Railway Society, 1992

42 *Stock Exchange Year Book 1972 - 1973*

43 Letter Alan Beresford to Frank Smith 21.8.1957

44 Annual Report of United Glass Ltd, 1965

45 *StHRep* 27.3.1981

46 Note dated January 1970 from United Glass Ltd to Information Management and Storage Ltd, at IM&S

47 Annual Report of United Glass Ltd, 1966

48 *BLN* 594

49 *BLN* 596

CHAPTER FOUR

PILKINGTON BROTHERS' SHEET WORKS

We now move westwards along the Ravenhead Branch to explore the district between the railway and the canal. Pilkington Brothers' Sheet Works eventually occupied the whole of the area and the present chapter is devoted to the development of the factory and its railway system.

The firm had its origins in the St Helens Crown Glass Works, founded in 1826 by a partnership which included William Pilkington, Peter Greenall and John William Bell [1]. Following the death of Peter Greenall in 1845, William and Richard Pilkington acquired control of the firm and successive generations of the family built up the company into the country's leading manufacturer of flat glass.

The original Crown Glass Works was extended and redeveloped almost continuously throughout the nineteenth century as demand went on rising. New processes were introduced and the name Sheet Works, or sometimes Sheet and Rolled Works, was adopted from the mid 1860s. Production of the out-dated crown glass, which had been the mainstay of the company in the early days, ceased in July 1872 [1].

A new works for the manufacture of plate glass, which we deal with in Chapter 10, was opened on a site near Gerard's Bridge in 1876. At the Sheet Works more and more property was acquired as adjacent factories closed down and their sites became available. By 1894, when the partnership was turned into a limited liability company, the the premises occupied some 300 acres.

In the early years of the twentieth century several other glass works in the St Helens area, which feature in later chapters, were bought up. All except the Ravenhead Plate Glass Works were closed down in order to eliminate competition. Meanwhile, the Sheet Works continued to be redeveloped to accommodate new methods of production and, until the outbreak of the second world war, neighbouring sites were still being acquired to provide additional factory and warehousing space.

Pilkington Brothers' first venture into coal mining was at the Green Lane Colliery, in Windle Township, which came into production in February 1845 [1]. Although the original intention was no doubt to provide a supply of fuel for the firm's factory, sales to outside customers soon became important. The St Helens Colliery, adjacent to the Crown Glass Works, which had lain derelict since 1844, was purchased in 1857 [2]. It was put into working order and coal was again being wound in 1861 [1]. In 1864, the partners started to sink the Alexandra Colliery at Ravenhead which we describe in Chapter 6.

There was discussion in 1868 about an amalgamation of the Pilkington colliery interests with those of Bournes and Robinson and Bromilow and Haddock [3], but nothing came of it. The question of a merger was again raised in 1875, this time with Bromilow and Haddock and with James Radley [4,5,6]. As a result, St Helens Collieries Ltd was registered on 12th July 1876 [1,7] to take over the assets of Bromilow and Haddock's Ravenhead Colliery Company and Pilkington Brothers' Alexandra and St Helens Collieries.

Most of the sand needed in the glass manufacturing process was obtained from local sources and for much of the nineteenth century was carted to the works by road. In 1880 the decision was taken to open out a new sandfield south of Rainford to supply both the Sheet Works and the Plate Works by rail. Although some sand was imported from Belgium after 1900, local production was maintained at a high level until 1978. Further information can be found in Part Two.

The Scene in 1849

In 1849, when the survey was made for the 1:1056 Town Plan, these developments were still in the future. The Crown Glass Works occupied only a small plot of land at the corner of Grove Street and Watson Street.

To the south, near Lower Grove Street, was the Ravenhead Glass Bottle Works of John Shaw and beyond this Bromilow and Haddock's Ravenhead Colliery, which we deal with in Chapter 5. The bottle works was on the site of an earlier flint glass factory opened by John William Bell in 1822 in the premises of a former iron foundry [1]. Shaw had taken over and converted the factory to bottle making following Bell's death in January 1838.

To the east, not far from the Ravenhead Branch of the Sankey Navigation, was the St Helens Colliery. This appears to have been sunk in the early years of the nineteenth century and in 1824 [8] was being worked by Clare and Haddock. The Deposited Plans for the St Helens and Runcorn Gap Railway [9], drawn up in 1829, show a short tramroad leading to an isolated pit some distance to the south.

The St Helens Colliery was put up for auction in 1844 [2], along with Clare and Haddock's Burtonhead and Union Collieries. There appears to have been little interest in the property and St Helens Colliery was not in use in 1849 when the Town Plan was surveyed.

The Town Plan shows the Ravenhead Branch of the St Helens Railway terminating at a junction with the private railway linking Ravenhead Colliery with a wharf at the lower end of Grove Street where coal was loaded on to canal barges. There were also short subsidiary branches serving the Crown Glass Works and the Ravenhead Bottle Works.

The St Helens and Runcorn Gap Railway Act of 1830 [10] had authorised construction of a line to the Ravenhead Plate Glass Works. The railway, built on a more northerly alignment than shown on the Deposited Plans [9], was opened as far as Ravenhead Colliery in December 1834 [11] and not extended beyond here until the early 1850s. The 1830 Act also authorised the branches to the Crown Glass Works and to St Helens Colliery, but it appears that these may have been completed by the owners of the establishments concerned rather than by the railway company.

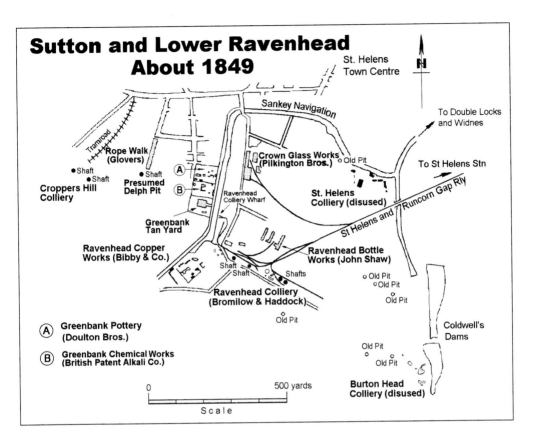

Sutton and Lower Ravenhead
About 1849

St. Helens Town Centre

To Double Locks and Widnes

To St Helens Stn

Sankey Navigation

Tramroad

Rope Walk (Glovers)

Shaft

Shaft

Croppers Hill Colliery

Shaft

Presumed Delph Pit

(A)

(B)

Crown Glass Works (Pilkington Bros.)

Old Pit

Ravenhead Colliery Wharf

St. Helens Colliery (disused)

St Helens and Runcorn Gap Rly

Greenbank Tan Yard

Ravenhead Copper Works (Bibby & Co.)

Shaft

Shaft

Shafts

Ravenhead Bottle Works (John Shaw)

Old Pit

Old Pit

Old Pit

Ravenhead Colliery (Bromilow & Haddock)

Old Pit

Coldwell's Dams

(A) Greenbank Pottery (Doulton Bros.)

(B) Greenbank Chemical Works (British Patent Alkali Co.)

Old Pit

Old Pit

Old Pit

0   500 yards

Burton Head Colliery (disused)

Scale

Developments 1849 to 1864

Considerable changes had taken place in the fifteen years between 1849 and 1864, when the Deposited Plans were prepared for the London and North Western Railway's direct line from Huyton to St Helens [12]. The new railway, authorised in 1865 [13], cut across the centre of the area, between Pilkington Brothers' Crown Glass Works and St Helens Colliery, and was largely on an embankment. By this date, the Crown Glass Works had more than doubled in size, but was still confined to a site at the corner of Grove Street and Watson Street [1,12]. Bridges and arches were provided under the new line to accommodate existing sidings and provide room for future expansion.

An alkali works had been erected on a plot of land between the lower end of Grove Street and the canal, formerly occupied by the wharf used by Bromilow and Haddock to load coal from Ravenhead Colliery. The works had its origins in a saltcake plant erected by Richard Watkins and John Parker Hall, on land leased by Watkins in 1851. Following the bankruptcy of Watkins and Hall in 1855, it had been bought by John Marsh of the Parr Alkali Works [2].

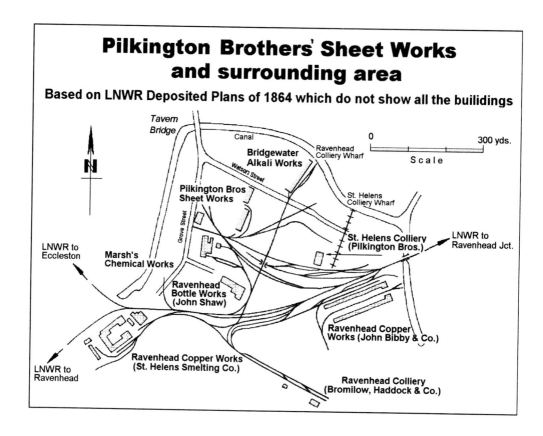

Pilkington Brothers' Sheet Works and surrounding area

Based on LNWR Deposited Plans of 1864 which do not show all the builidings

Land between Watson Street and the canal had been developed for industrial purposes and was occupied by the St Helens Ironworks, the Bridgewater Alkali Works and Bromilow and Haddock's new wharf. The St Helens Ironworks had been founded in 1859 as the Bridgewater Forge by Hadden William Todd and Richard Pilkington [2]. Following the retirement of Richard Pilkington in 1864, Charles Todd took his place and the firm changed its name to Todd Brothers [2]. An iron warehouse was later built alongside the works [14]. The Bridgewater Alkali Works dated from 1853 - 54 and had been built by Leathers, Watson and Wilson trading as the Bridgewater Smelting Company [2].

St Helens Colliery, which had been purchased by Pilkington Brothers in 1857, was located on the south side of Watson Street and had its own canal wharf, to the east of the one used by Bromilow and Haddock. Originally the line to the canal, presumably narrow gauge to accommodate pit tubs, crossed Watson Street on the level. In 1863, the arrangements were altered and a high level tubway was built between the colliery and the wharf. This cost £500 but saved an estimated 5d per ton on the 3000 tons shipped each year [15,16].

Just beyond the bridge carrying the Ravenhead Branch over the Burtonhead arm of the canal, there was Lyon's Peasley Glass Bottle Works. The works appears to have been established in the 1850s by a William Riley, who, however, was only in occupation for a short period [2]. It was taken over in the late 1850s by a partnership headed by J.H. Lyon, who moved here from Thatto Heath.

The rather complicated network of sidings serving the various factories is shown on Deposited Plans of 1864 mentioned previously [12]. The St Helens Railway's Ravenhead Branch had been extended to the Royal Colliery and the Plate Glass Works in 1851 or 1852. The Eccleston Branch, which left the Ravenhead line near Marsh's Crossing had been opened for traffic in March 1859. Additional sidings had been built to serve Pilkington's Crown Glass Works and this company's St Helens Colliery, while a line from the glass works, crossing Watson Street on the level, gave access to the St Helens Ironworks.

Shaw's Ravenhead Bottle Works, Marsh's Alkali Works and Lyon's Peasley Glass Bottle Works had also been provided with sidings, but in all cases the internal railway layout seems to have been on a minimal scale. For example, that at Shaw's works as late as 1875 consisted of a single siding, with two turntables giving access to the factory buildings [17].

The line from Ravenhead Colliery to Bromilow and Haddock's new canal wharf crossed the Ravenhead Branch of the LNWR, most of Pilkington Brothers' sidings and Watson Street on the level. Spurs gave access to the Bridgewater Alkali Works and to Pilkington Brothers' sidings.

Developments 1864 to 1876

The Alexandra Colliery at Ravenhead came into operation in 1867. Production here and at the St Helens Colliery was far in excess of the requirements of the glass works and there was a sharp rise in sales to outside customers.

The loading facilities at St Helens Colliery were evidently insufficient to deal with the increased shipments by canal and arrangements were made with Bromilow, Haddock and Company to use this firm's coal tip alongside the Bridgewater Chemical Works. The first cargo of Pilkington Brothers' coal went out from here on 15th February 1867 [18].

An office at Smeaton Buildings in Water Street was leased to deal with the Liverpool coal trade in June 1868 and two flats were chartered from William Mackay [19,20]. Further flats followed in September of the same year - ARGO, which was renamed ALEXANDRA, and ADMIRAL [21]. By January 1869 Pilkington Brothers had two flats which it owned and a further three were on charter [22,23].

Additional sidings were needed to handle the increased number of railway wagons being worked between the Sheet Works and the LNWR Ravenhead Branch. In 1864 one pair of sidings had sufficed [12] and these were extended in 1870 or thereabouts [24] when three additional loops were added.

Pilkington Brothers had hoped to have the use of an LNWR locomotive, as did some of the other St Helens firms, for the Alexandra Colliery traffic. The firm was unable to guarantee the minimum 74 wagons per day which the LNWR required [23,25,26] and by the beginning of 1869 had purchased a locomotive of its own [26].

The locomotive was apparently named ST HELENS, but apart from that nothing is known about it or its origins. It seems to have been something of a mixed blessing in the first few years and was often in need of repair.

In January 1869 the side rods broke because of bad track and had to be replaced by stronger ones [26]. The wheels needed turning in March 1869 [27] and it was thought that the locomotive might have to be sent away to have this done. In that case the partners considered trying to borrow Bournes and Robinson's spare engine, although the minutes do not say whether this actually happened.

The locomotive broke down in February 1870 [28] and repairs were needed again in May of the same year. These were expected to take several weeks [29,30] although the engine did not in fact return from what is described as "Sutton Shed" until October [31]. There is no reference to the hire of a replacement and it is assumed that horses were used as a temporary expedient. The locomotive was sent away again on 12th October 1872 for repairs estimated at £100 [32]. A replacement was to have been hired from the Ince Hall Coal Company at £2 2s 6d per day [33], but this fell through and as the minutes put it "so must bring out the horses" [32].

Further repairs were needed at the end of 1873. On this occasion it appears that Bournes and Robinson's spare locomotive SHERDLEY was borrowed and that it was damaged while with Pilkington Brothers. It was sent to Borrows' works at St Helens Junction for repairs and there was a dispute between Pilkington Brothers and Borrows about the cost [34,35].

Pilkington Brothers' locomotive was also involved in several accidents. At the beginning of 1870 it was damaged when it hit a pot carriage at the Glass Works which had been left insufficiently clear of the track [36]. The minutes record that in March 1870 there was "nearly an awful smash" when it was coming down from Alexandra Colliery [37]. In July 1871, the engine collided with a horse belonging to Bromilow and Haddock on one of the level crossings in the works [38]. Presumably the horse was hauling wagons from Ravenhead Colliery to the canal wharf over the line described earlier.

On several occasions the partners expressed concern about the locomotive. In April 1869 they wrote in the minutes "There is no doubt that the locomotive does a great deal of work, but so far seems a costly thing". At the end of 1873 the partners wrote to James Cross of Hutchinson's Trustees at Widnes enquiring about the working costs of locomotives there. The figure he gave was £15 0s 6d per week, including depreciation, wages, fuel, stores and maintenance, but whether this was a comfort to the partners was not recorded [35].

It seems probable that the main reason for purchasing the locomotive was to haul coal wagons over the LNWR line from Alexandra Colliery to the Sheet Works. Pilkington Brothers had tried to negotiate a rate of ¼d per ton for this traffic, but the minutes do not record if they were successful [39]. Other duties included shunting at the two collieries and within the Sheet Works, as well as working wagons over Watson Street to the St Helens Ironworks [40]. The locomotive was regarded as colliery property and was charged to the colliery account. The glass works and the ironworks paid the colliery for the use that they made of it, the former at a rate of £3 per week [41].

It appears that from about 1870 onwards coal from Alexandra Colliery to the Sheet Works and for shipment by canal was worked by LNWR locomotives, as must have been the case previously when Pilkington Brothers' own engine was under repair. The precise date when this change took place has gone unrecorded. It may have been in the summer of 1870 when a stationary engine was installed at Alexandra Colliery for shunting purposes [30,37,42]. Alternatively it may have been in October 1872 when Pilkington's locomotive went away for repairs and it was not possible to hire a substitute.

By January 1873 the locomotive was said to be working mainly for the glass works. It was transferred from the colliery account to the glass works account, the former being credited with its book value of £500. The colliery was to pay the glassworks £2 6s per day for its use, presumably at St Helens Colliery [43].

The colliery traffic called for a surprisingly large number of wagons, particularly as some were only used on the short haul between St Helens Colliery and the Glass Works. In January 1869 Pilkington Brothers owned 163 wagons. A further 54, presumably on hire purchase, became the property of the firm in January 1870 and 50 more in August 1870. About 70 wagons a day were being loaded and each wagon averaged 4 trips in 3 weeks [23]. In January 1871 the firm owned 213 wagons, of which about 13 were no good, so presumably a few had been disposed of in the meantime. It was decided to seek tenders for a further 50 wagons [44].

Another batch of wagons (either 25 or 50) was needed for the colliery in 1874. They seem to have been ordered from Whittle and Rushforth, whose tender was lower than that of Olive and Sons. That of the North of England Wagon Company was lowest of all but the wagons were not recommended by the colliery engineer as the woodwork was of poor quality [45].

At the end of 1874, with the Plate Works at Cowley Hill under construction and with extensions at the Sheet Works being considered, it was decided to purchase two additional locomotives. By this date Edward Borrows was established as a locomotive manufacturer at his Providence Foundry at St Helens Junction and his offer of £1325 each, with delivery in 6 months, was accepted [46,47,48].

As will be described in a later chapter, Borrows had developed a distinctive design of four-coupled locomotive, in which the water was carried beneath the boiler in a tank between the frames. These engines proved very popular with firms in and around St Helens as works shunters and, with one exception, all the locomotives purchased by Pilkington Brothers over the next 40 years, came from the Providence Foundry. The first of the new locomotives, named SUTTON, was not delivered until the autumn of 1875 [49] despite sharp letters and personal interviews with Borrows [50,51] about delays in completion. The second, WINDLE, arrived in August 1876 [52].

In the same month, Borrows submitted an estimate of £380 for repairing the old locomotive ST HELENS, but suggested making a third large engine taking ST HELENS in part exchange for £400 [52]. The matter hung fire until November 1877, when Borrows offered to make a new engine like SUTTON and WINDLE for £1300, allowing £380 for ST HELENS [53]. After further negotiation, Borrows agreed to allow £400 on the old locomotive and the order was placed for a new one [54]. This, named ST HELENS like its predecessor, was delivered in 1879.

Although the Board Minutes are not specific on this point, it appears that two of the locomotives were allocated to the Sheet Works, probably ST HELENS and SUTTON, with WINDLE at the Plate Works. No doubt there were transfers from one works to the other from time to time to cover for repairs and servicing.

Developments 1876 to 1900

Following the colliery amalgamation of 1876, Bromilow and Haddock's wharf was abandoned and the site taken over for an extension of the Bridgewater Alkali Works. The loading facilities at St Helens Colliery were adapted to deal with all shipments by canal and an overhead tubway was constructed in 1878 or the following year so that coal could be brought in tubs from the Ravenhead pits [55]. A painting of the Sheet Works in 1879, reproduced in Barker's The Glassmakers [1], illustrates the wooden viaduct which carried the tubway.

Construction of the tubway enabled the level crossing over the Ravenhead Branch of the LNWR to be abandoned and arrangements were made with the railway company to work coal traffic from Ravenhead Colliery to the Glass Works at a specially reduced rate of ½d per ton [55]. The northern part of Bromilow and Haddock's line, with its awkward level crossings over the Sheet Works sidings, was retained for the time being to provide access to the Bridgewater Alkali Works.

In 1875 and 1876 [56,57,58] negotiations were in hand to purchase John Marsh's Alkali Works. The premises were probably acquired by Pilkington Brothers after Marsh's bankruptcy at the end of 1878 [2] and the site was cleared to make way for clay sheds, a masons' shop and other ancillary plant. The railway connection to Marsh's works had been lifted by the LNWR in 1878 as there had been no traffic in the previous two years [59]. It was reinstated following the Pilkington take-over. As shown on the 25 inch map, surveyed in 1881, the Marsh site was also joined to the main works system by a level crossing over Grove Street. A second track was added over the level crossing in 1891 or 1892 to improve access between the Sheet Works and the timber yard [60].

On 1st January 1879 [61] Pilkington Brothers took possession of the Ravenhead Glass Bottle Works, at the lower end of Grove Street, where since 1866 Edward Cannington had been a partner with John Shaw [62]. The purchase had been negotiated in September 1875 [63], but completion had been deferred. This was to permit Pilkington Brothers to pay the purchase price of £13,500 in instalments and to allow time for Cannington, Shaw and Company to commission its new Sherdley Bottle Works.

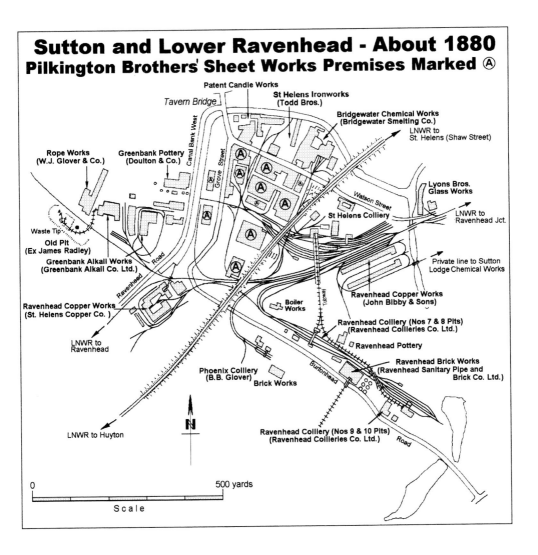

Sutton and Lower Ravenhead - About 1880
Pilkington Brothers' Sheet Works Premises Marked Ⓐ

Patent Candle Works

St Helens Ironworks
(Todd Bros.)

Tavern Bridge

Bridgewater Chemical Works
(Bridgewater Smelting Co.)

LNWR to
St. Helens (Shaw Street)

Rope Works
(W.J. Glover & Co.)

Greenbank Pottery
(Doulton & Co.)

Canal Bank West

Grove Street

Lyons Bros.
Glass Works

Watson Street

St Helens Colliery

LNWR to
Ravenhead Jct.

Waste Tip

Old Pit
(Ex James Radley)

Greenbank Alkali Works
(Greenbank Alkali Co. Ltd.)

Road

Private line to Sutton
Lodge Chemical Works

Ravenhead

Boiler
Works

Ravenhead Copper Works
(John Bibby & Sons)

Ravenhead Copper Works
(St. Helens Copper Co.)

Sutton

Ravenhead Colliery (Nos 7 & 8 Pits)
(Ravenhead Collieries Co. Ltd.)

LNWR to
Ravenhead

Ravenhead Pottery

Ravenhead Brick Works
(Ravenhead Sanitary Pipe and
Brick Co. Ltd.)

Burtonhead

Phoenix Colliery
(B.B. Glover)
Brick Works

N

Ravenhead Colliery (Nos 9 & 10 Pits)
(Ravenhead Collieries Co. Ltd.)

LNWR to Huyton

Road

0   500 yards

Scale

The Ravenhead Bottle Works and some adjacent housing were cleared to make way for sidings for the receipt of sand which, from early 1881, came from Rainford by rail [64-70]. Part of the site was also used for an extension to the cathedral plant and for new warehousing. A new connection between the LNWR Ravenhead Branch and the bottle works site was put in under an agreement with Pilkington Brothers dated 9th September 1885 [71].

In May 1884, the Bridgewater Alkali Works was put up for auction [1], presumably as the result of the bankruptcy in July 1878 [2] of J.K. Leathers, one of the principal partners. The site was acquired by Pilkington Brothers and construction of a new sheet glass plant, known as the Jubilee Works, was authorised in 1885 [72,73,74].

Sutton and Lower Ravenhead - About 1890
Pilkington Brothers' Sheet Works Premises Marked Ⓐ

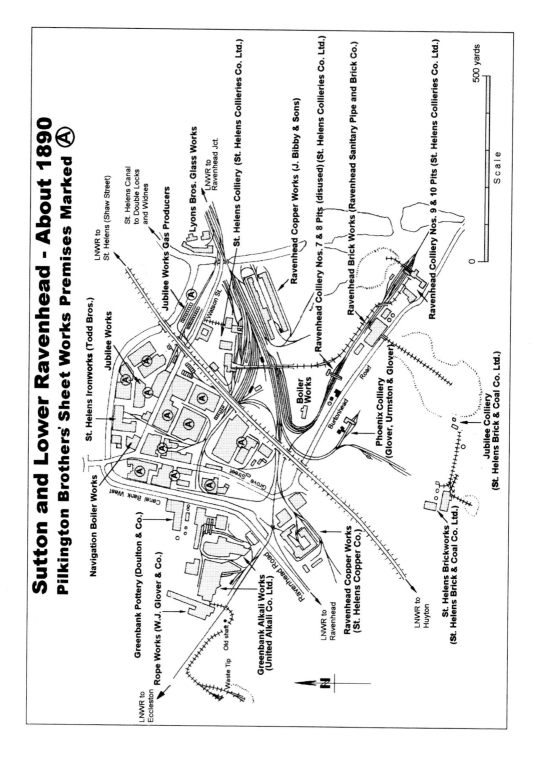

Plans were drawn up to provide a new rail access to the Jubilee Works which involved a bridge under the LNWR Huyton to St Helens line [75] and a bridge over the Burtonhead arm of the canal. An offer by Lyons Brothers to provide land for new sidings alongside the Ravenhead Branch was turned down on the grounds that the asking price of £4500 [76] was too high.

Negotiations with the LNWR continued over several years and the connection with the Ravenhead Branch, near Lyons' Glass Works but not on Lyons' property, was eventually provided under an agreement with the LNWR dated 12th November 1888 [77]. The level crossing over Watson Street, which had served the Bridgewater Alkali Works, was removed. It was replaced a new one further east which gave direct access from St Helens Colliery to the producers, where gas to fire the melting furnaces and the annealing furnaces at the Jubilee Works was manufactured from coal slack.

Within the older part of the works, the main exchange sidings with the LNWR, adjacent to those of the St Helens Colliery, were enlarged in the 1890s [78-83]. Five extra sidings were provided, the wagon shop was moved to a new site and the engine shed, which had only been constructed in 1885, was replaced.

Up to the end of 1881 one locomotive had been able to deal with all the work which was needed at the Sheet Works, but after that it was necessary to employ the spare engine as well [84]. With no stand-by locomotive now available at either the Sheet Works or the Plate Works, two more engines were ordered from Edward Borrows during 1882 and 1883 [68]. The first, RAINFORD, was delivered in 1883 and seems to have gone to the Plate Works. KNOWSLEY followed in 1884, presumably for the Sheet Works, although it may have been regarded as a spare engine to be used at either works.

In 1891 it was reported that there were six locomotives, one of which was under repair at Borrows' works. Three were allocated to the Sheet Works, two to the Plate Works and one to the colliery [79].

The reference to the colliery is at first sight puzzling, as the colliery property was under the control of a nominally independent company. It must be remembered, however, that Pilkington Brothers had a large financial interest in the St Helens Collieries Co Ltd and, as a result, there was some interchange of locomotives. As we shall see in Chapter 5, Pilkington Brothers Ltd took over the operation and maintenance of the colliery railway system early in the present century.

Although it is not possible positively to identify the locomotives mentioned in the 1891 minutes, it seem likely that SUTTON, WINDLE and the second ST HELENS were at the Sheet Works, with RAINFORD and KNOWSLEY at the Plate Works. There is some uncertainty about the engine at the colliery. As discussed in Chapter 5, there are two, if not three, possible candidates.

Another new locomotive was ordered from Borrows in January 1891 [79]. Delivered early in 1892, it was named ROBY. It appears to have been associated with the Plate Works from an early date, although it may also have employed at the Sheet Works for a time.

A view of part of the Sheet Works taken, probably before the first world war, from the waste heaps of Ravenhead Colliery. The LNWR Ravenhead Branch runs across the foreground, with a wooden building, probably the wagon repair shop, just inside the works boundary The wooden viaduct, carrying the tubway from Ravenhead Colliery, is on the right, with the headframe of St Helens Colliery clearly visible. The tall building on the left is the seven storey warehouse built in 1911 and in front of it can be seen the steel viaduct carrying the LNWR's Huyton and St Helens line over the Sheet Works tracks.
(Pilkington Brothers' Archives at IM&S)

Of the locomotives owned by Pilkington Brothers, it was recorded in 1895 that three were allocated to the Sheet Works accounts and two to the Plate Works. The sixth was regarded as a spare and the charges divided equally between the two works. Locomotives owned by the colliery company were evidently not included in these totals, although it was noted that sometimes one of the Pilkington engines was borrowed by the colliery [85].

The congestion at the Sheet Works grew worse, despite three locomotives being available. In April 1895 it was reported that the sidings were so full of wagons waiting to be unloaded that empty wagons for outgoing goods could not come into the works [86]. Traffic was very heavy and a few years later 43 or 44 wagons were being despatched each day from the packing department [87]. In addition, raw materials such as sand and saltcake as well as slack coal for the gas producers all had to be worked in.

HAZELS, the Chapman and Furneaux locomotive of 1899, was sold by Pilkington Brothers around 1923. It is seen here at the Aycliffe limestone quarry near Darlington, where it worked until 1951. *(Frank Jones)*

The available locomotives were kept working until late in the evening [88] and a decision was made to purchase two further engines to alleviate the situation. Both appear to have been intended for use at the Sheet Works.

In January 1897 Edward Borrows and Sons quoted a price of £1150 for one of the firm's well tanks [89]. It was decided to seek tenders from other manufacturers and although the price given by the Vulcan Foundry was lower, the design was not considered suitable [90]. The order was placed with Borrows [90] and the locomotive, named ECCLESTON, was delivered the following year.

For reasons which are not stated in the minutes, the second locomotive, HAZELS, was ordered from Chapman and Furneaux of Gateshead in 1899 at a cost of £1320 [91]. Perhaps the order book at the Providence Foundry was over full; perhaps Pilkington Brothers Ltd was sounding a warning that Edward Borrows and Sons would not get any future business unless prices were kept low.

Photographs from the 1950s show that HAZELS was generally similar in appearance to the Borrows locomotives but, unlike them, the valve gear was between the frames and the water was carried in short side tanks in front of the cab. It may have been rebuilt like this while it was with Pilkington Brothers Ltd, as there is a suggestion that it originally had a saddle tank.

Information about the wagons used at the Sheet Works during this period is incomplete. It is known that 80 old wagons lying at the colliery and no longer fit to be used on the main line were transferred to the glass works in February 1876 at a book cost of about £12 10s each [92].

Two coke wagons were hired from the Ditton Brook Iron Company in January 1878, the rental being 4/- per week [93]. In November 1879 there was discussion about converting old wagons lying at the colliery to transport salt cake at a cost of about £17 each [94]. In September 1887 it was recorded that Pilkington Brothers had 172 wagons [95].

Developments 1900 to 1914

More land north of Watson Street was obtained in 1890 when the lease on the Navigation Boiler Works expired. The works had been established in 1878 by David and John Forster. Later John Forster had become the sole owner and moved his business to Pocket Nook following the surrender of the Bridgewater Street lease [96].

The adjoining plot was taken over on 1st May 1897, after Pilkington Brothers Ltd had given six months notice to terminate Todd Brothers' lease [97]. The forge had closed in 1887 and Todd Brothers had then moved the caustic drum factory here, replacing an earlier works in Shaw Street acquired from W.H. Foster [14].

The Forster and Todd sites were redeveloped for extensions to the Jubilee Glass Works. The level crossing over Watson Street was retained to provide a connection with the original part of the Sheet Works.

In the 1890s Pilkington Brothers had been promoting the idea of closing the canal west of the junction with the Burtonhead arm [98,99,100], although later there were second thoughts. In 1902, the firm was considering the use of the canal as a lever against the LNWR in order to reduce rates [101], although nothing came of this idea.

In the event only the portion of the canal between the Tavern Bridge and the Ravenhead terminus was abandoned by the LNWR Act of 1898 [102]. Canal Street was built on the site and this enabled most of Grove Street to be closed. The land thus released was acquired by Pilkington Brothers Ltd and a new Head Office was built on part of it. The remaining works housing in Back Grove Street and Top Grove Street was also demolished at this time.

Between 1899 and 1902 [1] land in Greenbank, on the opposite side of Canal Street, was acquired. This included housing property in Pottery Street, Garden Street, High Street, St James Street and Liverpool Street [103,104] and Doulton's Greenbank Pottery.

The pottery had been founded by Thomas Harley in the early years of the nineteenth century and had been taken over by Doulton Brothers in about 1850 [2]. Under a Chancery Court order of 10th April 1891 Doulton and Company was obliged to sell the works to the neighbouring Greenbank Alkali Co Ltd within five years [2]. Presumably the United Alkali Company, as the successor to the Greenbank Alkali Company, was not interested in pursuing the matter and the Doulton property was sold to Pilkington Brothers Ltd instead.

116

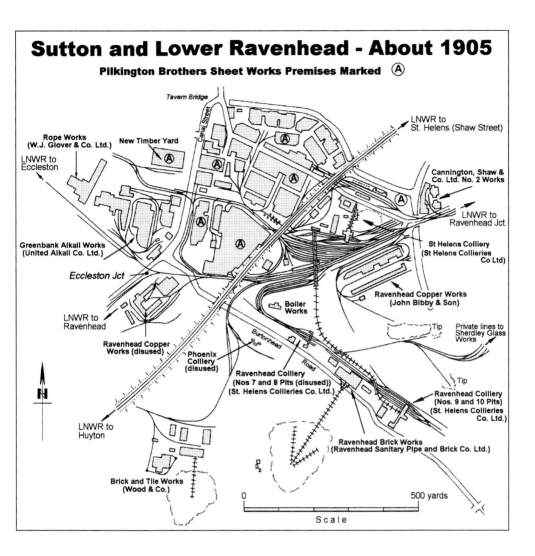

Sutton and Lower Ravenhead - About 1905

Pilkington Brothers Sheet Works Premises Marked Ⓐ

Tavern Bridge

Canal Street

LNWR to St. Helens (Shaw Street)

Rope Works (W.J. Glover & Co. Ltd.)

New Timber Yard

LNWR to Eccleston

Cannington, Shaw & Co. Ltd. No. 2 Works

LNWR to Ravenhead Jct.

Greenbank Alkali Works (United Alkali Co. Ltd.)

St Helens Colliery (St Helens Collieries Co Ltd)

Eccleston Jct

Boiler Works

Ravenhead Copper Works (John Bibby & Son)

LNWR to Ravenhead

Tip

Private lines to Sherdley Glass Works

Ravenhead Copper Works (disused)

Buttonhead Road

Phoenix Colliery (disused)

N

Ravenhead Colliery (Nos 7 and 8 Pits (disused)) (St. Helens Collieries Co. Ltd.)

Tip

Ravenhead Colliery (Nos. 9 and 10 Pits) (St. Helens Collieries Co. Ltd.)

LNWR to Huyton

Ravenhead Brick Works (Ravenhead Sanitary Pipe and Brick Co. Ltd.)

Brick and Tile Works (Wood & Co.)

0   500 yards

Scale

The Doulton site and the adjacent housing were cleared to make way for a new timber yard, together with box and crate making sheds which were built in 1903 and 1904 [104,105]. These were connected to the main works railway system by a line which crossed Canal Street on the level, for which permission was obtained from the St Helens Borough Council in 1900 [106].

Land now available within the main works boundary was used for extensions of the glass manufacturing plant and additional warehousing. The main contracts were let in 1905 [107,108] and the total cost was estimated at £46,800 [109]. There were also extensions to the clay sheds and the masons' shop [110], while a new fitting shop was opened in May 1907 [111].

Additional railway lines were provided to serve the new buildings and in 1907 a new line linking the old Ravenhead Bottle Works site and the wagon shops was authorised to improve the flow of traffic within the works [112].

Lyons Brothers' Glass Works, to the east of the Burtonhead arm of the canal, was acquired at the end of 1911. All the buildings were subsequently demolished, except those needed to store 1,000 tons of sand and straw [113].

There had been little change here since the 1870s, apart from the construction of some new furnaces. Lyons Brothers, which had become a limited company in 1886 [2], announced in October 1890 that it was to wind up and the employees were given their notice on 17th October [114]. The works was purchased by Cannington, Shaw and Co Ltd and restarted at the end of 1890 [115]. It became known as the No. 2 Works to distinguish it from the firm's main premises on the opposite side of the Ravenhead Branch and was closed in 1911 [62].

Alterations to the exchange sidings with the Ravenhead Branch were under consideration at the end of 1909, when a new gridiron was proposed [116,117]. There were further discussions in 1911 [118] and 1912 [119], when the intention seems to have been to utilise part of the Lyons Brothers site and to build a new bridge over the Burtonhead arm of the canal. In parallel, the LNWR would carry out improvements to the Ravenhead Branch. The scheme had to be modified to meet objections raised by St Helens Borough Council [120] and revised proposals were discussed with the railway company in 1913 [121,122]. Nothing had been agreed when the first world war broke out in 1914.

At the end of 1900 one locomotive was reported as working all night to place wagons at the warehouses for loading next morning [123] and clearly further additions to stock were needed. An order was placed with Edward Borrows in July 1904 for another well tank [124,125]. The locomotive, which cost £1,350, was delivered in the following year and was named WHEATHILL.

In 1905 SUTTON, built in 1875, was found to be too expensive to repair and a replacement was ordered from Borrows. The new locomotive was named SUTTON like its predecessor and was delivered later that year. In the meantime Borrows lent the firm another engine which he had on hand free of charge. The old SUTTON was not scrapped immediately as the Board thought that it would come in useful from time to time [126].

Two members of staff were sent to London in 1907 to inspect the locomotives which were on sale by the Metropolitan Railway after it had changed over to electric traction [127]. Although these were available at a knock down price of about £300 each, they were passenger engines with large diameter driving wheels and clearly unsuitable for shunting at the Sheet Works.

WINDLE needed repairs in 1908 but it was decided not to proceed as the cost was not justified [128], and it is apparent that the second ST HELENS was also withdrawn from service around this time. Two new locomotives were ordered from Borrows in May [128] and were delivered in the following year. They took the names of the previous engines, WINDLE and ST HELENS.

WHEATHILL, delivered by Edward Borrows and Sons in 1905. Photographed at the Sheet Works on 23rd July 1950. (C.A. Appleton)

The Board Minutes [128] record that with these additions to the stock there would be five 15 inch engines at the Sheet Works, four working and one spare. Although the individual locomotives were not identified, it appears that they comprised HAZELS, WHEATHILL. the second SUTTON, the second WINDLE and the third ST HELENS. If this surmise is correct, it would suggest that ECCLESTON had been sent to work at Ravenhead Colliery as implied in the Industrial Railway Society lists.

There was talk about ordering another locomotive in 1914, as the Ravenhead Works had borrowed the Sheet Works spare engine. However it was decided not to proceed, as it would be possible to hire a locomotive if the need arose [129,130].

During this period the minutes are generally silent about the wagons used by the firm, although some small scraps of information appear from time to time. In 1904 fifteen or twenty more wagons were needed and it was considered to be cheaper to purchase than hire. A price of £67 each had been quoted [131].

The question of 20-ton wagons for the sand traffic from Rainford was raised in 1905. The Ince Wagon Company had given a price of £76 each, but those from Haydock at £82 each were preferred. It was decided to offer Haydock £79 [132]. Although the minute is not specific, the implication is that wagons were being manufactured at Richard Evans and Co Ltd's Haydock Workshops for sale to outside customers as well for use by the colliery company.

119

In 1906, a further twenty five wagons were required. The Ince Wagon Company had quoted £72 each for 15-ton wagons, but it was decided to seek an alternative quotation from a Midland company [133]. More sand wagons were needed in 1908 and a member of the firm's staff was sent to Chorley to see what could be obtained second hand [134].

Developments 1914 to 1939

In 1918, towards the end of the war, Pilkington Brothers Ltd had made an attempt to acquire the St Helens Foundry site from Robert Daglish and Co Ltd. The intention was that the premises would be leased to George Varley to manufacture cast iron shell cases which were needed by the Ministry of Munitions. It is also apparent that Pilkington Brothers had an eye to post war expansion of the glass works and the closure of the canal east of Tavern Bridge. In the event, Robert Daglish and Company was not prepared to release the property at an acceptable price and the deal fell through [135-139].

The first major acquisition of the post war period was the the Greenbank Alkali Works of the United Alkali Co Ltd which we deal with in Chapter 5. The works was located on the south side of the Pilkington Brothers' timber yard and crate making shops. Negotiations had been in progress since 1917 [140-143] and the purchase was finally settled early in 1921 [144]. According to the Sidings Schedules, Pilkington Brothers took possession in January 1922.

The buildings were demolished and the site cleared to make way for a new wagon shop and for extensions of the joiners' shops. One of the connections between the alkali works and the LNWR, at 98 yards from Eccleston Junction, was transferred to Pilkington Brothers under an agreement of 7th September 1923. The other, at 320 yards, was removed. The internal railway system was extended to link up with that at Pilkington Brothers' existing timber yard.

With a view to providing a second crate yard, Pilkington Brothers Ltd entered into negotiations with W.J. Glover and Co Ltd about the purchase of its rope works, which adjoined the Greenbank site. The intention was that Glovers would move to the derelict London and Manchester Plate Glass Works site at Sutton Oak which Pilkingtons were trying to dispose of [145]. The deal fell through as Glovers asked too high a price [146]. According to the Sidings Schedules, the second crate yard was eventually constructed on the Greenbank site and was brought into use on 18th January 1937, replacing that at the Ravenhead Works.

Further room for expansion became available with the closure of St Helens Colliery. Coal winding ceased here in the early 1920s, although the colliery was not formally abandoned, according to the Mines Lists, until 1931. The site was quickly cleared, partly for extra siding accommodation and partly for additional glass making plant. A drawn sheet tank was erected here in 1925 and a warehouse in 1933 [110]. At the same time there was redevelopment of the older part of the works, where two new tanks were built in 1931 and 1933 respectively [110].

The final acquisition of this period was Bibby's Copper Works, on the south side of the Ravenhead Branch opposite to the Sheet Works sidings. Purchase of the site had first been discussed in 1900, [147,148] when a move to Widnes was being considered. However, the asking price was too high and it was not until around 1920 that Pilkington Brothers Ltd took over, following the closure of the works. Pilkingtons used the premises for storage, with some of the original copper works buildings on the south side of the site being retained for several years as warehouses [1,110].

In the immediate post war period improvements to the Sheet Works railway system were again considered and capital expenditure for this purpose of £2,300 was authorised in September 1919 [149]. By 1920 a comprehensive series of proposals had been drawn up [150] which included a modification of the 1913 scheme. This was intended to improve the general traffic facilities on the Ravenhead Branch and the costs would therefore be borne jointly by the company and the LNWR.

The proposed works comprised :

(a) A fan of sidings on the St Helens Colliery site
(b) A mixing room and reception sidings on the Lyons' Glass Works site
(c) Alterations to Watson Street to avoid the three level crossings
(d) A double line over the canal bridge

In addition it was intended to improve the internal railway system by :

(a) Providing two through roads by the Rolled Plate Crate Repair Shops
(b) Removing the wagon shops and engine shed to the St Helens Colliery site and laying down a short length of sidings in their place
(c) Providing additional sidings between the St Helens Colliery site and the existing exchange sidings
(d) Extending the line through Bibby's Yard into the Ravenhead Colliery sidings
(e) Providing a line from the Crate Yard to the Siberia Warehouse for empty wagons

These schemes were modified subsequently. St Helens Colliery did not close as early as expected and it was later found that proposed sidings on the colliery site, intended to accommodate 150 wagons, would in any case have proved to be too long to be worked satisfactorily [151]. The connection between Bibby's Yard and the Ravenhead Colliery sidings was completed by 1926 and is shown on the revised 25 inch map surveyed in that year. The curve linking the crate yard with the main exchange sidings, which involved a level crossing over Canal Street, had also been completed by 1926, but was removed before 1939 [110].

The engine shed was retained in its original location but, as we have already related, the wagon shops were replaced by a new building on the Greenbank Alkali Works site in 1924 [110]. This then permitted the construction of two extra through sidings and an additional dead end siding where the old wagon shops had been located [110,152]. Extra sidings were also laid in to serve the new glass plant and warehouse on the St Helens Colliery site.

CORONATION, built by the Hunslet Engine Company to the Kerr, Stuart Moss Bay design, at the Sheet Works on 10th August 1958. (J.A. Peden)

Rearrangement of the sidings at Lyons' Yard were still under discussion in 1925 [153] and 1926 [154], but was put in hand shortly afterwards. A double track connection between the Jubilee Glass Works and the LMSR was built by Pilkington Brothers Ltd on the north side of Watson Street; this required the construction of a new bridge over the disused Burtonhead arm of the canal. The improvements on the Ravenhead Branch , including a new double track bridge over the canal, were carried out by the railway company.

On the locomotive side, two members of staff were sent to Stoke on Trent in March 1919 to inspect what was considered to be a suitable locomotive which was available at the works of Kerr, Stuart and Company [155]. As a result four of that firm's Moss Bay class four-coupled saddle tanks were purchased. VICTORY, FAIRFIELD and THE GROVE were for use at the Sheet Works and Ravenhead Colliery, while ROSEBANK went to the Plate Works.

Two four-coupled well tanks arrived in 1921, named KELVIN and PATIENCE. By this time, Edward Borrows and Sons had gone out of business and the drawings and patterns had been acquired by H.W. Johnson and Company, which completed the locomotives at Rainford. The story goes that PATIENCE was so named because Pilkington Brothers had been kept waiting a long time before it was delivered. KELVIN was transferred to the Plate Works early in 1922 [156] and perhaps was only temporarily at the Sheet Works.

HAZELS, which was surplus to requirements and also of a non-standard type, was sold in 1923, to H.W. Johnson and Company. It was resold to the Aycliffe Lime and Limestone Co Ltd, near Darlington.

There was no further change to the locomotive stock until 1937, when No 3, a well tank built by Borrows in 1883, was transferred from the Ravenhead Works [157]. It did not see much service at the Sheet Works, being broken up there in the following year [157]. Perhaps it was only needed as a stop gap until CORONATION arrived in 1937. This was a four-coupled saddle tank from the Hunslet Engine Company to the same design as the Kerr Stuart locomotives.

There was apparently a shortage of wagons immediately after the first world war. In 1919 a hundred were purchased second hand from the LNWR, although there was some delay in obtaining delivery [158]. The Wigan colliery firm, Crompton and Shawcross Ltd, offered to sell Pilkington Brothers 150 of its wagons in January 1921, but a decision was deferred because there were likely to be plenty at a cheaper price in the future [144].

PATIENCE and CORONATION at the Sheet Works engine shed on 23rd July 1950. The photograph is taken looking towards the Ravenhead Branch which runs beyond the fence behind the shed. In the foreground is the beginning of the fan of sidings where traffic was exchanged with British Railways. (C.A. Appleton)

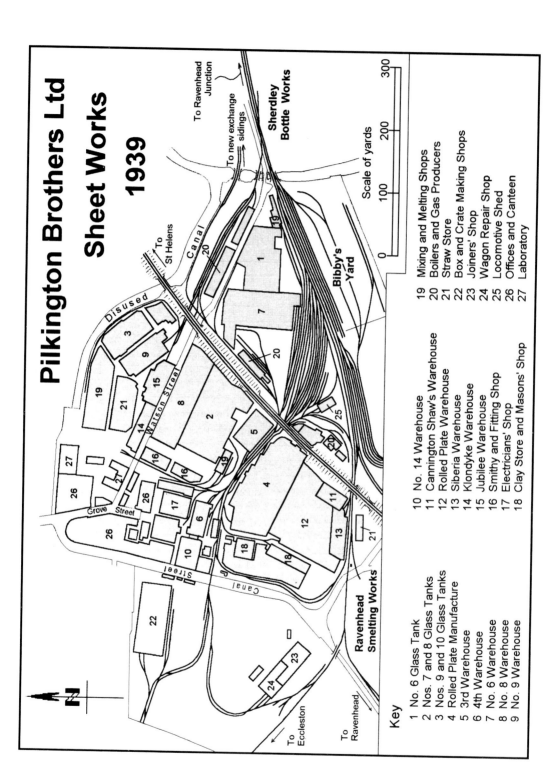

Pilkington Brothers Ltd
Sheet Works
1939

To Ravenhead Junction

To new exchange sidings

Sherdley Bottle Works

Scale of yards

0   100   200   300

To St Helens

Disused

Canal

Bibby's Yard

Watson Street

Grove Street

Canal Street

Ravenhead Smelting Works

To Eccleston

To Ravenhead

N

Key

1 No. 6 Glass Tank
2 Nos. 7 and 8 Glass Tanks
3 Nos. 9 and 10 Glass Tanks
4 Rolled Plate Manufacture
5 3rd Warehouse
6 4th Warehouse
7 No. 6 Warehouse
8 No. 8 Warehouse
9 No. 9 Warehouse
10 No. 14 Warehouse
11 Cannington Shaw's Warehouse
12 Rolled Plate Warehouse
13 Siberia Warehouse
14 Klondyke Warehouse
15 Jubilee Warehouse
16 Smithy and Fitting Shop
17 Electricians' Shop
18 Clay Store and Masons' Shop
19 Mixing and Melting Shops
20 Boilers and Gas Producers
21 Straw Store
22 Box and Crate Making Shops
23 Joiners' Shop
24 Wagon Repair Shop
25 Locomotive Shed
26 Offices and Canteen
27 Laboratory

124

The Sheet Works 1939 to 1996

War time conditions between 1939 and 1945 put an end to any plans for further expansion at the Sheet Works. Part of the plant was turned over to the manufacture of munitions and production of glass remained at a relatively high level to replace windows damaged by bombing.

During the late 1940s and 1950s, the flat glass trade continued to boom but production could largely be met by existing plant at the Sheet Works. The only additional property acquired during this period was the works of St Helens Smelting Co Ltd. The agreement in respect of the sidings here was transferred to Pilkington Brothers Ltd as from 31st December 1959 [159].

A major alteration to the railway system was the reorganisation of the trackwork on the north side of Watson Street. A start had been made in the late 1930s when the Burtonhead arm of the canal was filled in and a new line was built north of Lyon's Yard to connect with the Ravenhead Branch. In the post war period the layout was extended and a bank of eleven through sidings were provided to exchange traffic with British Railways, thus bringing to fruition a scheme which had been first mooted in 1907 [160].

A busy scene in the Sheet Works sidings, probably in the late 1950s, when rail traffic was at its peak. The United Glass Bottle Manufacturers' Sherdley Works is on the left beyond the Ravenhead Branch. The waste tips in the far distance on the right are those of the now closed Sherdley Colliery. (Pilkington Brothers' Archives)

In the late 1950s, rail traffic was at peak levels. An article published early in 1958, but presumably based on information obtained the previous year [161] stated that the Sheet Works handled, on average, 1800 incoming and outgoing wagons each week. Nine locomotives were employed, although not all would have been in service at any one time. In addition to the administrative staff to control traffic movements and liaise with British Railways, there were eight full time drivers, eight shunters, two locomotive cleaners and a shed cleaner.

The complement of nine locomotives included five well tanks from the pre war period - WHEATHILL, the second SUTTON, the second WINDLE, the third ST HELENS and PATIENCE. VICTORY and CORONATION had been joined by a third similar engine, ECCLESTON, which came from the Hunslet Engine Company in 1947. Finally there was SENTINEL No. 1, delivered in 1957 after a visit by a demonstration locomotive.

SENTINEL No. 1 had been equipped for oil firing when new and most of the remaining locomotives were converted to comply with the Clean Air Act. The first to be dealt with was WHEATHILL in May 1957. This conversion was apparently not satisfactory and the engine was scrapped by Todd Bros on 10th February 1958. PATIENCE, VICTORY, ECCLESTON and WINDLE were treated later in 1957 and appear to have been more successful.

SUTTON and ST HELENS remained as coal burners and were taken out of service in 1958. They stood out of use at the Sheet Works until broken up by Todd Brothers in 1960 [162].

A Barclay locomotive, presumably PROGRESS from Pilkington Brothers' Ravenhead Works and perhaps here in a temporary role, was noted from a passing train on two occasions in November and December 1958. There is also a note in the Industrial Railway Society lists that the Hawthorn, Leslie locomotive, REX, was transferred from the Plate Works in 1960. It apparently did not last long at the Sheet Works and was believed to have been scrapped in the same year.

DH1, DH2 and DH3, all four-coupled diesel hydraulic machines built by the Yorkshire Engine Company, were delivered in May 1960, February 1961 and July 1961 respectively. By early 1962 only one of the steam locomotives was in use each day and, with the continuing run down of rail traffic, the diesels took over entirely soon afterwards.

PATIENCE and VICTORY were taken out of traffic in the middle of 1960 and were cut up by Todd Bros late in 1961 [162]. WINDLE worked until 28th May 1960 and stood in the engine shed until December. It was then decided to present it to the Middleton Railway Preservation Society.

Opposite above. SENTINEL No.1 dismantled, with the boiler taken out for repair, photographed at the Sheet Works on 10th August 1958. (J.A. Peden)

Opposite below. DH3, one of the three Yorkshire Engine Company's diesel locomotives used at the Sheet Works. The photograph was taken at the Haydock yard of Lowton Metals on 11th October 1977. (A.J. Booth)

WINDLE had been converted back to coal firing by July 1961 and the steam brake and some other parts off PATIENCE were fitted. It was later taken to the wagon shops where it was repainted and was presented to the Society at a formal ceremony on 17th October 1961 [163].

An aerial photograph of around 1950, looking east, with the Sheet Works occupying most of the foreground. The St Helens to Huyton railway runs diagonally across, with the new plant of the 1930s beyond. On the opposite bank of the canal are the chimney and buildings of the Brooklands lead works. The Ravenhead Branch cuts across the right hand half of the picture. In the foreground, on the near side of the branch, are the main exchange sidings with the Sheet Works, while on the far side sidings occupy the site of Bibby's Copper Works. Beyond here is the Sherdley Glass Bottle Works, where some expansion has already taken place on to the McKechnie site, as indicated by the building with the white roof. In the distance, past the canal and the St Helens to St Helens Junction railway, the Kurtz Alkali Works has been replaced by the new gas works. Beyond, in the far distance, the white buildings and the chimney are on the site of the Hardshaw Brook Alkali Works. (Pilkington Brothers' Archives at IM&S)

CORONATION was taken out of service shortly afterwards and was subsequently scrapped. ECCLESTON and SENTINEL No. 1 lasted until about 1964. The Sentinel had not been regarded as successful and was not liked by the drivers. It had had to be returned to the makers for alterations shortly after it had been delivered, as the clearance above the track was too low [163].

A fourth diesel No. 7 SAXON arrived about 1964 from the Pilkington Brothers Ltd's Kirk Sandall Works, near Doncaster, and there is also a note that THE SCHOLES was temporarily here from the sand wash at Old Mill Lane in 1965 and 1966.

By 1972 much of the track in the works was no longer in use. Four of the exchange sidings adjacent to the former St Helens Colliery site and two of the new sidings north of Watson Street had been lifted by that year. The track in Bibby's Yard had also been removed, except for two sidings serving the oil terminal which we describe later.

DH3 was sold to Lowton Metals Ltd for scrap around the end of 1972 and taken to this firm's yard at Ashton in Makerfield to be cut up. DH1 and DH2 continued in service until rail traffic finished around the end of July 1981 and went to Steamport, Southport, towards the end of the following year. The fate of SAXON is not known.

Epilogue

The float process came into commercial production in the early 1960s and as a result much of the manufacture of sheet glass has been transferred to other works. The Sheet Works now operates on a much reduced scale and only makes cathedral glass and a range of special products transferred from the Ravenhead Works.

Many of the peripheral properties have been disposed of and the works is now confined to the area bounded by Watson Street, Canal Street and the site of the Ravenhead Branch railway. Watson Street itself has been reconstructed and now forms part of the new road network. North of this the land that was formerly part of the Sheet Works is now occupied by a hotel. One of the glass houses of the Jubilee Works, adjacent to "The Hotties", so called because Pilkington Brothers once used the canal here for cooling water, is in course of restoration as a historical monument.

The once busy Ravenhead Branch was closed around the end of 1983 or early in 1984, with the exception of a single line which was left in between Ravenhead Junction and Pilkington Brothers' oil terminal, on the site of Bibby's Copper Works. The terminal had been opened at the end of 1968 following the signing of a contract with Shell Mex and BP Ltd for the supply of 300,000 tons of fuel oil per year.

This terminal, which supplied the Sheet Works and later the new Greengate Works, and similar facilities near Gerard's Bridge Junction to serve the Cowley Hill Works, were capable of handling 1,000 tons at a time in block trains of 100-ton tank wagons [164]. The trains ran about twice each week [165] and the tank wagons were placed in position by the British Rail train engine.

There were considerable alterations in 1992 brought about by the construction of a new road which ran across the stub end of the Ravenhead Branch. The remaining part of the branch was closed on 22nd June and the old oil terminal taken out of use [166]. A new oil terminal was built on an adjacent site in Bibby's Yard and served by a steeply graded spur from the Huyton to St Helens line. This new rail connection was brought into use at the end of October 1992 [165,166].

LOCOMOTIVE SUMMARY

Pilkington Brothers' Sheet Works

Partnership including William Pilkington, Peter Greenall and William Bell 1826 to 1845
Pilkington Brothers 1845 to 1894
Pilkington Brothers Ltd from 1894
Pilkington Brothers plc from 1981
Pilkington plc from 1987

ST HELENS
Purchased at end of 1868 or early in 1869
Taken by Edward Borrows in part exchange for new loco in 1879

SHERDLEY
On loan from Bournes and Robinson, end of 1873

SUTTON New Scrapped after Feb 1905	0-4-0WT OC	EBS	4	1875	13"x20"	3' 6"
WINDLE New Scrapped 1908	0-4-0WT OC	EBS	5	1876	13"x20"	3' 6"
ST HELENS New Scrapped about 1909	0-4-0WT OC	EBS	9	1879	13"x20"	3' 6"

RAVENHEAD   0-4-0WT OC   EBS   1880
Appears in Industrial Locomotive Society List as new to Pilkington Brothers but is not mentioned in Pilkington Bros Minutes
Possibly used at Ravenhead Colliery. See text and Chapter 5

ECCLESTON   0-4-0WT OC   EBS   36   1898   15"x20   3' 6"
New
Possibly used at Ravenhead Colliery from about 1908 to early 1920s
Later at Ravenhead Works and scrapped there in March 1941

HAZELS	0-4-0T	OC	CF	1189 1900	14"x19"	3' 2"

New

Sold about 1923 to H.W. Johnson and Co, Rainford and resold to Aycliffe Lime and Limestone Co Ltd

WHEATHILL	0-4-0WT	OC	EBS	47 1905	15"x20"	3' 6"

New

Converted to oil firing May 1957

Scrapped by Todd Bros, February 1958

SUTTON	0-4-0WT	OC	EBS	49 1905	15"x20"	3' 6"

New

Withdrawn from service April 1959

Scrapped 1960

WINDLE	0-4-0WT	OC	EBS	53 1909	15"x20"	3' 6"

New

Converted to oil firing Nov 1957

Withdrawn from service May 1960

Repaired and reconverted to coal firing and presented to Middleton Railway Preservation Society 17.10.1961

To HE for repairs August 1962, then to Middleton Railway Preservation Society

ST HELENS	0-4-0WT	OC	EBS	54 1909	15"x20"	3' 6"

New

Withdrawn from service April 1959

Scrapped 1960 by Todd Bros

FAIRFIELD	0-4-0ST	OC	KS	4025 1919	15"x20"	3' 3"

New

Used at Ravenhead Colliery as well as Sheet Works

At Ravenhead Colliery on 1.1.1947 and transferred to NCB soon afterwards

For later history see Chapter 5

THE GROVE	0-4-0ST	OC	KS	4146 1919	15"x20"	3' 3"

New

Used at Ravenhead Colliery as well as Sheet Works

At Ravenhead Colliery on 1.1.1947 and transferred to NCB soon afterwards

For later history see Chapter 5

VICTORY	0-4-0ST	OC	KS	4148 1920	15"x20"	3'3"

New

Used at Ravenhead Colliery as well as Sheet Works

At Sheet Works on 1.1.1947 and not transferred to N C B

Scrapped at Sheet Works in about 1962

PATIENCE	0-4-0WT OC	HWJ	57	1921	15"x20"	3' 6"

New
Converted to oil firing 1957
Withdrawn from service mid 1960
Scrapped by Todd Bros latter part of 1961

KELVIN	0-4-0WT OC	HWJ	58	1921	15"x20"	3' 6"

New
To Plate Works February 1922

CORONATION	0-4-0ST OC	HE	1891	1937	15"x20"	3' 3"

New
Converted to oil firing by September 1957
Withdrawn from service 1961
Scrapped in about 1964

No. 3	0-4-0WT OC	EBS	17	1883		

Ex Ravenhead Works 1937
Scrapped at Sheet Works 1938

ECCLESTON	0-4-0ST OC	HE	3447	1947	15"x20"	3' 3"

New
Converted to oil firing by September 1957
Scrapped about 1964

	4wTGVB	S	9575	1954	200HP	

On trial from makers, mid 1955

SENTINEL No.1	4wTGVB	S	9612	1957	200HP	3'2"

New, oil fired
Scrapped in about 1964

PROGRESS	0-4-0ST OC	AB	1465	1916	14"x22"	3'5"

From City Road Works, noted at Sheet Works in Nov and Dec 1958

No.1 REX	0-4-0ST OC	HL	3933	1937	14"x22	3'6"

From City Road Works 1960
Scrapped at Sheet Works 1960

DH 1	0-4-0DH	YE	2677	1960	220HP	

New, delivered 7.5.1960
To Steamport, Southport about December 1982

DH 2	0-4-0DH	YE	2820	1960	170 HP	

New, delivered 6.2.1961
To Steamport, Southport about December 1982

DH 3	0-4-0DH	YE	2838	1961	170HP	

New, delivered 7.6.1961
To Lowton Metals Ltd, Haydock about December 1972

No. 7 SAXON   0-4-0DE   RH   433679 1960   Class 200DE
    Ex Kirk Sandall Works, in about 1964
    Scrapped or sold

THE SCHOLES   4wDM   RH   299104 1950   Class 88DS
    Ex Mill Lane Sand Wash 1965
    Returned to Mill Lane Sand Wash 1966

References to Chapter 4

1   *The Glassmakers Pilkington 1826 - 1976*, T.C. Barker, Weidenfeld and Nicolson, London, 1977

2   *A Merseyside Town in the Industrial Revolution St Helens 1750 - 1900*, T.C. Barker and J.R. Harris, Frank Cass & Co Ltd, London, 1959

3   Pilkington Bros General Board Mins, 22.10.1868, at IM&S

4   Ibid 24.9.1875

5   Ibid 30.12.1875

6   Ibid 10.3.1876

7   WO 14.7.1876

8   *History, Directory and Gazetteer of the County Palatine of Lancaster*, Edward Baines, Liverpool, 1824 and 1825

9   LRO PDR 188

10 11 Geo 4; cap lxi

11 *The St Helens Railway*, J.R. Tolson, The Oakwood Press, 1982

12 LRO PDR 799

13 28 & 29 Vic cap cccxxiii; 5th July 1865

14 *History of Todd Bros (St Helens and Widnes) Ltd*, Murray Todd, no imprint, no date, about 1948, at StHLH A36.1(P)

15 Pilkington Bros General Board Mins 19.2.1863

16 Ibid 26.2.1863

17 Ibid 28.5.1875

18 Ibid 14.2.1867

19 Ibid 21.5.1868

20 Ibid 26.6.1868

21 Ibid 18.9.1868

22 Ibid 19.10.1868

23 Ibid 21.1.1869

24 Ibid 23.12.1869

25 Ibid 28.2.1868

26 Ibid 28.1.1869

27 Ibid 25.3.1869

28 Ibid 16.2.1870

29 Ibid 12.5.1870

30 Ibid 1.6.1870

31 Ibid 19.10.1870

32 Ibid 10.10.1872

33 Ibid 5.9.1872

34 Ibid 18.12.1873

35 Ibid 7.1.1874

36 Ibid 2.2.1870

37 Ibid 15.3.1870

38 Ibid 1.8.1871

39 Ibid 28.2.1868

40 Ibid 14.11.1871

41 Ibid 13.5.1869

42 Ibid 8.6.1870

43 Ibid 31.1.1873

44 Ibid 5.1.1871

45 Ibid 30.12.1874

46 Ibid 22.10.1874

47 Ibid 5.11.1874

48 Ibid 13.11.1874

49   Ibid 24.8.1875

50   Ibid 11.6.1875

51   Ibid 24.6.1875

52   Ibid 4.8.1876

53   Ibid 8.11.1875

54   Ibid 14.11.1877

55   Ibid 9.10.1877

56   Ibid 22 and 24.2.1875

57   Ibid 10.3.1876

58   Ibid 6.5.1876

59   Ibid 5.12.1878

60   *StHNews* 22.8.1891

61   Pilkington Bros General Board Mins 10.1.1879

62   *Sherdley - Peasley Glass Works 1877 - 1977*, United Glass Ltd pamphlet, xerox copy at StHLH A 37.8 (P)

63   Pilkington Bros General Board Mins 14.9.1875

64   Ibid 25.2.1880

65   Ibid 5.2.1880

66   Ibid 12.1.1883

67   Ibid 12.6.1883

68   Ibid 31.7.1883

69   Ibid 12.6.1884

70   Ibid 8.8.1884

71   LNWR Sdgs Diag 174; 12.1916

72   Pilkington Bros General Board Mins 17.2.1885

73   Ibid 3.3.1885

74   Ibid 5.5.1885

75   Ibid 24.3.1885

76   Ibid 18.9.1884

77   LNWR Sdgs Diag 172; 12.1916

78   Pilkington Bros General Board Mins 23.12.1890

79   Ibid 13.1.1891

80   Ibid 29.4.1891

81   Ibid 16.7.1891

82   Ibid 17.11.1895

83   Ibid 8.12.1895

84   Ibid 6.12.1881

85   Ibid 22.1.1895

86   Ibid 7.4.1895

87   Ibid 7.12.1898

88   Ibid 17.2.1898

89   Ibid 17.4.1897

90   Ibid 11.5.1897

91   Ibid 1.8.1899

92   Ibid 24.2.1876

93   Ibid January 1873

94   Ibid 27.11.1879

95   Ibid 29.9.1879

96   *A History of Forster's Glass Co Ltd*, no author, no publ, nd, about 1969, at StHLH A 37.8

97   Pilkington Bros General Board Mins 27.10.1896

98   Ibid 19.11.1890

99   Ibid 13.12.1890

100 Ibid 19.11.1891

101 Ibid 4.2.1902

102 61 & 62 Vic cap ccxxiv; 12th August 1898

103 *StHNews* 22.8.1902

104 Pilkington Bros General Board Mins 20.1.1903

105 Ibid 15.5.1903

106 *StHNews* 24.3.1900

107 Pilkington Bros General Board Mins 29.5.1905

108 Ibid 20.7.1905

109 Ibid 12.12.1905

110 Plan of Pilkington Bros Sheet Works, 1939, unnumbered Plan at IM&S

111 Pilkington Bros General Board Mins 4.4.1907

112 Ibid 15.1.1907

113 Ibid 14.11.1911

114 *StHNews* 21.10.1890

115 *StHNews* 31.12.1890

116 Pilkington Bros General Board Mins 30.11.1909

117 Ibid 9.12.1909

118 Ibid 4.1.1911

119 Ibid 4.12.1912

120 Ibid 14.2.1913

121 Ibid 22.10.1913

122 Ibid 4.11.1913

123 Ibid 12.12.1900

124 Ibid 14.6.1904
125 Ibid 26.7.1904
126 Ibid 23.2.1905
127 Ibid 10.1.1907
128 Pilkington Bros Plate Board Mins 22.5.1908, at IM&S
129 Pilkington Bros General Board Mins 21.4.1914, at IM&S
130 Ibid 8.6.1914
131 Ibid 13.9.1904
132 Ibid 7.3.1905
133 Ibid 10.1.1906
134 Ibid 28.4.1908
135 Ibid 8.4.1918
136 Ibid 19.5.1918
137 Ibid 28.5.1918
138 Ibid 1.7.1918
139 Ibid 28.8.1919
140 Ibid 5.11.1917
141 Ibid 13.11.1917
142 Ibid 8.4.1918
143 Ibid 18.6.1918
144 Ibid 7.1.1921
145 Ibid 20.11.1925
146 Ibid 12.2.1926
147 Ibid 30.8.1900
148 Pilkington Bros General Board Mins 6.11.1900

149 Ibid 2.9.1919
150 Ibid 9.4.1920
151 Ibid 28.1.1921
152 Ibid 24.10.1924
153 Ibid 9.10.1925
154 Ibid 4.3.1926
155 Ibid 18.3.1919
156 Cowley Hill Works Capital Expenditure Requisitions, 1912 - 1927, IM&S PB 657
157 Letter E.M.S. Wood to Frank Smith 21.5.1956
158 Pilkington Bros General Board Mins 21.11.1919
159 Note on Line Plan of St Helens Railway, LNWR, Rugby, 1871, 2 chains to 1 inch at BRPB, Manchester Office
160 LNWR drg 21073, dated 28.10.1907, at IM&S PB 269.21
161 Article on Cross and Borrows Locomotives, in StHRep 1958
162 Letter E.M.S. Wood to Bernard Roberts 17.11.1961
163 Letter E.M.S. Wood to Bernard Roberts 16.4.1962
164 Information provided to the authors by J.M. Tolson
165 BLN 695
166 BLN 698

CHAPTER FIVE

SUTTON AND LOWER RAVENHEAD

In this chapter we deal with firms which occupied premises to the south and west of Pilkington Brothers' Sheet Works. As we have already noted, many of the sites were later taken over by Pilkington Brothers and much of the information which we present here complements that in the previous chapter. Because of the interconnected history and geography of the various sites, we have not attempted to provide a separate series of maps and the reader is referred to those in Chapter 4.

We start with the territory to the south of the Sheet Works, beyond the Ravenhead Branch railway, which was largely given over to coal mining and brick making. We then move to the west, to the neighbourhood of the the Ravenhead terminus of the canal. A copper works was established as early as 1779 and other industries, which included a pottery, a rope-walk and an alkali works, followed in the first few decades of the nineteenth century.

The coal industry had a long history, operations on a commercial scale being started in the 1760s and 1770s by entrepreneurs such as John Mackay and Thomas Case [1]. By the early years of the nineteenth century, the Haddock family featured prominently. Here, as in other parts of the St Helens coalfield, they operated through a series of interlocking partnerships with other well known colliery proprietors such as the Caldwells, the Bromilows and the Clares. The Deposited Plans for the St Helens and Runcorn Gap Railway [2], prepared in 1829, show that, west of the Burtonhead arm of the canal, coal production was centred on three sites.

The St Helens Colliery has already been described in Chapter 4. It was probably sunk about 1800 and was being worked by Clare and Haddock in 1824. It was out of use from 1844 until it was taken over by Pilkington Brothers in 1857.

Burtonhead Colliery was situated near the terminus of the Burtonhead arm of the canal and never seems to have had a rail connection. The pits here had been acquired by Thomas West following Jonathan Case's financial problems in the late 1770s [1]. By 1825 Burtonhead Colliery was being worked by Thomas Caldwell [3] and at some date after 1834 [4] it was taken over by Clare, Haddock and Company. It was put up for auction in 1844 [1], along with the firm's St Helens and Union Collieries, and like them remained unsold.

Ravenhead Colliery came into the possession of the Haddock family in 1818 [1] and subsequently passed to Bromilow, Haddock and Company [3]. There were several changes in the membership of the partnership, for example in 1840 [5] and again in 1850 [6]. An associated firm, Bromilow, Haddock and Partners, owned the Knights Grange Salt Works at Winsford in Cheshire.

Ravenhead Colliery up to 1900

The 1849 1:1056 Town Plan identifies the position of a series of pits which formed the Ravenhead Colliery along a north-west south-east axis from the canal terminus. The earliest pits, nearest the canal, seem to have become disused by this date. Only what the 1952 6 inch Geological Map describes as Nos.7 and 8 Pits, south of the connection with the St Helens Railways' Ravenhead Branch, were obviously active.

The Town Plan shows a railway connecting the pits with a wharf on the canal adjacent to Lower Grove Street. It seems likely that this had originally been a horse worked tramroad, but had been converted to standard gauge shortly after the opening of the Ravenhead Branch of the St Helens Railway in 1834.

As described in the previous chapter, this wharf was replaced by new facilities for loading barges which were established at a point between the Bridgewater Alkali Works and St Helens Colliery. A railway was constructed from Ravenhead Colliery to the new wharf which crossed the Ravenhead Branch, the sidings leading to Pilkington Brothers' works and Watson Street on the level. The old wharf and the railway leading to it were abandoned and the canal side site was later occupied by Marsh's Alkali Works.

The date when these changes were made has not been recorded, but was probably around 1850. They had certainly been completed by 1864, when the Deposited Plans were prepared for the Huyton to St Helens Railway of the LNWR [7]. The plans also show that a direct rail connection had been provided between Ravenhead Colliery and the Ravenhead Copper Works, which enabled coal to be delivered to the works without payment of toll to the LNWR.

The Ravenhead Colliery Co Ltd was registered on 5th September 1871 [8], with D. Bromilow, H.G. Bromilow and James Haddock as directors along with Edward Turner, H.J. Whiteley, David Gamble and G.W. Bates. The new company took over Bromilow and Haddock's collieries at Ravenhead and Parr as well as the Knights Grange salt works.

There was a further change of ownership in 1876 when the St Helens Collieries Co Ltd was registered on 12th July [9,10]. This brought together the coal mining interests of Pilkington Brothers at the St Helens and Alexandra Collieries and those of the Ravenhead Colliery Company. The Knights Grange Salt Works appears to have been sold to Joseph Verdin and Sons or possibly to W. and R. Hickson [11] and became the property of the Salt Union Ltd in 1888.

By 1881, when the survey was made for the first edition of the 25 inch map, the colliery company's railway had been extended along the north side of Burtonhead Road to Nos.9 and 10 Pits. These were near the site of Clare and Haddock's Burtonhead Colliery and the new sinkings may have been started in the 1870s. The Mines Lists show Benjamin Blake as working at Burtonhead in 1873 and 1874, followed by James Haddock in 1875 and 1876. No.11 Pit was sunk nearby at a later date and No.9 Pit was subsequently dispensed with.

The 25 inch map also shows the high level tubway which had been authorised by the Pilkington Board towards the end of 1877 [12] and probably completed in 1878. This linked the Ravenhead Nos.9 and 10 Pits with St Helens Colliery and there was also a branch serving Nos.7 and 8 Pits. It enabled Ravenhead coal to be loaded on to barges at the St Helens Colliery wharf and eliminated the need for the level crossing over the LNWR Ravenhead Branch.

Although coal from Ravenhead Colliery to Pilkington's Sheet Works now had to be worked round by the LNWR, a special rate of ½d per ton had been negotiated [12]. Coal to other neighbouring works could avoid travelling over LNWR tracks and thus escape paying any toll. In 1881 the direct link to the old Ravenhead Copper Works was still in existence and lines had been built across the waste land east of the colliery to the Sutton Lodge Alkali Works and the Peasley Glass Bottle Works. There was also a connection from the colliery sidings to the new copper works of John Bibby and Sons which, however, had been taken out by 1891 when the survey was made for a revision of the 25 inch map.

Information about the locomotives employed at Ravenhead Colliery during the nineteenth century is extremely scanty and unfortunately the minute books of the St Helens Collieries Co Ltd are no longer available. It is known that a locomotive was sent to Cross and Company's works for repairs in July 1869 [1], before the St Helens Collieries Co Ltd took over. Horses were evidently used as well, perhaps when the locomotive was not available. As we have already seen, a horse belonging to Bromilow and Haddock was involved in an accident with Pilkington's locomotive at one of the level crossings in July 1871 [13].

The first edition of the 25 inch map, surveyed in 1881, marks what is clearly an engine shed adjacent to the sidings serving Nos.9 and 10 Pits. It seems unlikely that there was more than one locomotive at the colliery at this period, as it was the practice to borrow an engine from the Sheet Works when the need arose [14].

The Industrial Locomotive Society lists include a four-coupled well tank named RAVENHEAD, said to have been built by Borrows about 1880 for Pilkington Brothers. This engine cannot be accounted for at any of the firm's glass works and it is possible that it may have been purchased for use at Ravenhead Colliery. The partnership maintained a tight control over the affairs of St Helens Collieries Ltd and Pillington Brothers may well have been the nominal owner, as was the case with the Kerr Stuart locomotives at a much later date.

Another RAVENHEAD is illustrated in *The Chronicles of Boulton's Siding* [15] which had certain features suggesting that it had been built by the Lilleshall Iron Company of Oakengates in Shropshire. Allthough the locomotive had evidently passed through the hands of Isaac Watt Boulton; no date is given nor is there any information about the purchaser. A heavily retouched photograph of what may be the same engine exists in the Pilkington archives and is reproduced here. There are certain similarities and what points of difference are evident may have been the result of rebuilding. Unfortunately there is nothing to confirm that the photograph was taken at the colliery and it is quite possible that the locomotive was associated with Ravenhead Plate Glass Works.

The photograph of the mystery locomotive RAVENHEAD, found amongst a collection of railway pictures in the archives. Was it used at Ravenhead Colliery or at Ravenhead Plate Glass Works ?

(Pilkington Brothers Archives)

Ravenhead Colliery 1900 to 1947

By 1906, when the survey was made for the second edition of the 25 inch map, Ravenhead Nos.7 and 8 Pits had closed and the spur from the overhead tubway which served them had been dismantled. The direct rail link with the Ravenhead Copper Works had also disappeared. The locomotive shed had been moved and was now located alongside the old screens of Nos.7 and 8 Pits.

The Mersey trade was evidently still flourishing at this time and there are references to boxes for the transport of coal. These containers were carried three or four at a time on flat wagons and were used extensively by collieries in South Lancashire. It is not clear whether they had been employed by the St Helens Collieries previously, but in 1908 the Pilkington Board authorised the manufacture of 75 container boxes and noted that a further 25 were needed [16]. Construction of a jetty at Birkenhead was authorised in 1913 to enable coal brought there in boxes to be shipped more expeditiously [17].

Pilkington Brothers' minutes at the end 1908 also record that the colliery railways were to be taken over by the glass works and put in order [18]. Presumably maintenance had been rather neglected.

The Industrial Railway Society's list suggests that the locomotive ECCLESTON was transferred from the Sheet Works to Ravenhead Colliery at an unknown date. Perhaps, like the railways, the previous locomotive was also in poor condition and ECCLESTON was sent to replace it as part of the shake-up of 1908 and 1909.

ECCLESTON appears to have moved to the Ravenhead Plate Glass Works later, probably after the delivery of new locomotives in 1919. As mentioned in the previous chapter four saddle tanks of the maker's Moss Bay class, named VICTORY, FAIRFIELD, THE GROVE and ROSEBANK, were obtained from Kerr, Stuart and Company of Stoke. ROSEBANK was sent to the Plate Works at Cowley Hill. Of the others, one was normally employed at the Sheet Works and two at Ravenhead Colliery. Often the Sheet Works locomotive could be found working at the colliery while one of the colliery engines was under repair at the Sheet Works. Latterly at least, all three were regarded as the property of Pilkington Brothers Ltd [19].

FAIRFIELD, one of the four Moss Bay class locomotives purchased by Pilkington Brothers Ltd, which was used at Ravenhead Colliery. Photographed in National Coal Board days on 22nd May 1959.

(J.A. Peden)

Reconstruction of Ravenhead Colliery started in 1922. Underground tunnels were driven to connect with the St Helens Colliery workings, enabling all coal to be wound at Ravenhead Nos.10 and 11 Pits. Modernisation of the surface plant was completed by 1925 and deepening of No.10 Pit three years later [20]. The Mines Lists record that winding ceased at Alexandra Colliery on 30th May 1925, with St Helens Colliery closing at about the same time. At this period 72% to 75% of the output went to Pilkington Brothers' two main glass works and about 20% was sold to outside customers, while some 5% was used in the colliery boilers [20].

The revised 25 inch map, surveyed in 1926, shows that the screening plant at Ravenhead Colliery had been enlarged and that there had been some improvements to the railway layout. The overhead tubway to St Helens Colliery had been dismantled, although some portions of the viaducts were still in place over the Ravenhead Branch and over the tracks near the reconstructed screens.

A new site for tipping waste had been brought into use west of Burtonhead Road, replacing the earlier tips north of the colliery. The new tip was served by an aerial ropeway and also a single track railway which crossed Burtonhead Road by means of a bridge. The tip was also used by Pilkington Brothers for the disposal of waste from the Sheet Works and the ropeway was owned and operated by the firm until October 1939, when it was transferred to the colliery company [19].

A merger with neighbouring colliery companies was discussed by Pilkington Brothers' Board in 1939 [21]. Possible schemes were still being considered in 1944 [22-26], but were overtaken by events when the coal industry was nationalised on 1st January 1947.

Ravenhead Colliery 1947 to 1968

Ravenhead Colliery was absorbed into the No.3 (St Helens) Area of the North Western Division of the National Coal Board. It was included in the newly formed West Lancashire Area on 1st January 1961 when the North Western Division was restructured. Under a further reorganisation on 26th March 1967, it became part of the North Western Area.

Ravenhead Colliery was gradually run down, the number of employees falling from over 1,000 in 1947 to 477 in April 1968 [27]. The ropeway to the tip across Burtonhead Road was dismantled in the early 1950s and dumper trucks used instead to move the waste. The ropeway was operated by Pilkington Brothers Ltd up to 31st January 1950 [19] and had been used by the firm for rubbish disposal until a few months previously [19].

On vesting day two of the Kerr, Stuart locomotives, FAIRFIELD and THE GROVE were at the colliery, but were still under the ownership of Pilkington Brothers Ltd. They were not handed over to the National Coal Board until March or April 1947 [19].

The Ravenhead Colliery locomotives, which had previously been overhauled at the Sheet Works, were now sent to the Area Workshops at Haydock when needing repairs. A number of other locomotives were moved to Ravenhead, sometimes on a temporary basis.

GARSWOOD, a four-coupled saddle tank built by Manning, Wardle and Company in 1900 and taken over by the National Coal Board from Richard Evans and Co Ltd, was transferred from Haydock around 1950. It was taken out of service at the end of 1956 and broken up at Ravenhead towards the end of 1957.

GARSWOOD was replaced by ALLENBY, a four-coupled saddle tank built by Andrew Barclay Sons and Company in 1919, which arrived from Sutton Manor Colliery in November 1956. FAIRFIELD, which needed a new boiler, was then taken out of service early in 1957 and COLLINS GREEN was sent as a temporary replacement.

COLLINS GREEN had been built by Peckett and Sons of Bristol in 1933 for the Collins Green Collieries Co Ltd. It had originally been known as LEES EVANS but was later renamed BOLD NO 2. After overhaul at Haydock Works, when it acquired the name COLLINS GREEN, it was sent to Ravenhead at the end of 1958. The locomotive returned to Haydock in April 1959, by which time FAIRFIELD was back in service.

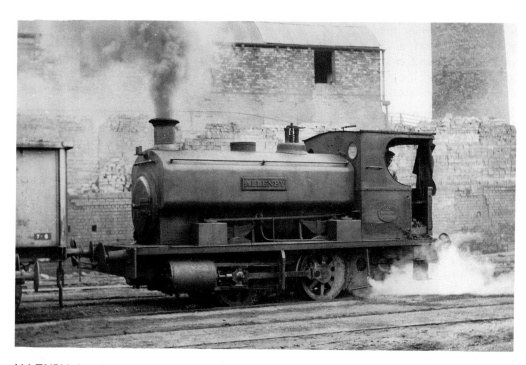

ALLENBY hard at work in the colliery yard on 21st May 1957, with Ravenhead Brickworks in the background. The siding serving the brickworks can just be seen behind the locomotive.

(J.A. Peden)

THE GROVE was sent to Haydock for a major overhaul early in 1959 and returned late in 1959 or early in 1960. This then released ALLENBY, which in April 1961 was transferred to Haydock, ostensibly for repairs. These were not carried out and the locomotive remained out of use at Haydock until it was cut up for scrap in June 1965.

FAIRFIELD was under repair again in 1961, having been sent to Haydock in February. Its place at Ravenhead was taken by BOLD, which arrived from Haydock during the previous month. BOLD, a sister locomotive to COLLINS GREEN, had been built by Peckett and Sons in 1927 and had just been given an overhaul at Haydock.

FAIRFIELD had returned to Ravenhead by March 1962 after a spell in the store of reserve locomotives set up by the West Lancashire Area of the National Coal Board at Ince Moss Colliery near Wigan. At the same time, its sister engine THE GROVE was laid aside and remained at Ravenhead in a derelict condition for several years until it was finally broken up in July 1965. COLLINS GREEN was also back at Ravenhead by March 1962 and thereafter most of the work seems to have been done by this locomotive and BOLD, with FAIRFIELD usually the spare engine.

BOLD went by road to Walkden Yard for overhaul in August 1965 and on arrival there it was found that the repairs would be very much more protracted than anticipated. With one, or perhaps both, of the Ravenhead locomotives in a poor shape, WESTWOOD was hastily taken out of store, given a quick repair and despatched to St Helens in November 1965. WESTWOOD was a four-coupled saddle tank built by Hudswell, Clarke and Company in 1913 for Platt Brothers and Co Ltd's Moston Colliery and had effectively been the spare locomotive for the Manchester Area and later the East Lancashire Area of the National Coal Board.

A view of Ravenhead Colliery, looking north west, on 7th August 1971, before the surface buildings were dismantled The headframes of Nos.10 and 11 Pits are prominent in the background, while to the right are the screens and washery. Although coal production had ceased some three years before the photograph was taken, the washery had been retained temporarily to treat coal brought in by road from neigbouring pits.
(P.G. Hindley)

BOLD returned to Ravenhead in October 1966 and thereafter it appears that neither FAIRFIELD nor COLLINS GREEN did much work. By mid 1967 both were reported to be out of use. FAIRFIELD was sent to Walkden Yard in September 1967 and was broken up there a year later, while COLLINS GREEN lingered on in a derelict state at Ravenhead, with various fittings removed to keep BOLD in operation.

Ravenhead Colliery closed on 18th October 1968 [28]. The washery remained in operation for several years after that, dealing with coal from other collieries in the district, but only road transport was used.

WESTWOOD was scrapped at Ravenhead in November 1968 followed by BOLD in May 1969. COLLINS GREEN was apparently overlooked and remained in the engine shed, becoming more and more derelict with the passing years. By October 1972 an adjoining dirt tip had slipped and encroached on the shed. In May 1973 the dirt tip had slipped further and it was reported that the locomotive lay amongst a tangle of the wreckage of the engine shed, forced upwards at an angle of 45 degrees by the rubble. The remains were finally broken up in July 1973.

Ravenhead Brick Works

The Ravenhead Brick Works was located alongside Burtonhead Road, between the Ravenhead Colliery Nos.7 and 8 Pits and Nos.9, 10 and 11 Pits. It seems to have been established around 1850 by Horn and Kelly [29], who are shown as manufacturers of bricks and stoneware pipes at Ravenhead in directories from 1864 to 1871 [30,31,32]. The Ravenhead Sanitary Pipe and Brick Co Ltd was registered in 1875 [33] to take over the works, with David Horn as manager [34]. Manufacture of pipes was given up around 1880 and thereafter the firm concentrated on brick making [29]. The name of the firm was later changed to the Ravenhead Brick Co Ltd.

Clay was obtained on the opposite side of Burtonhead Road, from opencast workings which eventually covered an area of some twelve acres. The clay was conveyed in tubs up an inclined plane to the pug mills, passing over Burtonhead Road on a bridge.

The works was served by a single short siding from the Ravenhead Colliery internal railway system and traffic seems to have been worked to and from the main line by the colliery locomotives. Later, it appears that the firm may also have made use of the siding on the south side of Burtonhead Road which had formerly served the Phoenix Colliery. An LNWR Siding Diagram of 1916 [35] shows the main line connection leading to what is described as the Ravenhead Brick and Tile Company.

We have been unable to trace any locomotive associated with the Ravenhead establishment. This is in contrast to the works at Upholland, taken over in 1908 from the Upholland Brick and Tile Co Ltd, where the firm used its own locomotives [36].

Ravenhead Brick Co Ltd was taken over by Roughdale Brickworks Ltd [37] around 1960 and the works was later closed. The clay pits were filled up in the 1970s with chemical waste cleared from the dumps of the Kurtz and Hardshaw Brook Works adjacent to Jackson Street [38]. Some of the brickworks buildings still remain at the time of writing.

Ravenhead Chemical Works

There was a short lived vitriol works on a site adjacent to the Ravenhead Brick Works. It appears to have been established in the late 1870s, but apart from a few fragmentary references, little is known about it.

In June 1880 the Pilkington partners were discussing a proposed rail link, on land near Ravenhead Colliery, between the chemical works and the glass works [39] but this does not seem to have been taken further. The Ravenhead Chemical Works was not a success and it was put up for auction on 29th November 1883 by order of the mortgagees [40].

Phoenix Colliery

Phoenix Colliery is of more recent origin than those which we have so far described and was located on the opposite side of Burtonhead Road to the Ravenhead Nos.7 and 8 Pits. It was started in 1872 by Benjamin Bradshaw Glover [1] and first appears in the Mines Lists for 1873 when it was shown as "sinking".

The ownership changed to Glover, Urmston and Glover in 1886. The two pits are variously described as Phoenix and Sutton between 1883 and 1884, Phoenix Nos.1 and 2 in 1885 and 1886 and Phoenix No.1 and Sutton No.2 subsequently. A small brickworks associated with the colliery is shown on the 1881 and 1891 25 inch maps, but had been demolished by the time that the survey was carried out for the second edition of the map in 1906.

There was a serious fire on 23rd November 1892, when the surface buildings and the screens, all of wooden construction, were reduced to ashes [41,42,43]. The Mines Lists indicate that No.2 Pit had already ceased production in 1890 and is shown as "not working" until 1893, when it was apparently abandoned. No.1 Pit continued in use for a few more years and was closed at the end of April 1895 [44]. The whole of the plant was auctioned on 6th February 1896 [45].

Phoenix Colliery had a rail connection which crossed Burtonhead Road on the level and joined the Ravenhead Branch at a point 995 yards from Ravenhead Junction. In view of the very restricted railway layout at the colliery, it is doubtful whether a locomotive was employed and no record of one has been found. It is more likely that horses were used to haul the wagons to and from the main line.

As previously noted, an LNWR siding diagram of 1916 [35] shows this connection as leading to the Ravenhead Brick and Tile Company's premises and records an agreement with Dicconson and Company dated 13th July 1899. The implication of these statements is not known. It may be that the Ravenhead Brick Company used the siding to load outgoing wagons. It may be that the firm was intending to open a new works here, but that certainly never happened. The 25 inch map surveyed in 1906 shows the derelict buildings of the Phoenix Colliery on the site and by 1926, when the 25 inch map was revised, the Phoenix Foundry had been built in their place.

The foundry was the property of William Woodcock and Sons Ltd, a firm established in 1919 by a former partner in the Brookfield Foundry [46]. It continued in use until 1972 and in December of that year the premises were put up for sale [47]. The site was cleared to make way for Pilkington Brothers' Greengate Glass Works, on which construction started in 1977 [48].

The Old Teapot Brick & Tile Works

The St Helens Brick and Tile Works was situated to the south of the Phoenix Colliery and was in existence prior to the survey for the first edition of the 25 inch map in 1881. It became the property of the St Helens Brick and Tile Co Ltd, registered on 8th February 1884, which also took over the Alltami Colliery Co Ltd's Argoed Hall Estate at Northop in Flint [49]. The company was reformed as the St Helens Coal and Fireclay Co Ltd on 11th October of the same year [50]. This second company was ordered to be wound up by a court order on 24th May 1886 [51]. A third company, the Liverpool and St Helens Brick Co Ltd, took over, probably around 1890, as the revised 25 inch map of 1891 shows what is called the Liverpool and St Helens Brick Works.

There was a series of small coal mines associated with the works. The Jubilee Colliery first appears in the Mines Lists for 1888 when it was being worked by the Jubilee Colliery Company. In 1890 to 1893 the colliery is shown, apparently incorrectly, under the ownership of the St Helens Brick and Coal Co Ltd. The Liverpool and St Helens Brick and Coal Co Ltd, again seemingly not quite the correct title, is shown as working the Frodsham Mine here between 1894 and 1900.

A valuation of the Liverpool and St Helens Brick Company's property in 1895 provides a description of the works and its associated colliery at that time [52]. The brickworks comprised three brick making sheds, a 16 chambered semi-Hoffman kiln and three circular kilns. Power for the machinery was supplied from a 35 hp horizontal engine, which no doubt also worked the winding drum hauling the clay wagons from the pit. There were two traction engines and their wagons, seven horses and their carts and sixteen railway wagons.

The pottery was leased from the Midland Pottery Company and included four large circular kilns. The colliery lease had 16 years to run and comprised about ten Cheshire acres. Coal was mined from the Yard, New and Furnace seams at a depth of 60 yards.

There is a hint that the brickworks may have been provided with a rail connection prior to 1881. The 25 inch map surveyed in that year shows a railway track from the Ravenhead Branch crossing Burtonhead Road alongside that serving Phoenix Colliery and then terminating short of the works. This possibly indicates that the works was not in use at the time of the survey or perhaps the sidings were still under construction.

The revised 25 inch map of 1891 again shows the track crossing Burtonhead Road and stopping short of the brickworks. The impression is that in the intervening ten years the line had extended as far as the works and there is what appears to be an engine shed in the sidings west of Burtonhead Road. Probably the map was surveyed in the period following the failure of the St Helens Coal and Fireclay Co Ltd in 1888 and before the resumption of production under the new owners.

It seems clear that the Liverpool and St Helens Brick Co Ltd restored the railway system serving the works soon afterwards. A few years later, in 1898, the firm was seeking to put in a standard gauge line from the works to the colliery, no doubt to replace the existing narrow gauge tubway. Application was made to the St Helens Borough Council for permission for a level crossing over the public footway from Burtonhead Road to Knobstick Hall, when it was stated that the firm wanted to take its locomotive over the crossing twice a day [53]. Approval was not immediately forthcoming and it appears that the proposal was dropped.

The locomotive in question was probably a four-coupled saddle tank built by the Hunslet Engine Company of Leeds in 1885, the only one which we have found recorded as being used at the works. It was supplied new to the public works contractor James Firbank and had passed through the hands of a Mr W. Webster before coming to St Helens. The manufacturer's records show that spare parts were supplied to the Liverpool and St Helens Brick Company in May 1898; by December 1900 the locomotive had been resold and was working at the West Norfolk Farmers Chemical Company

Around the turn of the century, the brickworks and colliery were purchased by Wood and Company, which firm also appears to have taken over the lease of the Midland Pottery. There was a further change of ownership in the 1920s when the property was acquired by J.J. Bate and Son Ltd which promoted its business activities under the name "The Old Teapot"

In 1935 the works, still trading as "Wood and Company - The Old Teapot Brickworks - John J. Bate and Son Ltd proprietors", was producing all kinds of bricks, including some which were supplied to Liverpool Cathedral. The pottery, opened some 40 years previously, had evidently been purchased outright by J.J. Bate and Son Ltd around 1930. At one time specialising in stoneware jam jars, it was now turning out teapots, fireplace tiles and fancy vases [46,54].

Coal mining continued in a small way. The Mines Lists show the Frodsham Mine as being worked intermittently by Wood and Company between 1901 and 1907. Nos.3 and 4 Pits at Wood's New Mine were opened up in 1913 but operations were suspended in 1922 and 1924 respectively.

Mining was resumed in 1928 under the auspices of J.J. Bate and Son Ltd, though still on a small scale, with typically four or five men underground. Wood's Old Teapot No.3 Pit is shown in the Mines Lists and the Colliery Year Books from 1928 to 1941 and Old Teapot No.4 Pit from 1938. Old Teapot No.5 Pit seems to have been opened up about 1940 and the Earthy Delph Pit in 1941. Both had closed temporarily by 1944 but were never reopened.

BRITISH NO.1 working at the Old Teapot Brick and Tile Works in pre-war days. The locomotive came second hand to St Helens from Cardiff.
(Industrial Railway Society H.W. Robinson Collection)

The railway layout used by the Liverpool and St Helens Brick Co Ltd remained virtually unchanged during the period that the works was in the hands of Wood and Company and later J.J. Bate and Son Ltd.

According to an old employee who was interviewed in 1938, Wood and Company had at one time employed a vertical boiler locomotive with the name of AUNT or something similar. It is tempting to associate this with the locomotive named ANT used at the Ince Forge at Wigan. This was one of three steam tram engines purchased by the Ince Forge Company from the Bury, Rochdale and Oldham Tramways Company in 1905. Two were offered for sale in 1907 and one appears to have later had connections with a brick and tile works [36], but unfortunately we have no firm evidence of any St Helens connection.

Whatever locomotive was used in the early days, it must have been taken out of service by 1920. The Sidings Schedules record an agreement of 21st July 1920 with Wood and Company under which the United Alkali Company's locomotive from the Greenbank Works would travel over the Ravenhead Branch to shunt at the brick works on payment of a fee of £2 on 31st December each year. A further note in the Sidings Schedules dated December 1921 records that Messrs Wood and Co had now purchased a locomotive of its own, a move that was probably precipitated by the closure of the Greenbank Works.

We presume that the locomotive purchased in 1921 was the four-coupled saddle tank built by Andrew Barclay Son and Company of Kilmarnock which survived at the Old Teapot Works for many years. It had been built in 1895 and passed through the hands of several owners, mostly in Scotland, before coming to St Helens.

The Barclay was followed by another second hand locomotive, which came in 1929 from Cudworth and Johnson Ltd, the Wrexham dealers. This was a four-coupled saddle tank built by Peckett and Sons of Bristol in 1903 for the British Wagon Co Ltd's works at Port Tennant, near Swansea. It carried its original name, BRITISH No.1, while at St Helens.

The Old Teapot Works survived the second world war, although by the 1950s visitors came away with the impression of minimal activity. Its railway was out of use by this time and the locomotives had disappeared, presumably for scrap. The works continued to appear in directories up to 1966 [37] but seems to have finally closed a year or two later. In 1974 the Old Teapot clay pits were being filled with alkali waste from the tips off Jackson Street [38] and the site is now occupied by the Greengate Works of Pilkington Brothers Ltd

Ravenhead Old Copper Works

Copper smelting at Ravenhead goes back to the eighteenth century, when the Parys Mining Company leased land from John Mackay in September 1779. The works, which was located on the south side of the Ravenhead Branch of the canal near the terminal basin, started production in 1780 [1].

The Parys Mining Company's works closed down in 1815 [1] and in 1829 or 1830 a new establishment was opened on a nearby site by the St Helens Smelting and Copper Company, which changed its name to the Ravenhead Copper Company in 1834 [55]. This second works was taken over in 1838 [55] by John Bibby and Company, the Liverpool shipowners. Copper ore from South America was carried as ballast in the firm's vessels and a smelting works had previously been operated at Seacombe on the Wirral [1].

John Bibby and Company's works had no rail connection when the 1:1056 Town Plan of St Helens was surveyed in 1849 and must have relied entirely on canal transport for its supplies of imported ores. A siding seems to have been provided when the St Helens Railway Company extended its Ravenhead Branch to the Royal Colliery and Ravenhead Plate Glass Works in 1851 or 1852. The agreement with David Bromilow relating to the construction of the line covered the tolls to be charged for the conveyance of coal to the copper works from the Royal Colliery and Ravenhead Colliery [56].

The site was vacated by John Bibby and Company, which moved in the early 1860s to a new factory. This was located on the south side of the Ravenhead Branch Railway, opposite Pilkington Brothers' Sheet Works and we deal with its history later in the chapter. Bibby's original works, usually referred to subsequently as the Ravenhead Old Copper Works, was taken over in 1866 or 1867 [55] by the St Helens Smelting Company. This firm, which was unconnected with the St Helens Smelting and Copper Company of the 1830s, had been forced to move from its original premises at Sutton Oak after an injunction for nuisance [1].

149

Deposited Plans, drawn up in 1864, for the LNWR Huyton to St Helens line [7] show a series of sidings within the copper works, connecting with the Ravenhead Branch. There was also a private line linking the works with Ravenhead Colliery which enabled coal from there to be delivered to the works without paying tolls to the LNWR.

The St Helens Copper Co Ltd took over in 1875 [55], but the works and its railway layout were little changed when the surveys were made in 1881 and 1891 for the 25 inch maps. The only addition was a short length of line which passed under the Ravenhead Branch and linked the works with the canal. This was taken up later, following the abandonment of the canal west of Tavern Bridge in 1898.

Ravenhead Old Copper Works closed around 1900 and is shown as disused on the second edition of 25 inch map, revised in 1906. It was purchased in 1913 by yet another St Helens Smelting Company [57], which had been established in the early years of the present century to operate a metal recovery plant on the former St Helens Chemical Company's site at Pocket Nook. What was now known as the Ravenhead Smelting Works was re-equipped for the extraction of antimony and like materials and was in full production by 1916.

The sidings were retained by the new owners and a revised sidings agreement with the LNWR was signed on 26th July 1915 [35]. We have found no record of any locomotive used at the Ravenhead Smelting Works. It is quite likely that shunting was performed by horses and later by road tractors.

The St Helens Smelting Co Ltd was registered on 31st October 1918 [57] and the Pocket Nook Works closed shortly afterwards [58]. Successive editions of the 25 inch map indicate that additional buildings were erected at Ravenhead. Eventually, in 1958, the firm amalgamated with Associated Lead Manufacturers Ltd. Production was transferred to Newcastle upon Tyne and the Ravenhead Works was closed [58]. The premises were taken over by Pilkington Brothers Ltd, presumably for storage and warehousing, and the sidings agreement was transferred as from 31st December 1959 [59].

Bibby's Copper Works

As noted above, John Bibby and Company moved in the early 1860s to new premises on a previously undeveloped site on the south side of the Ravenhead Branch. At the same time, or perhaps a few years later, the name of the firm was changed to John Bibby and Sons.

The new works was provided with a siding connection to the Ravenhead Branch at a point 500 yards from Ravenhead Junction and by 1881, when the survey was made for the first edition of the 25 inch map, there was a sizeable internal railway network. The private tracks joined up with those of the Sutton Lodge Chemical Company by means of a single line which was carried over the Burtonhead arm of the canal on a draw bridge. There was also a direct connection to the sidings of the Ravenhead Colliery, which enabled coal to reach the works without paying a toll to the LNWR.

Bibby's works remained largely unchanged over the years. Successive 25 inch maps show little alteration to the internal railway system, except for the direct connections to the Sutton Lodge Works and to Ravenhead Colliery which had been removed by 1891.

As early as 1900 the firm had suggested selling the works to Pilkington Brothers Ltd as it was considering moving production to Widnes [60]. Evidently the asking price was too high [61] and the St Helens works continued in operation until about 1920. The site was then taken over by Pilkington Brothers Ltd and its later history has been described in Chapter 4.

Very little information has come to light about the locomotives employed by John Bibby and Sons and the only reference which has been found is in the Industrial Locomotive Society's lists. Here it is recorded that Edward Borrows and Sons supplied one of its four-coupled well tanks to the firm around 1900. The subsequent fate of this locomotive is not known.

Greenbank Alkali Works

The Greenbank Alkali Works was situated on the west side of the canal near the Ravenhead terminus. Its origins go back to around 1835, when Samuel and William Thompson Clough opened a small   factory in what had previously been Bevan and Rigby's soap works [1]. The Cloughs were bankrupt at the end of 1841 [1] and the works was leased to Thomas Spencer and Josiah Churchill from 1st June 1844. A year or two later Spencer and Churchill began to trade as the British Patent Alkali Company, a name which was retained when Messrs Evans, Harmer and Jennings took over the lease in May 1847 [1].

The British Patent Alkali Co went out of business in 1856 and the property was purchased by the St Helens Alkali, Blue Vitriol and Metal Co Ltd in 1857. This firm was wound up in 1863 and the works was taken over by the Greenbank Alkali Company in 1867. The works was mortgaged to Henry Menzies of Liverpool in 1870 and eventually passed into the control of his two sons [1]. The Greenbank Alkali Co Ltd was registered on 21st December 1877 [62] to take over the alkali works and its associated collieries.

The Patent Alkali Company applied to the St Helens Railway in April 1851 for a siding connection and this was agreed on payment of £200. A bridge over the canal, or more probably the end of the terminal basin, was required for which construction contracts were let on 18th August 1851 [56]. The line into the works was presumably completed early in the following year and seems to have joined the extension of the Ravenhead Branch in the vicinity of Marsh's Crossing. The first 150 yards or so appear to have been incorporated into the Eccleston Branch, which came into operation in March 1859. A new connection was installed immediately to the west of the bridge over the Ravenhead Branch of the canal, at 98 yards from Eccleston Junction, although the agreement was not signed until 28th February 1866 [63]. A further connection was provided at a point 320 yards from Eccleston Junction under an agreement dated 30th November 1881 [63].

In addition to the standard gauge sidings, the company operated a narrow gauge tramway to take waste material to tips on the opposite side of the Eccleston Branch, which was crossed by a bridge. The trucks on the tramway were presumably pulled by horses or pushed by men as the system seems too small to have required a locomotive. The 25 inch map surveyed in 1881 shows tipping near the shaft of James Radley's former colliery, between the sand lodges belonging to the British Plate Glass Company and the railway. By 1891 the tramway had been extended to tips near the old Cropper's Hill Pits.

Probably no standard gauge locomotive was needed until the expansion of the Greenbank Works in the 1870s. In December 1876 the firm advertised for a four-wheeled tank engine with 10 inch cylinders, nearly new or of the latest construction [64]. The next we know is that in July 1884 Andrew Barclay, Sons and Company of Kilmarnock supplied spare parts for a four-coupled saddle tank named GREENBANK, which had originally been built by the rival firm of Barclays and Company at the River Bank Works in Kilmarnock.

The Greenbank Alkali Ltd became part of the United Alkali Co Ltd on its formation in November 1890 and the works remained in operation until 1921 [65]. The premises were then purchased by Pilkington Brothers Ltd [66] and the subsequent history of the site has been described in the previous chapter.

A locomotive named GREENBANK, which may or may not have been the one referred to earlier, was here in 1919 [67]. As noted above, it was this engine which travelled over a short portion of the Ravenhead Branch for a few months in 1920 and 1921 to shunt at Wood's Brickworks. It is not known for certain what happened to GREENBANK after the works closed, although there is an unconfirmed suggestion in the Industrial Railway Society list that it was transferred to the United Alkali Company's Hardshaw Brook Works.

W.J. Glover & Company's Rope Works

The rope works of W.J. Glover and Company was situated immediately to the west of the Greenbank Alkali Company's premises. The rope-making firm had been founded in 1818 and had moved here in the 1830s [1]. For a time James Bromilow, the colliery proprietor, was a partner with Glover at the Greenbank Rope Works.

Successive large scale maps show a continual expansion of the premises throughout the nineteenth century as the demand for hemp and later iron and steel ropes went on rising. Nevertheless, the rope works remained without a rail connection throughout its existence. An agreement was made on 5th January 1898 with the London and North Western Railway for the provision of a siding from the Eccleston Branch which ran past the end of the works. A note in the Sidings Schedules dated 17th April 1901 records, however, that the siding was not put in, that the scheme was abandoned and the agreement cancelled.

As mentioned in the previous chapter, Pilkington Brothers Ltd had in 1926 hoped to take over the rope works for a new crate yard, in exchange for land at Sutton Oak. The scheme fell through and Glovers remained on the Greenbank site until 1989, when the works closed [68].

Cropper's Hill Colliery

Radley's colliery, which featured in a possible take over by Pilkington Brothers in the 1860s, was located between Glover's rope works and Cropper's Hill. A plan of the Ravenhead Estate [69] marks two pits adjacent to the Eccleston Branch and two more between Cropper's Hill and what later became Borough Road.

The first mention which we have found of the colliery is in 1845, when it was being worked by the firm of Bromilow, Jones and Brown [70]. By 1847 it had been taken over by Bromilow, Oldham and Brown. The latter partnership was dissolved on 17th April 1847 [71] According to Barker and Harris [1] James Radley took over in 1850 although George Saul appears to have been in occupation in the intervening period [72] The Mines Lists show Radley at the Cropper's Hill and Union Collieries until 1865 when the pits were drowned out [73]

A short tramroad, presumably worked by animal power, ran from the Cropper's Hill pits to what was probably a landsale yard on the Liverpool Road. The line is shown on the Deposited Plans for the Eccleston Branch, dated November 1852 [74], but presumably had been constructed some years previously.

There was some further small scale mining between 1874 and 1879 by Meadowcroft and Barton and by 1881 one of the Cropper's Hill pits nearest to the Eccleston Branch was being used to provide a water supply, presumably for industrial use. As noted earlier, the area surrounding the Cropper's Hill pits was later used by the Greenbank Alkali Company to tip chemical waste.

Pilkington Brothers' Greengate Works

The most recent development in the district covered by the present chapter has been the construction of the Greengate Works by Pilkington Brothers Ltd. With the float process of glass manufacture firmly established at Cowley Hill, further production facilities were needed and it was decided to build a new plant on a different site.

As mentioned earlier, a start had been made in 1974 to fill in the clay pits along Burtonhead Road. Construction of the Greengate Works began in 1977 and all remains of the Old Teapot Works, the Phoenix Foundry and the Greengate Brickworks were obliterated. The first production line, the UK 5 Plant, was started in 1981, followed by the UK 6 Plant, which was opened by the Duke of Edinburgh in 1992 [75].

No rail connections were provided for the Greengate Works, road transport being used to bring in raw materials and to take out finished products. Only fuel oil still arrives by rail, being piped from the oil terminal at Bibby's Sidings, described in the previous chapter.

LOCOMOTIVE SUMMARY

Ravenhead Colliery

Bromilow, Haddock and Co until September 1871
Ravenhead Colliery Co Ltd September 1871 to July 1876
St Helens Collieries Co Ltd July 1876 to 31.12.1946
National Coal Board from 1.1.1947
    No.3 (St Helens) Area, North Western Division 1.1.1947 to 31.12.1960
    West Lancashire Area, North Western Division 1.1.1961 to 25.3.1967
    North Western Area from 26.3.1967
Colliery closed 10.10.1968

The following locomotives were possibly used at Ravenhead Colliery, but confirmation is lacking - see text. :

RAVENHEAD   0-4-0WT OC   EBS
    Shown in Industrial Locomotive Society List

RAVENHEAD   0-4-0ST OC
    Mentioned in *The Chronicles of Boulton's Siding* (Ref 15)
    Possibly made by Lilleshall Company

RAVENHEAD   0-4-0ST OC
    Photograph in Pilkington archives at Information Management and Storage Ltd
    Possibly the Lilleshall locomotive in a rebuilt form

The following locomotives owned by Pilkington Brothers Ltd were used at Ravenhead Colliery from time to time :

ECCLESTON   0-4-0WT OC   EBS   36   1898
    Ex Sheet Works, possibly around 1908
    To Ravenhead Works, possibly in early 1920s

FAIRFIELD   0-4-0ST OC   KS   4025 1919   15"x22" 3'3"
    New to Pilkington Brothers Ltd
    At Ravenhead Colliery on 1.1.1947
    To NCB early in 1947

THE GROVE   0-4-0ST OC   KS   4146 1919   15"x22" 3'3"
    New to Pilkington Brothers Ltd
    At Ravenhead Colliery on 1.1.1947
    To NCB early in 1947

VICTORY   0-4-0ST OC   KS   4148 1920   15"x22" 3'3"
    New to Pilkington Brothers Ltd
    At Sheet Works on 1.1.1947

Locomotives used by National Coal Board at Ravenhead Colliery

FAIRFIELD   0-4-0ST OC   KS   4025 1919   15"x22" 3'3"
    Ex Pilkington Brothers Ltd early in 1947
    Repaired at Ravenhead and new boiler fitted between early 1957 and late 1958 or
      early 1959
    To Haydock for repairs 2.1961, thence to Ince Moss 12.1961
    Returned to Ravenhead by 3.1962
    Out of use at Ravenhead by 7.1967
    To Walkden Yard 9.1967 and scrapped there 9.1968

THE GROVE   0-4-0ST OC   KS   4146 1919   15"x22" 3'3"
    Ex Pilkington Brothers Ltd early in 1947
    To Haydock for repairs early 1959. Returned late 1959 or early 1960
    Noted derelict at Ravenhead 3.1962
    Scrapped at Ravenhead 7.1965

GARSWOOD   0-4-0ST OC   MW   1486 1900   12"x18" 3'0"
    Ex Haydock about 1950
    Scrapped at Ravenhead at end 1960

ALLENBY   0-4-0ST OC   AB   1625 1919   14"x22" 3'5"
    Ex Sutton Manor Colliery 11.1956
    To Haydock 4.1961

COLLINS GREEN   0-4-0ST OC   P   1762 1933   14"x22" 3'2½"
    Ex Haydock Shops at end 1958.
    To Haydock 4.1959
    Ex Bold Colliery by 3.1962
    Out of use at Ravenhead by.7.1967
    Scrapped at Ravenhead 7.1973

BOLD   0-4-0ST OC   P   1737 1922   14"x22" 3'2½"
    Ex Haydock 1.1961
    To Walkden Yard for repairs 7.1965, returned 10.1966
    Out of use at Ravenhead by 10.1967
    Scrapped at Ravenhead 5.1969

WESTWOOD   0-4-0ST OC   HC   1036 1913   16"x24" 3'8"
    Ex Walkden Yard 11.1965
    Scrapped at Ravenhead 11.1968

Old Teapot Brick and Tile Works

Owners before 1884 not known
St Helens Brick and Tile Co Ltd February 1884 to October 1884
St Helens Coal and Fireclay Co Ltd October 1884 to May 1886
Liverpool and St Helens Brick Co Ltd about 1890 to about 1900
Wood and Co about 1900 to 1920s
J.J. Bate and Son Ltd from 1920s
Works closed probably in 1960s

| | 0-4-0ST OC | HE | 385 | 1885 | 9"x14" | 2'8½" |

Ex works 19.10.1885 to J. Firbank, contractor, named EDENBRIDGE.
At Liverpool and St Helens Brick Co Ltd by 5.1898
At West Norfolk Farmers Manure Co Ltd, South Lynn, by 12.1900

0-4-0T GVB

Named ANT or AUNT - see text

| | 0-4-0ST OC | AB | 754 | 1895 | 10"x18" | 3'0" |

Rebuilt AB 1912
Ex Gavin Paul and Co, Vogrie Colly, Fushiebridge after 11.1918
Scrapped in early 1950s

BRITISH No.1   0-4-0ST OC   P   976   1903   12"x18"   3'0"
    Class R1
    Ex British Wagon Co, Port Tennant, via Cudworth and Johnson, dealers, Wrexham, 1929
    Out of use by 1936,
    Scrapped early 1950s

Bibby's Copper Works

John Bibby and Company, later John Bibby and Sons, from early 1860s to about 1920
Premises acquired by Pilkington Brothers Ltd

| | 0-4-0WT OC | EBS | 40 | About 1900 |

Probably new to John Bibby and Sons
Scrapped or sold

Greenbank Alkali Works

British Patent Alkali Co from about 1845 to 1856
St Helens Alkali, Blue Vitriol and Metal Co 1857 to 1867
Greenbank Alkali Co Ltd 1867 to November 1890
United Alkali Co Ltd from November 1890
Works closed 1921
Premises acquired by Pilkington Brothers Ltd

GREENBANK   0-4-0ST OC   Bys   12"
   Here by July 1884
   Presumably the same GREENBANK here in June 1919
   Scrapped or sold (Industrial Locomotive Society list says to Hardshaw Brook Works)

References to Chapter 5

1   *A Merseyside Town in the Industrial Revolution - St Helens 1750 to 1900*, T.C. Barker and J.R. Harris, Frank Cass & Co Ltd, London, 1959
2   LRO PDR 188
3   *History, Directory and Gazetteer of the County Palatine of Lancashire*, Edward Baines, Liverpool, Two vols 1824 and 1825
4   *National Commercial Directory for the Counties of Chester, Cumberland, Durham and Lancashire*, James Pigot and Co, Manchester, 1834
5   *LG* 6.10.1840
6   *LG* 22.11.1850
7   LRO PDR 799
8   *MJ* 16.9.1871
9   *The Glassmakers - Pilkington 1826 - 1976*, T.C. Barker, Weidenfeld and Nicolson, London, 1977
10   *WO* 14.7.1876
11   CRO DIC/SU 9/1
12   Pilkington Bros General Board Mins 9.10.1877 - at IM&S
13   Ibid 1.8.1871
14   Ibid 13.1.1891
15   *The Chronicles of Boulton's Siding*, A.R. Bennett, Locomotive Publishing Co Ltd, London, 1927
16   Pilkington Bros General Board Mins 29.12.1908
17   Ibid 12.2.1913
18   Ibid 29.12.1908
19   IM&S File PB 358/43
20   Notes referenced G A N 1950 in Raw Materials File at IM&S
21   Pilkington Bros General Board Mins 20.7.1939
22   Ibid 30.3.1944
23   Ibid 24.5.1944
24   Ibid 24.7.1944
25   Ibid 28.9.1944
26   Ibid 30.11.1944

27 *Ravenhead Collliery*, Colliery Profiles, National Coal Board, Western Area, Public Relations Dept, nd

28 *StHRep* 12.10.1968

29 *StHChron* 3.5.1889

30 *Royal National Commercial Directory of Lancashire*, Isaac Slater, Manchester, 1864

31 *Royal National Commercial Directory of Lancashire*, Isaac Slater, Manchester, 1869

32 *Directory and Historical Sketches of St Helens and District*, P. Mannex and Co, Preston, 1871

33 *Industry in South Lancashire*, South Lancashire Development Corporation, publ Ed Burrows and Co Ltd, Cheltenham and London, nd , about 1970

34 *Directory of Warrington, Wigan, St Helens, etc*, John Worall, Oldham, 1876

35 LNWR Sdgs Diag 175, dated 12.1916

36 *Industrial Railways of the Wigan Coalfield, Part One*, C.H.A. Townley, F.D. Smith and J.A. Peden, Runpast Publishing, Cheltenham, 1991

37 *County Borough of St Helens Directory*, Blair Publications Ltd, Blackpool,1966

38 *StHRep* 27.9.1974

39 Pilkington Bros General Board Mins 29-6-1880, at IM&S

40 *StHNews* 10.11.1883

41 *LMerc* 23.12.1892

42 *StHNews* 24.12.1892

43 *LMerc* 24.12.1892

44 *WO* 27.4.1895

45 *BC* 1.2.1896

46 *St Helens Commercially Considered*, St Helens Corporation, 1935

47 *StHRep* 8.12.1972

48 *StHRep* 5.10.1979

49 *Iron* 22.2.1884

50 *Iron* 24.10.1884

51 *Register of Defunct and Other Companies Removed from the Stock Exchange Year Book*, Stock Exchange Year Book Publishing Co Ltd, 1959

52 *Valuation of brickworks and pottery and colliery worked in association therewith*, dated 22.3.1895, at IM&S PB 624

53 *StHNews* 21.5.1898

54 *Daily Dispatch* 20.11.1934

55 *A Directory of the Chemical Works of St Helens 1820 - 1889*, J.D. Turton, C. Kay and P. Meara, Halton Historical Publications No 15

56 Information supplied to the authors by Mr J.M. Tolson

57 *A History of Antimony Smelting in St Helens*, Peter Hampson, 1994, Typescript at StHLH A 36.1 HAM (P)

58 *StHRep* 13.12.1958

59 Line Plan of St Helens Railway, LNWR, Rugby, 1871, 2 chains to 1 inch, at BRPB, Manchester Office

60 Pilkington Bros General Board Mins 30.8.1900

61 Ibid 6.11.1900

62 *Iron* 5.1.1878

63 LNWR Sdgs Diag 177, dated 12.1916

64 *CG* 22.12.1876

65 CRO DIC/UA 12/20

66 Pilkington Bros General Board Mins 7.1.1921

67 CRO DIC/UA 11/1/11

68 *StHRep* 30.3.1989

69 IM&S PB 147/135

70 *LG* 12.12.1845

71 *LG* 24-9-1847

72 *Royal National Classified Commercial Directory of the County of Lancashire*, Isaac Slater, Manchester, 1851

73 Pilkington Bros General Board Mins 25.1.1865

74 LRO PDR 195

75 Information supplied to the authors by Ms Stobbs of IM&S

CHAPTER SIX

RAVENHEAD

We now move to the western outskirts of the town which were served by the Ravenhead Branch of the St Helens Railway. Between Thatto Heath and the Prescot Turnpike, the coal seams lay at a shallow depth and no doubt some mining had taken place since the earliest times. Exploitation on a commercial scale dates from the purchase of the Ravenhead Estate by John Mackay in the 1760s and the coal industry expanded rapidly in the early years of the nineteenth century under a number of other proprietors. Glass making had likewise been carried on in a small way around Thatto Heath in the early part of the eighteenth century but the foundations of the modern industry were not laid until the 1770s, when the Ravenhead Plate Glass Works was established [1].

The 1830 Act [2] which incorporated the St Helens and Runcorn Gap Railway included powers to construct a branch to the Plate Glass Works. As we have described earlier, this was not completed as planned and was opened in 1834 only as far as Ravenhead Colliery. The extension of the line beyond here was instigated by David Bromilow and Company, whose Royal Colliery was situated near to the Plate Glass Works. In March 1844 the firm wrote to the proprietors of the works about building a line of its own which would pass through their land [3]. Although negotiations dragged on until 1845 nothing appears to have come of them.

The next we hear is in 1848, when the St Helens Railway Minutes [4] record that an agreement about a branch to the Royal Colliery had been signed with David Bromilow and Company in April of that year. Land had been earmarked for the line and is shown as "railway" on a plan dated 1849 [5]. For most of its course the line ran alongside Ravenhead Road, the private road which connected the Plate Glass Works to the Ravenhead terminus of the canal.

Construction of the line was to be undertaken by the railway company. The colliery company would pay £150 to the railway company to offset costs and a further £150 would come from tolls. These were fixed at 1d per ton on coal from the Royal Colliery to the Plate Glass Works, which would also be connected to the new line, and 2d per ton to the Ravenhead Copper Works. The railway company also agreed to carry coal from Bromilow's Ravenhead Colliery to the Copper Works, subject to a haulage charge of ½d per ton over and above the standard toll [4].

The plans were finalised and land purchased in March 1850 [4] from Mrs Fraser's estate. However, the scheme was modified in the following May when it was found that, by purchasing a small additional plot of land, it was possible to dispense with a bridge and reduce the severity of the curves [4]. No record has been found of the date when the line was opened for traffic. Presumably it was sometime during 1851 or 1852.

159

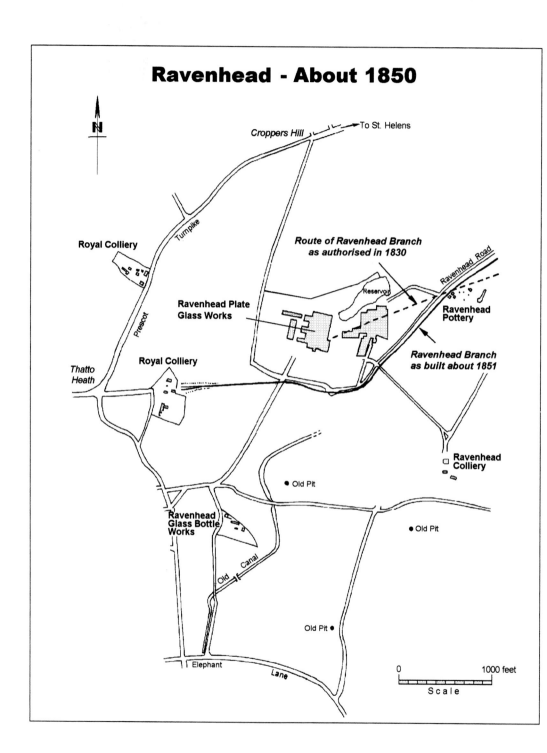

Ravenhead - About 1850

N

To St. Helens

Croppers Hill

Turnpike

Royal Colliery

Prescot

Route of Ravenhead Branch as authorised in 1830

Ravenhead Road

Reservoir

Ravenhead Plate Glass Works

Ravenhead Pottery

Ravenhead Branch as built about 1851

Thatto Heath

Royal Colliery

Ravenhead Colliery

● Old Pit

Ravenhead Glass Bottle Works

● Old Pit

Old Canal

Old Pit ●

Elephant Lane

0   1000 feet

Scale

The Ravenhead Plate Glass Works

Construction of the Ravenhead Plate Glass Works was started in 1773 [1] under the auspices of the Governor and Company of the British Cast Plate Glass Manufacturers, incorporated by Act of Parliament in April of that year [6]. The plant, which came into production in 1776 [7], was the first in the country to manufacture high quality glass by casting and subsequently grinding and polishing.

The statutory powers were renewed in 1798 [8], when 'Cast' was dropped from the title, and again in 1819 [9]. The property was leased to Thomas Cockburn, William Blake and Turner Grant on 26th May 1841 [10] and a joint stock company, 'The Governor and Company of British Plate Glass Manufacturers', was set up by Royal Charter on 24th September 1842 [10]. A new partnership with the title of the British Plate Glass Company took over the lease on 21st September 1843 [10], which was assigned to new partners on 6th December 1850. There was a further assignment to Edward Robert Sullivan on 31st December 1860 which was confirmed by Act of Parliament in 1862 [11].

A short private canal, about half a mile long, was constructed to link the works with Thatto Heath. It was completed before the end of the eighteenth century and, according to Hadfield and Biddle [12], is shown on maps of 1793 and 1795. The canal appears to have been used to bring in the large quantities of coal which were needed as fuel, but may also have served to carry some of the finished glass to the turnpike road.

When extra land was leased by the Governor and Company from Thomas Eccleston in October 1792, the landowner reserved the right to lay down self acting inclines [13]. These were presumably intended to provide the means of transporting coal from mines on the Eccleston Estate to the Ravenhead terminus of the canal, or perhaps to the Plate Glass Works itself. There is, however, no evidence of any tramroad in the vicinity of the works, either on the Deposited Plans of 1829 [13] for the St Helens and Runcorn Gap Railway or on the 1849 Estate Plan referred to earlier.

The connection to the St Helens Railway dates from the completion of the Ravenhead Branch extension to the Royal Colliery or shortly afterwards. By the 1860s, although the casting hall had been extended and new buildings had been erected in other parts of the factory, the Ravenhead Plate Glass Works was only served by two short sidings [14]. This was still the position in 1865 when a plan of the works [15] was made for Sir Edward Sullivan, Mr Sievewright and Mr Crossley. These three had entered into a fresh lease [16,17] of the works from the Trustees and Directors of the British Plate Glass Company on 21st June 1864.

An inventory [18] prepared in 1865 in connection with the lease lists 62 yards of track to the new glassworks and 32 yards to a new warehouse. There were also 74 yards of 11ft gauge track in the New Casting Hall and a 3ft 6in gauge line from the New Casting Hall through the Old Casting Hall into the Rough Cutting Room, used for conveying pot carriages and roller carriages. There is no mention of a locomotive and none would have been needed bearing in mind the very limited length of the sidings.

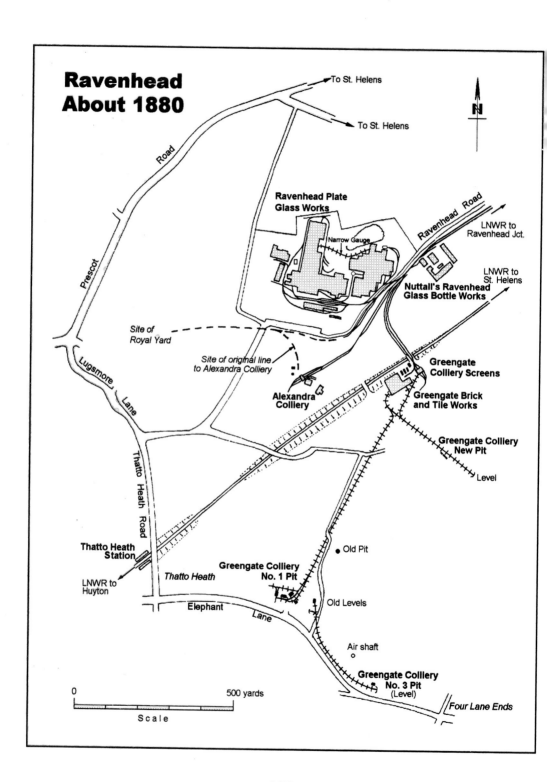

Ravenhead
About 1880

N

To St. Helens

To St. Helens

Road

Prescot

Ravenhead Plate
Glass Works

Narrow Gauge

Ravenhead Road

LNWR to
Ravenhead Jct.

LNWR to
St. Helens

Nuttall's Ravenhead
Glass Bottle Works

Site of
Royal Yard

Site of original line
to Alexandra Colliery

Lugsmore Lane

Alexandra
Colliery

Greengate
Colliery Screens

Greengate Brick
and Tile Works

Greengate Colliery
New Pit

Level

Thatto Heath Road

Old Pit

Thatto Heath
Station

LNWR to
Huyton

Thatto Heath

Greengate Colliery
No. 1 Pit

Old Levels

Elephant   Lane

Air shaft

0   500 yards

Scale

Greengate Colliery
No. 3 Pit
(Level)

Four Lane Ends

Ownership of the works changed again in 1868, when a new 99 year lease was drawn up with the London and Manchester Plate Glass Company [7]. This firm was already well established at the plate glass works at Sutton Oak which we describe in Part Two.

The new company set about a programme of expansion and modernisation. This included the provision of a standard gauge railway system serving all parts of the works. It is known that the firm purchased a four-coupled well tank from Edward Borrows in 1883 and circumstantial evidence suggests that this was used at Ravenhead. It carried the number 3, Nos. 1 and 2 presumably being the earlier locomotives used at the Sutton Oak Works. What appears to be a 2-road engine shed is shown on the 25 inch map surveyed in 1891 but we have found no record of a second locomotive at Ravenhead. Perhaps the shed was built to house two locomotives in anticipation of extra traffic.

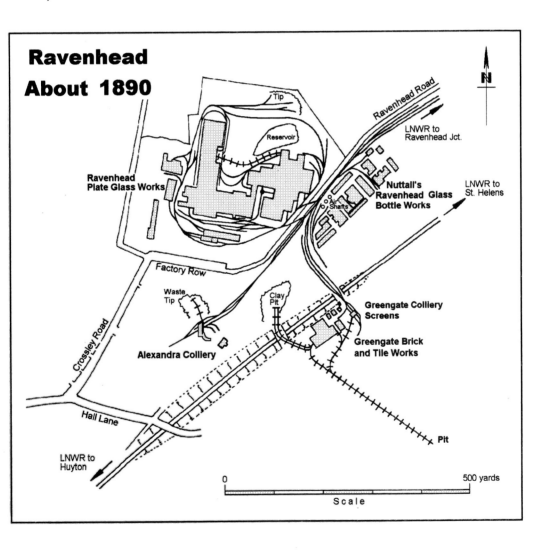

By 1894 the London and Manchester Plate Glass Company Ltd was in financial difficulties and both the Sutton Oak and Ravenhead Works had been closed. On 20th September the shareholders voted to liquidate the company [19] and in December the Chancery Court gave permission to dispose of the Ravenhead Works [20]. The lease was transferred on 10th April 1895 [21] to a new firm named the British Plate Glass Co Ltd.

Again there were extensions to the works, with the addition of an extra casting hall and new grinding sheds. The standard gauge railway system was extended to serve the new plant [22]. The well tank, No 3, appears to have been taken over by the new owners.

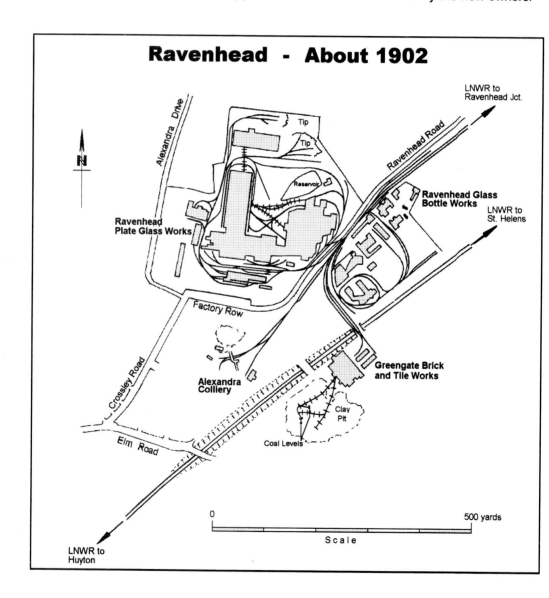

A maker's photograph of the 3ft 6in gauge locomotive CASTING HALL No.1
(J.A. Peden Collection)

The 3ft 6in gauge railway system was also enlarged and by 1901 was stated to run from the Extension Casting Hall to the Extension Grinding Room and to the Old Grinding Shed [22]. A small locomotive, CASTING HALL No.1, was purchased from the Hunslet Engine Company of Leeds. It was delivered on 15th November 1895 and put to work on 27th November [23].

The British Plate Glass Co Ltd seems to have quickly run into financial difficulties. The works was up for sale in 1901 and was purchased by Pilkington Brothers Ltd for £100,000 in the autumn of that year [24]. Plate glass manufacture was run down and replaced by sheet glass plant. The final casting of plate glass took place some time during the first world war but the finishing processes had ceased somewhat earlier, in 1908 or 1909 [7]. After that the site does not seem to have been fully utilised and part of the premises was turned into an orthopaedic hospital in 1916 for the treatment of wounded soldiers [25].

The last reference to the narrow gauge locomotive, CASTING HALL No.1, is in October 1902 [26]. By 1906, when the survey was made for the second edition of the 25 inch map, the narrow gauge lines had been removed. The standard gauge system continued to operate under Pilkington ownership. The locomotive, presumably No.3, was stated to be in bad order towards the end of 1902 [27] but must have been repaired. Possibly a locomotive was transferred temporarily from the Sheet Works to take its place while it was away.

165

A second locomotive came to Ravenhead following the purchase by Pilkington Brothers Ltd of the Sutton Oak Works in 1905. It is recorded that two small four-coupled well tanks were built by Edward Borrows about 1875 for the London and Manchester Plate Glass Company and it was presumably one of this pair which found its way to Ravenhead. In May 1908 it was reported that the 10 inch locomotive acquired from Sutton was under repair at Borrows' works at an estimated cost of £350, leaving one 12 inch engine, presumably No.3, at Ravenhead [28,29].

The subsequent history of the locomotive from Sutton is hard to unravel. As will be described in Part Two, the former London and Manchester works at Sutton Oak was taken over by the Ministry of Munitions in January 1916 for the inspection of shell casings and other material. The Ministry is known to have requisitioned a locomotive from Pilkington Brothers Ltd for work at Sutton Oak and it appears that this may have come from the Ravenhead Works.

The locomotive which had been requisitioned was returned to Pilkington Brothers Ltd at the end of 1919 [30] and was apparently sent to the Ravenhead Works, where it was known as WINKLE. The name may have been given to it while it was with the Ministry of Munitions, as the telegraphic address of the depot at Sutton was also 'Winkle'. An old locomotive driver told the authors that WINKLE was maker's number 2. However, some lists give it as Borrows' No.1.

DAPHNE, a four-coupled saddle tank built by Peckett and Sons of Bristol in 1889, arrived at Ravenhead around 1922 or 1923. It had been acquired second hand by Pilkington Brothers Ltd for use in connection with the abortive Garden Village scheme at Eccleston, which we deal with in a later chapter, but it seems to have been regarded as Ravenhead Works property. It was presumably DAPHNE that was referred to when the Pilkington Board approved the purchase of a locomotive for Ravenhead in September 1919 at a cost of £1058 [31].

Two further locomotives KNOWSLEY and ECCLESTON were transferred to the Ravenhead Works at unknown dates. KNOWSLEY, a four-coupled well tank built by Borrows in 1884, came from the Plate Works at Cowley Hill. ECCLESTON, which seems to have been employed at Ravenhead Colliery for a time, had possibly gone from the colliery to the Sheet Works before coming to Ravenhead.

It appears that WINKLE was broken up in the early 1920s together with another old locomotive, RAVENHEAD, which the authors were told was scrapped soon after the arrival of DAPHNE. Like WINKLE, RAVENHEAD is also something of a mystery. As mentioned in the previous chapter there were several rather nebulous locomtives which bore this name and the engine at the Ravenhead Works may have been one of these.

The locomotive shed was rebuilt in 1921 following a fire [32]. It was reroofed and altered to accommodate an extra locomotive and the 3 ton steam crane which had been purchased in 1919 [33]. A year or two later, the connections between the works railway system and the LNWR Ravenhead Branch were relocated and a new line was built across Ravenhead Road to give direct access to Alexandra Colliery [34].

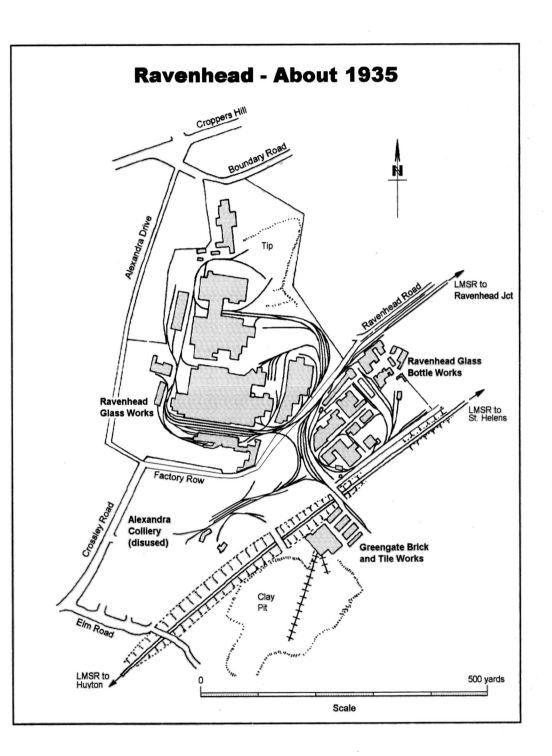

Ravenhead - About 1935

Croppers Hill

Boundary Road

N

Alexandra Drive

Tip

LMSR to
Ravenhead Jct

Ravenhead Road

Ravenhead Glass
Bottle Works

Ravenhead
Glass Works

LMSR to
St. Helens

Factory Row

Crossley Road

Alexandra
Colliery
(disused)

Greengate Brick
and Tile Works

Clay
Pit

Elm Road

LMSR to
Huyton

0   500 yards

Scale

By 1930, the Ravenhead Works was manufacturing cathedral glass and miscellaneous items such as accumulator containers, shades and later glass insulators and glass bricks [7]. Many of the older parts had been demolished and replaced by new buildings, while some, such as the original casting hall, had been re-equipped with modern machinery. A plan [35] of this period shows that the internal railway system had been extended and many of the awkward sidings and loops replaced.

KNOWSLEY was broken up at Ravenhead in October 1936 [36]. No.3, the ex London and Manchester Plate Glass Company's locomotive was sent to the Sheet Works in 1937 and subsequently scrapped there [36]. ECCLESTON lasted until 1941 when it was also broken up at Ravenhead [36].

The first diesel locomotive arrived in February 1937. Named RAVENHEAD, it was a four-coupled 80hp machine with mechanical drive, built by John Fowler and Company of Leeds. Along with DAPHNE it provided the motive power for the Ravenhead Works railway throughout most of the war years.

Immediately after the second world war, part of the Ravenhead site was taken over for the construction of a new factory for Fibreglass Ltd, a Pilkington Brothers' subsidiary. Production of flat glass ceased in 1976 [7] and afterwards the whole of the site was devoted to the manufacture of glass fibre and associated products. New head offices for the Pilkington Brothers Group were opened on an adjacent plot of ground in 1964 and a glass museum added later.

The entrance to the works on 21st August 1971, taken from Ravenhead Road, with the connection to British Railways in the foreground.   *(J.A. Sommerfield)*

ROF 9 No.5 on 6th May 1956.   *(Industrial Railway Society Bernard Mettam Collection)*

The diesel locomotive RAVENHEAD was transferred to Pilkington Brothers' glass works at Pontypool in South Wales about 1945 and two additional steam locomotives were obtained in 1946 from the Ministry of Supply. These retained their original numbers, ROF 9 No.3 and ROF 9 No.5, whilst at Ravenhead. Both had been built in 1941, the former by Hudswell, Clarke and Company of Leeds and the latter by Robert Stephenson and Hawthorns Ltd. PROGRESS a four-coupled saddle tank built by Andrew Barclay Sons and Company of Kilmarnock in 1916, and obtained second hand by Pilkington Brothers Ltd in 1942, was transferred from the Plate Works in about 1953.

The final acquisitions were two four-coupled 200hp diesel electric locomotives built by the Yorkshire Engine Company of Sheffield. ALEXANDRA, later named J B M, came new to Ravenhead in August 1957. CROSSLEY, later A H D, built in 1958, arrived in June 1959 after some months of use at the Cowley Hill Works. Two of the steam engines were then taken out of service. ROF 9 No.3 was broken up in 1957. PROGRESS, which may have spent a short period at the Sheet Works, was scrapped about January 1959.

The other two steam locomotives were kept in reserve for a few years in case of breakdown of the diesels [37]. ROF 9 No.5 was scrapped in April 1969 by Richardson Metals Ltd. DAPHNE, which had been at Ravenhead for more than forty years, went to a children's playground at Skelmersdale in 1966. By November 1987 it had moved to the Fleetwood Locomotive Centre Ltd at Wyre Dock. From about August 1994 it has been on display at Tarzan's Restaurant, St Annes on Sea.

Rail traffic continued at Ravenhead on a diminishing scale until late 1983 or early 1984. The two diesel locomotives were sold around March 1984 to United Glass Containers Ltd for use at its Peasley Glass Works.

The Royal Colliery

The earliest pits at the Royal Colliery were located near the toll bar on Prescot Road in Croppers Hill. They were sunk soon after 1830 by members of the Bromilow family [1] who for a time traded under the name of the Eccleston Coal Company [38,39]. The Royal Colliery later expanded on to a second site located about a quarter of a mile further from St Helens and on the opposite side of the Prescot Road, near the Plate Glass Works. The original pits seem to have relied entirely on road transport but, as we have seen earlier, this second site had a rail connection from about 1851 or 1852 onwards.

The Royal Colliery is shown in the occupation of David Bromilow and Company in the Mines Lists from 1853-54 to 1859, when coal production appears to have ceased. The plant was put up for auction on 1st and 2nd April 1861 [40,41,42]. The sale included 50 coal wagons to hold 4 to 5 tons each and the railway connection was also mentioned. There is no reference to a locomotive in the advertisements, the railway layout evidently being too small to require one. The colliery itself was put up for sale on 3rd September 1861 [43].

Bromilow's second Royal Colliery, at the end of the Ravenhead Branch, or at least the surface property there, was leased by Pilkington Brothers for use as a landsale yard. Coal from the latter's St Helens Colliery was conveyed over the branch, much of it apparently going from there by road to Prescot and neighbouring places.

At the end of 1863 [44] Pilkington Brothers were complaining about the tolls charged for this traffic by the LNWR but, in spite of this, there were plans [45] to move the landsale yard to a position alongside the main road. The cost of making the new yard and providing an engine house, weighing machine and 200 yards of new railway was estimated at £200.

It is not clear if the work was carried out as there was a dispute with the landowner, a member of the West family, about the rent which was to be charged. There was also a wrangle with the railway company and the British Plate Glass Company about the track leading to the yard. The land occupied by the line had been leased by the Plate Glass Company to the railway company, which was under an obligation to restore the site when the colliery closed. Pilkington Brothers hoped that the railway company could be persuaded to pay the Plate Glass Company for the cost of restoration without actually carrying out the work. In this way Pilkington Brothers would be able to obtain a fresh lease from the Plate Glass Company at a reduced price [45].

Use of the Royal Yard was in any case not necessary after Pilkington Brother's nearby Alexandra Colliery came into production in 1868. Minutes of February and October 1869 relate to clearing old rails from the Royal Yard [46,47] and in October 1870 it was decided to dispose of the land [48].

The Royal Colliery reappears in the Mines Lists in 1875 under the name of John Cross, who also established a firebrick works nearby. The West Lancashire Collieries and Fireclay Works Co Ltd, which was registered on 31st January 1877 [49], took over this property and the Gillars Green Colliery at Eccleston. Cross, as we shall see later in the present chapter also had an interest in the Greengate Brick and Tile Works and its associated coal pits.

We have been unable to identify the location of this later Royal Colliery. It is unlikely that Cross reopened the pit near Pilkington Brothers' one time coal yard. More probably his operations were on or close to the site of Bromilow's earlier workings nearer to St Helens.

The plant at the Royal Colliery was advertised for sale on 20th December 1878 [50] and afterwards the property seems to have reverted to John Cross. His name appears in the Mines Lists from 1878 to 1883. Between 1884 and 1886 the occupier is shown as the Victoria Coal and Fireclay Company, after which the Royal Colliery seems to have finally closed. It does not appear in the 1886 and subsequent lists, but what is referred to as the Royal Colliery, and also as the old colliery near the toll bar, was later used to provide a water supply for Pilkington Brothers' works [51,52].

The Alexandra Colliery

Following the success of the St Helens Colliery which was reopened in 1857, Pilkington Brothers decided to expand their mining activities. They declined an offer by W.P. Radley to purchase his pits at Croppers Hill and at the Delph, near the Crown Glass Works [53,54,55]. In December 1863 they decided to sink a new colliery of their own on a site at Ravenhead near the Plate Glass Works at an estimated cost of £3,500 including machinery [44]. The perceived advantages were that there would be a great saving in wagon hire and transport costs, that access could be gained to the Royal Yard without being charged by the railway company, that the Rainhill district would be more accessible, that production costs would be 3d per ton cheaper than at St Helens Colliery and that the workings would not be much troubled by water.

In March 1864 a pumping engine was purchased second hand at Chorley [45] and by September both this and a winding engine had been put to work [56]. It was not until December 1867, shortly before production started, that it was decided to name the new sinking Alexandra Colliery [57].

As described in Chapter 4, Pilkington Brothers purchased their first locomotive, ST HELENS, at the end of 1868 or early in 1869. As well as hauling coal trains between Alexandra Colliery and the Sheet Works, St HELENS evidently carried out a certain amount of shunting at the colliery. In 1870, when the locomotive was out of service for a lengthy overhaul, it was decided to install a stationary engine to move the wagons in the colliery sidings [58] and this was in operation by 8th June [59]. An engine from the mixing room at the Sheet Works was considered suitable [60], but we do not know whether this was actually used.

The original rail access to the Alexandra Colliery was over a back shunt from the line leading to the Royal Yard and this was later replaced by a direct connection from the Ravenhead Branch. It appears [61] that the LNWR had purchased additional land for this purpose, but in the event the new connection was built on Pilkington Brothers' property. The changes are shown on the first edition of the 25 inch map surveyed in 1881 and were probably made in 1875. Pilkington Brothers' minutes refer to "a new curve to the colliery", which we assume to be the Alexandra, for which expenditure was authorised in March 1875 [62]. The contract was let to Edward Borrows, who incurred the displeasure of the partners over his failure to finish the work on time. It seems to have been eventually completed at the beginning of July 1875 [59,63].

The portion of line in front of Factory Row, provided in the first instance to gain access to the Royal Colliery and retained to serve Alexandra Colliery, was no longer required and the lease of land on which it was built was given up by the London and North Western Railway. The land purchased by the LNWR for its own direct connection to Alexandra Colliery was sold to Pilkington Brothers under an agreement of 2nd November 1908 which related to the widening of the Ravenhead Branch [64].

The second edition of the 25 inch map, surveyed in 1906, shows that the layout of the sidings within the colliery yard had been simplified, apparently around 1900. There were further changes to the connection with the Ravenhead Branch, probably immediately after the first world war, when the sidings leading from the colliery were moved on to a new alignment to the south of the earlier one. A new direct curve to the Plate Glass Works was constructed in 1922 or 1923 at the cost of the Ravenhead Works [34].

The colliery itself seems to have changed little over the years. It was taken over by the St Helens Collieries Co Ltd on the amalgamation of Pilkington Brothers' coal mining interests and those of the Ravenhead Colliery Co Ltd in June 1876. The Mines Lists state that winding ceased on 30th May 1925 and one of the pits was subsequently used as a pumping station at least until 1968.

Greengate Colliery and Brick and Tile Works

Greengate Colliery was located on the south side of the Huyton and St Helens line. Its origins are somewhat obscure. It was on the site of earlier workings which are marked as Ravenhead Colliery on the first edition of the 6 inch map, surveyed in 1846 and 1847.

According to Barker and Harris [1] Greengate Colliery was opened about 1869 by a William Walmesley, but it is not shown in the Mines Lists until 1872, when the occupier is given as John Cross and Co Ltd. There was a siding, however, which ran between the colliery and the Ravenhead Branch as early as 1864 and which is shown on the Deposited Plans for the Huyton and St Helens line [65]. The new line was in a cutting at this point and a bridge was provided to accommodate the colliery siding.

The siding over the LNWR was retained by later owners to give access to the new developments. These included a brick and tile works which was probably erected during John Cross' period of occupation.

After 1872, possibly as a result of the alterations to the connection with Alexandra Colliery, wagons from Greengate Colliery had to pass over a short portion of Pilkington Brothers' line to reach the Ravenhead Branch. The Pilkington Minutes record that this was covered by a legal agreement with J. Cross of Atherton and Cross, who had to pay £5 per annum for the privilege [66].

John Cross and Co Ltd is last shown in the Mines Lists for 1876. The property then passed to the Greenbank Colliery Company Ltd, a subsidiary of the Greenbank Alkali Co Ltd of which the Menzies family were the proprietors. The alkali company must have had some interest in the colliery prior to that, as there are several references to the Menzies in Pilkington Brothers' minutes.

In March 1875, runaway wagons at the Alexandra Colliery smashed some of Menzies' wagons, which the minutes add tersely "shouldn't have been there" [67]. In the same month in what seems to have been a separate incident, a Greengate Colliery wagon was damaged. Because of the agreement with the colliery company, Pilkington Brothers escaped paying compensation [67].

Perhaps because of these accidents, the London and North Western Railway was, in May 1875, canvassing the idea of erecting a signal box at Ravenhead, half the costs for which were to be shared by Pilkington Brothers, John Cross and the Menzies. Pilkington Brothers told the LNWR that they were satisfied with the existing arrangements and nothing more was heard of the scheme [68].

The Greengate property was put up for auction on 17th April 1882 by the Greenbank Alkali Company, which was stated to be discontinuing its coal interests [69,70]. The first edition of the 25 inch map, surveyed in 1881, shows that by this date a system of narrow gauge lines had been built to connect with a number of small mines, over half a mile away near Elephant Lane. These were used to bring coal to the Greengate site, where some was loaded into standard gauge wagons and some used as fuel at the brickworks. No information has survived about how these narrow gauge railways were operated, but it seems likely that the coal was conveyed in pit tubs, probably attached to an endless chain driven by a stationary engine.

The auction sale in April 1882 must have fallen through as the Mines Lists show the Greenbank Alkali Co Ltd, incorrectly described as the Greenbank Alkali Works Ltd, as continuing in occupation until 1889, though the colliery was not working in 1888 and 1889. Greenbank Alkali Co Ltd became part of the United Alkali Co Ltd in November 1890 and the colliery and brickworks were transferred to the Greengate Brick and Tile Co Ltd.

By 1891, when the 25 inch map was resurveyed, most of the earlier coal and clay pits had been abandoned, as had the greater part of the narrow gauge railway system. An opencast clay pit had been opened up to the north of the LNWR line and was connected to the works by a tramway or tubway which crossed the main line on a new bridge. Coal mining continued in a small way until 1894, after which the firm disappears from the Mines Lists.

Subsequently the brickworks passed into the hands of J.J. Bate, who seems to have purchased the property in December 1901 [71]. Mining was resumed at what is described as the Greengate Park Colliery in 1902 but coal production ceased again, according to the Mines Lists, in 1907.

In July 1919 [71], the Greengate Brickworks was acquired by Pilkington Brothers Ltd to provide a supply of materials for the Garden Village project, which we describe in a later chapter. Mr J.J. Bate was kept on by the new owners as manager [72], but left later that year [73,74,75]. As we have seen in Chapter 5, he was also associated with the 'Old Teapot' Works.

Prior to the take-over, wagons had been hauled to and from the Ravenhead Branch by horses. This was still the situation in 1921 when Pilkington Brothers Ltd was taken to task by the London and North Western Railway Company for failing to load the wagons to full capacity [76]. In a letter of 3rd October, the firm pointed out that the horses could not deal with fully loaded wagons. However, there was a small locomotive named WINKLE, weighing 17 tons 16 cwt, which could be used if the LNWR would confirm that the bridge was strong enough [76]. The LNWR replied that the bridge needed to be strengthened.

The matter was left in abeyance until, on 23rd April 1923, Pilkington Brothers made further enquiries about the use of a larger locomotive, weighing 28 tons 10 cwt [76]. Presumably this was the Peckett DAPHNE which we have described earlier. On this occasion, the LNWR agreed to strengthen the bridge at a maximum cost of £225 to Pilkington Brothers. Thereafter, one of the locomotives from the Ravenhead Works seems to have been used to take wagons to and from the brickworks [76].

With the curtailment of the garden village scheme, Pilkington Brothers Ltd tried to dispose of the Greengate Brickworks in 1934, but was unsuccessful [77,78,79]. It was still the firm's property in May 1943, when Greengate was reported to be one of the only two brickworks in St Helens still in operation. Because of the loss incurred in brick manufacture the plant was partly shut down but it was decided to continue production on a limited scale in the hope of recovering losses after the war [80].

Rail traffic appears to have finished after the second world war. On 15th January 1957 [76] Pilkington Brothers Ltd wrote to British Railways seeking permission to lift the railway track over the bridge and build up the roadway to make it suitable for lorries.

The Greengate Works was taken over by by Roughdales Brickworks Ltd in January 1962 [81] and was closed a few years later. The site was absorbed into the Pilkington Brothers Ltd's new Greengate plant.

Nuttall's Ravenhead Glass Bottle Works

The Ravenhead Glass Bottle Works was located on the south side of the Ravenhead Branch near the sidings serving the Greengate Brickworks. It was established by a partnership headed by Francis Dixon-Nuttall and came into production in the Spring of 1873 [82].

The first edition of the 25 inch map, surveyed in 1881, shows two short sidings, provided under an agreement with the LNWR dated 24th January 1876 [83], leading into the works. By the time that the 25 inch map was resurveyed in 1891, the works had more than doubled in size and now extended as far as the tracks leading to the Greengate Colliery and Brickworks. Extra siding capacity had been provided within the works and the connections with the LNWR had been altered under an agreement dated 14th January 1889 [83]. Also shown on the 1891 map, near where the Greengate sidings joined the Ravenhead Branch, were a ventilating shaft and fan engine house. We have been unable to discover whether these were associated with the Alexandra Colliery or one of the other collieries in the neighbourhood.

There were further extensions around 1900, almost doubling the size of the factory again. The second edition of the 25 inch map, surveyed in 1906, shows that all the vacant land up to the boundary of the LNWR Huyton and St Helens line was now occupied and that an extensive network of internal railway tracks had been established.

It appears that the firm's first locomotive was obtained at this time, as an agreement with the LNWR, dated 15th February 1902, refers to the firm's engine working on the Ravenhead Branch [84]. No information has survived about it and the earliest record we have is of THE KING, a four-coupled well tank which was purchased from Edward Borrows around 1905. A similar locomotive named THE QUEEN came in 1907 from the same manufacturer.

THE QUEEN, one of the two well tanks supplied by Edward Borrows to Nuttall's Ravenhead Works.   *(J.A. Peden Collection)*

Nuttall and Co Ltd, which had taken over from the original partnership, amalgamated with Cannington, Shaw and Co Ltd on 31st March 1913 [85] to form United Glass Bottle Manufacturers Ltd. The Ravenhead Works continued under the new ownership with little outward change. On the railway side, THE KING was transferred to the firm's Charlton Works, near London, in 1922 and remained there until February 1967. It was then acquired by the Industrial Locomotive Preservation Group and put into store at Robertsbridge in Kent, where it remained until the end of 1969. It is now with a preservation society at Fleetwood, by coincidence the same group which, for a time, owned DAPHNE, the Peckett from Pilkington Brothers' Ravenhead Works.

THE QUEEN was thereafter the only locomotive to be allocated to the Ravenhead Works until after the second world war, although no doubt engines were made available from the United Glass Bottle Manufacturer's Sherdley Works to cover periods when it was out of service. In 1950 or perhaps a year to two earlier, THE QUEEN was sent to the Sherdley Works where it was given a thorough overhaul. It returned to Ravenhead where it was noted in August 1952. THE QUEEN was back at Sherdley in June 1953, but reappeared at Ravenhead, where it was seen in May 1955. It was broken up at Ravenhead in March 1958.

No.5 PEASLEY at the United Glass Botttle Manufacturers Ltd's Ravenhead Works, on 19th April 1958. By this date it was no longer in use and had been brought out of the engine shed, where it was stored, so that it could be photographed.   *(J.A. Peden)*

As described in Chapter 3, several of the locomotives traditionally associated with the Sherdley Works were sent to Ravenhead during this period. SUTTON LODGE was seen working here in June 1953, but went back to Sherdley. PEASLEY was also noted at Ravenhead in June 1953 and seems to have remained here, being scrapped in 1959. SHERDLEY was observed at Ravenhead in May 1955 and again does not appear to have returned to Sherdley. It was broken up in March 1958.

None of the steam engines at Ravenhead probably saw much service after the arrival of a four-wheeled diesel locomotive in 1957. This was a 117hp machine with a mechanical drive which came new from F.C. Hibberd and Co Ltd of Park Royal, London, and was named RAVENHEAD.

United Glass Ltd was registered on 1st March 1959 to act as a holding company [85] and the Ravenhead Bottle Works was transferred to a subsidiary, Ravenhead Glass Ltd [86]. In March 1965 a start was made on reconstructing and extending the works, which was turned over to the manufacture of glass tableware [87]. The factory is still in production at the time of writing, although rail traffic ceased in the early 1970s and RAVENHEAD was sold to Lowton Metals Ltd, Stockport in May 1974.

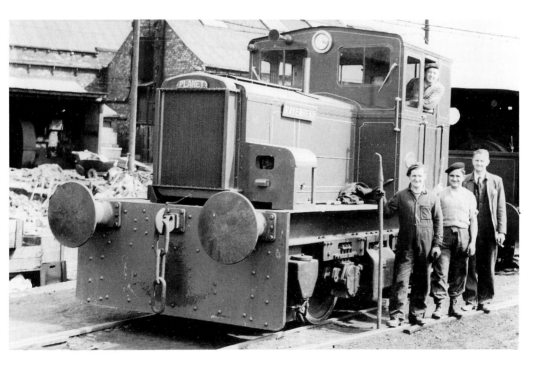

The diesel locomotive, RAVENHEAD, was delivered to the United Glass Bottle Manufacturers' Ravenhead Works in 1957 as a replacement for the steam locomotive PEASLEY. It is seen here with its crew on 19th April 1958. (J.A. Peden)

LOCOMOTIVE SUMMARY

Ravenhead Glass Works

Various Statutory and Joint Stock Companies 1773 to 1868 (see text)
London and Manchester Plate Glass Co Ltd 1868 to 1894
British Plate Glass Co Ltd 1895 to 1901
Pilkington Brothers Ltd 1901 to about 1976
Site shared with Fibreglass Ltd from about 1945 to about 1976
Site taken over completely by Fibreglass Ltd about 1976

3ft 6in gauge

CASTING HALL No.1   2-2-0ST IC   HE   641 1895
   New in November 1895
   Scrapped or sold, probably around 1905

Standard Gauge

No.3   0-4-0WT OC   EBS   17 1883   12"(?)
   Probably new to Ravenhead Works
   To Sheet Works in 1937 and later scrapped there

                      0-4-0WT OC   EBS
   Possibly EBS 2 of about 1875 (see text)
   Ex Sutton Oak Works by 1908
   Possibly requisitioned by Ministry of Munitions for use at Inspection Bond 1201, Sutton Oak
   Presumably the same locomotive which was at Ravenhead Works in early 1920s named WINKLE
   Presumed scrapped about 1923

RAVENHEAD
   Stated to have been scrapped in early 1920s
   See text and Chapter 5 for possible identity

DAPHNE   0-4-0ST OC   P   737 1899 14½"x18" 3'1½"
   Class W4
   From Tytherington Stone Co Ltd, Falfield, to Garden Village scheme, about 1920
   Ex Garden Village scheme to Ravenhead Works about 1923
   To children's playground at New Church Farm Play Area, Skelmersdale, about 1966
   By November 1987 at Fleetwood Locomotive Centre Ltd at Wyre Dock
   From about August 1994 on display at Tarzan's Restaurant, St Annes on Sea

KNOWSLEY   0-4-0WT OC   EBS   19 1884   15"x20" 3'6"
   Transferred from Cowley Hill Plate Works
   Scrapped in 1937

Name	Type		Builder	Works No.	Year	Cylinders	Wheels
ECCLESTON	0-4-0WT OC	EBS		36	1898	15"x20"	3'6"

Transferred probably from Sheet Works, previously at Ravenhead Colliery
Scrapped in 1941

| RAVENHEAD | 0-4-0DM | JF | | 21457 | 1937 | 80HP | |

New February 1937
To Pontypool Road Works, about 1945

| ROF 9 No.3 | 0-4-0ST OC | HC | | 1722 | 1941 | 14"x22" | 3'4" |

Ex Ministry of Supply in 1946
Scrapped in 1957

| ROF 9 No.5 | 0-4-0ST OC | RSH | | 7046 | 1941 | 14"x22" | 3'6" |

Ex Ministry of Supply in 1946
Converted to oil firing by March 1962
Scrapped April 1969 by Richardson Metals Ltd, St Helens

| PROGRESS | 0-4-0ST OC | AB | | 1465 | 1916 | 14"x22 | 3'5" |

Ex Cowley Hill Plate Works about 1953
Possibly transferred to Sheet Works at end of 1958
Scrapped about January 1959

| J B M | 0-4-0DE | YE | | 2653 | 1957 | 200HP | |

Formerly ALEXANDRA
New, delivered 1.8.1957
To United Glass Containers Ltd, Peasley Works, about March 1984

| A H D | 0-4-0DE | YE | | 2730 | 1958 | 200HP | |

Formerly CROSSLEY
Ex City Road Works about June 1959
To United Glass Containers Ltd, Peasley Works, about March 1984

Ravenhead Glass Bottle Works

Nuttall and Co 1873 to 1913
United Glass Bottle Manufacturers Ltd 1913 to March 1959
Ravenhead Glass Ltd from March 1959

| THE KING | 0-4-0WT OC | EBS | | 48(?) | 1906(?) | 10"x18" | 3'1" |

Presumed new to Ravenhead Glass Bottle Works
To Charlton Works, London, 1923

| THE QUEEN | 0-4-0WT OC | EBS | | 50 | 1907 | 12"x20" | 3'2½" |

New
To Sherdley Works about 1950 and returned by August 1952
To Sherdley Works by June 1953 and returned by May 1955
No. 4 from about 1952
Scrapped March 1958

| SUTTON LODGE | 0-4-0ST OC | HC | 564 | 1900 | 13"x20" | 3'3" |

Temporarily transferred from Sherdley Works and noted at Ravenhead in June 1953
No. 1 from about 1952

| PEASLEY | 0-4-0ST OC | P | 763 | 1899 | 14"x20" | 3'2½" |

Transferred from Sherdley Works by June 1953
No. 5 from about 1952
Taken out of service by mid 1958 and scrapped early 1959

| SHERDLEY | 0-4-0ST OC | HC | 251 | 1883 | 13"x20" | 3'3" |

Transferred from Sherdley Works by May 1955
Scrapped March 1958

| RAVENHEAD | 4wDM | FH | 3863 | 1957 | 117HP |

New
To Lowton Metals Ltd, Stockport May 1974

An aerial photograph of Ravenhead taken probably in the late 1930s. Pilkington Brothers' Works occupies most of the foreground. Nuttall's Bottle Works lies beyond Ravenhead Road and the branch railway. In the distance, on the far side of the St Helens and Huyton line, there are two brickworks and their associated clay pits; in the centre left is the Old Teapot Works, while the Greengate Works is to the right.

(Pilkington Brothers Archives at IM&S)

References to Chapter 6

1   *A Merseyside Town in the Industrial Revolution   St Helens 1750 - 1900,* T.C. Barker and J.R. Harris, Frank Cass & Co Ltd, London, 1959

2   11 Geo 4 cap lxi; 29th May 1830

3   British Plate Glass Co - Rough Minutes of Committee - IM&S BPG 7

4   Information supplied to the authors by Mr J.M. Tolson

5   Particulars of Ravenhead Estate, the Property of the Late Colonel and Mrs Fraser - Sale by Auction 30th October 1849 - IM&S PB 147/91

6   13 Geo III cap xxxviii

7   *The Glassmakers Pilkington 1825 - 1975,* J.R. Harris, Weidenfeld and Nicolson, London, 1977

8   38 Geo III cap xvii; 7th May 1798

9   59 Geo III cap v; 23rd March 1819

10 Preamble to 25 Vic cap xvi; 16th May 1862

11 25 Vic cap xvi; 16th May 1862

12 *The Canals of North West England,* C. Hadfield and G. Biddle, David and Charles, Newton Abbot, 1970

13 Lease T. Eccleston to Governor and Company, dated 11th Oct 1792, in Dicconson papers at LRO, quoted in *Railways of the St Helens Coalfield down to 1830,* by J.R. Harris - at StHLH A 35.7 (P)

14 Plan of Ravenhead Works dated 1860 IM&S PB 147/35

15 Plan of Ravenhead Works dated 1865 IM&S PB 147/103

16 Lease dated 21st June 1864 - IM&S PB147/101

17 Counterpart lease dated 14th Nov 1865 IM&S PB 147/103

18 Attached to IM&S 147/103

19 *StHNews* 24.9.1894

20 *StHNews* 22.12.1894

21 IM&S PB 147/123

22 Plan of Ravenhead Works 1901 - IM&S PB 269/45

23 Board of Trade Boiler Explosion Report 1278, 1901

24 Pilkington Bros Ltd General Board Minutes 6.9.1901

25 IM&S PB 1/1080 Draft note dated 21st October 1920.

26 Pilkington Bros Ltd General Board Minutes 3.10.1902

27 Pilkington Bros Ltd Plate Board Minutes 25.9.1902

28 Ibid 7.5.1908

29 Ibid 22.5.1908

30 IM&S File PB1/1080

31 Pilkington Bros Ltd General Board Minutes 2.9.1919

32 Capital Requisitions, Ravenhead, 8.12.1920 - IM&S PB 628

33 Ibid 23.6.1919

34 Ibid 30.6.1922

35 Ravenhead Works Plan of about 1936 at IM&S

36 Letter E.M.S. Wood to Frank Smith 21.5.1956

37 Letter E.M.S. Wood to Bernard Roberts 27.11.1961

38 *Royal National Commercial Directory and Topography of Lancashire,* Isaac Slater, Manchester, 1848

39 *Royal National Classified Commercial Directory and Topography of Lancashire,* Isaac Slater, Manchester, 1851

40 *MJ* 16.3.1861

41 *WO* 30.3.1861

42 *MG* 30.3.1861

43 *WO* 30.8.1861

44 Pilkington Bros General Board Minutes 24.12.1863

45 Ibid 17.3.1864

46 Ibid 25.2.1869

47 Ibid 25.10.1869

48 Ibid 24.10.1870

49   *Iron* 17.2.1877
50   *MG* 14.12.1878
51   Pilkington Bros Ltd General Board Minutes 9.5.1905
52   Ibid 15.8.1905
53   Pilkington Bros General Board Minutes 19.3.1863
54   Ibid 26.3.1863
55   Ibid 21.5.1863
56   Ibid 2.9.1864
57   Ibid 10.12.1867
58   Ibid 1.6.1870
59   Ibid 8.6.1870
60   Ibid 2.3.1870
61   Plan of repairs to Ravenhead Road, nd, about 1908 - IM&S 655/1
62   Pilkington Bros General Board Minutes 24.3.1875
63   Ibid 24.6.1875
64   Line Plan of St Helens Railway, LNWR, Rugby, 1871, 2 chains to 1 inch, at BRPB, Manchester Office
65   LRO PDR 799
66   Pilkington Bros General Board Minutes 16.2.1872
67   Ibid 24.3.1875
68   Ibid 28.5.1875

69   *WO* 1.4.1882
70   *MG* 15.4.1882
71   Documents relating to sale by Bate to Pilkington - IM&S PB 2/13
72   Pilkington Bros Ltd General Board Minutes 10.7.1919
73   Ibid 7.10.1919
74   Ibid 21.11.1919
75   Ibid 12.12.1919
76   *The "WINKLE" File* - Extracts from the Bridge Files of British Railways Civil Enginering Dept. Copy in possession of Mr John Ryan
77   Pilkington Bros Ltd General Board Minutes 22.3.1934
78   Ibid 28.11.1934
79   Ibid 28.8.1935
80   Ibid 27.5.1943
81   *StHRep* 9.12.1961
82   *StHNews* 31.12.1898 - Review of year item dated 12.3.1898
83   LNWR Sdgs Diag 176, dated 12.1916
84   Endorsement on Line Plan of 1871 Reference 64
85   *Stock Exchange Year Book* 1972-1973
86   United Glass Ltd - Annual Report, 1965
87   *StHRep* 27.3.1965

CHAPTER SEVEN

THE ECCLESTON BRANCH

We continue our exploration of the district to the west of St Helens town centre along the Eccleston Branch railway. When the line was opened in 1859, it served Pilkington Brothers' Eccleston Glass Works at Boundary Road and continued as far as Gillar's Green, where it was hoped to open out a new colliery. In the 1870s additional sidings were constructed at Boundary Road to give access to a short lived alkali works and to Doulton Brothers' Brick Works and Pottery. At the turn of the century St Helens Corporation established its electricity works on the alkali factory site. Many of the other sidings were taken over by coal merchants for unloading incoming wagons and were still in active use until the branch closed in October 1967.

Mining at Gillar's Green did not develop as quickly as expected and the colliery there was not sunk until the early 1870s. It finally closed in 1910. After that there seems to have been little traffic beyond Boundary Road Sidings, except perhaps for a small amount of inwards coal for the landsale yard at Home Farm Lane, until the Pilkington Garden Village Scheme after the first world war. When that was abandoned about 1922, Boundary Road again became the effective terminus of the line until sidings were laid near Home Farm Lane, by now renamed Holme Road, in the early 1930s to serve the new Triplex factory.

The events leading up to the construction of the Eccleston Branch were far from simple and it is worthwhile giving an outline here. The branch proper was built under parliamentary powers obtained in 1853 [1]. These authorised the St Helens Railway to construct a line, as shown on the Deposited Plans of 1852 [2], from the termination of the Ravenhead Branch as completed in 1834 to a point about 30 yards west of Home Farm Lane.

The Deposited Plans, however, did not quite tally with the facts. The St Helens Railway Company's line from the 1834 terminus at Ravenhead Colliery Sidings to the Royal Colliery and the Plate Glass Works, if not actually open for traffic, must have been in an advanced stage of construction when the Plans were drawn up. There was also a short spur from the line to the Royal Colliery which gave access to the Greenbank Alkali Works, for which contracts had been placed in August 1851.

Thus the Eccleston Branch in reality commenced at a junction with the Ravenhead Branch extension at a point near Marsh's Crossing, sometimes referred to in railway company documents as Eccleston Junction. The first 150 yards or so of the branch appears to have incorporated part of the siding laid in to serve the Greenbank Works.

Because of geological faulting, there was a small area at Gillar's Green where the coal seams came to the surface and, although there had been some mining since the 1750s, a rail connection was essential if the colliery was to be fully exploited. In 1846 the St Helens Railway Company put forward a scheme for a line from Gerard's Bridge to join the Grand Junction's proposed Huyton and St Helens Railway. There were discussions with the landowner, Samuel Taylor, about a spur to serve the colliery but these came to nothing as the St Helens Company's Bill was withdrawn due to opposition from the Grand Junction [3].

With the Eccleston Branch now under construction thoughts again turned to a link with Gillar's Green, situated about a mile from the authorised terminus of the branch at Home Farm Lane. Beyond here the line was continued as private railway, built under an agreement dated 4th March 1857 [4] between Samuel Taylor and the St Helens Company. The land needed was made available by Taylor, who must have contributed to the construction costs, as he was allowed to keep half the revenue from the traffic over the line until he had recouped his estimated outlay of £1,500 [3]. Under the agreement the line was to be worked and maintained by the railway company for both passenger and goods traffic, with coal being carried at the same rates as other collieries in St Helens. Provision was also made for a branch to Charles Scarisbrick's colliery, if required. This would have crossed Taylor's property to join the Gillar's Green line. Under the 1857 agreement [4], Taylor was to lease the land which was needed at £10 per Cheshire acre and to allow the Scarisbrick coal to pass free of toll.

The whole of the Eccleston Branch, including the extension to Gillar's Green, was completed early in 1859 and a locomotive made a trial trip over the line on 2nd March [5]. A passenger train service was never operated over the line and it is not clear what goods traffic there was beyond the sidings at Boundary Road at this time. The branch to Scarisbrick's colliery was never built and, as mentioned earlier, the colliery at Gillar's Green was not sunk until the early 1870s.

The only tunnel on the St Helens Railway was located on the Eccleston Branch where the line passed under Cropper's Hill. Soon after the opening this fell in and had to be repaired [6]. There was another collapse on 25th June 1894, which caused the colliery at Gillar's Green to be stopped until the line could be reopened [7].

Doulton and Company's Liverpool Road Works

Doulton Brothers and Company, as noted in Chapter 5, had since about 1850 occupied the Greenbank Pottery in Canal Bank [8], which specialised in the manufacture of glazed earthenware pipes [9]. The firm acquired a plot of land between Cropper's Hill Road and Boundary Road, on the south side of the Eccleston Branch, probably in the mid 1870s, for its new Liverpool Road Works. Brickmaking equipment was installed and clay pits were opened up which also supplied raw material to the Greenbank factory.

The Greenbank Pottery was sold to Pilkington Brothers towards the end of the century and the partnership, latterly known as Doulton and Company, was turned into a limited liability company around 1900 [10,11] Acccording to Barker and Harris, manufacture of glazed pipes was transferred to the Liverpool Road Works [9]. Production is said to have started in 1896, while bricks ceased to be made there after 1906 [9].

Although contemporary maps mark an opencast clay pit, connected to the production plant by narrow gauge inclines, there was also an underground clay level. The Mines Lists show that this was in operation intermittently from the early 1880s to 1912, when it was stated to be worked out.

The Liverpool Road Works was taken over by Ellistown Pipes Ltd and transferred to a subsidiary company, Doulton Vitrified Pipes Ltd. It closed at the outbreak of the second world war and the stock on hand was sent to Royal Ordnance Factories at Risley and Kirkby which were then being constructed [12].

The works was served by a short siding which was provided under an agreement between the LNWR and Doulton and Company dated 30th April 1877. This appears to have continued in use until the works closed. In 1946 part of the site was taken over by the St Helens Industrial Co-operative Society to serve as a coal yard. The siding was retained for incoming coal delivered by rail. The Sidings Schedules record that the siding was transferred to its new owners on 10th October 1946 but that the agreement with the Co-operative Society was not completed until 19th July 1959. It is not known if the siding survived until the closure of the Eccleston Branch in 1967, although this seems likely.

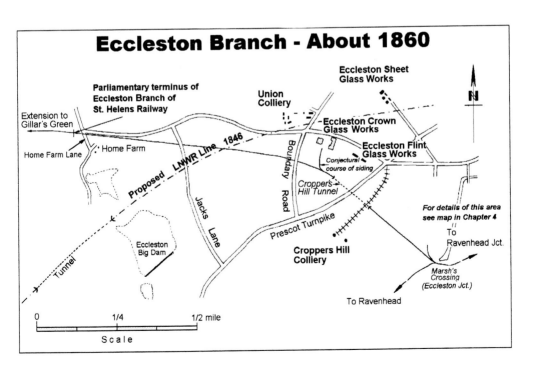

The Boundary Road Sidings

On the north side of the Eccleston Branch, opposite to Doulton's pottery, there were several short sidings which gave access to a variety of industrial premises. The first to be provided was probably that to serve the Eccleston Crown Glass Works. The works, situated at the corner of what is now Boundary Road and Eccleston Street, was set up early in 1792 by Mackay, West and Company [13]. After passing through the hands of several owners, it became the property of Pilkington Brothers in 1853 [13].

The siding was probably contemporary with the opening of the Eccleston Branch in 1859 and appears also to have served a landsale yard for coal coming from Pilkington Brothers' St Helens Colliery. Pilkington Brothers' minutes record that the Eccleston Coal Yard was unprofitable and in February 1863 it was resolved to close it [14]. Further evidence that the siding serving the Eccleston Glass Works was in use at an early date comes from a minute of October 1863 referring to a dispute with the railway company over rates for traffic to Eccleston from the Sheet Works [15].

Production of rolled plate glass, which had formerly been made at Eccleston, was transferred to the Sheet Works in 1869 [13]. By 1872, all glass production had ceased at Eccleston and the glass cone had been demolished. Pilkington Brothers retained a small part of the works for stained glass manufacture and other special products [13]. Other parts of the premises were let out.

As early as 1866 vacant land was leased by Pilkington Brothers to James Varley for the erection of an iron foundry [9]. When Varley moved elsewhere, the premises were let to Baron and Cook , who assigned the lease for at least part of the site in May 1878 to W.H. Foster, who is described as a corn merchant [16]. The Sidings Schedules record that by December 1878 the remaining part of the foundry had been taken over by John Windus. Following the death of Joseph Windus, the Eccleston Foundry Co Ltd was registered on 15th March 1882 to take over from his executors [17].

A corn mill was erected on another part of the Eccleston Glass Works site. The Sidings Schedules, in a note dated December 1878, show the mill was occupied by J.& J. Melling. They also record that the Mellings became insolvent, that the mill passed into the hands of a Liverpool Bank and that the premises had been let to a Mr Potts to gain access to his private coal yard.

The revised 25 inch map shows that by 1891 most of the mill site had been redeveloped as a caustic drum factory, with one small building still in use as a mill. It was presumably this building which was later occupied by John Thornton and Co Ltd, a Huddersfield firm that moved here about 1907 to make cloth and felt hearthrugs [18].

The siding which had previously served the corn mill and Mr Potts' coal yard was later taken over by H.J. Lyon. A Mr Craven, also presumably a coal merchant, appears at Lyon's Siding in 1912 and again in 1938 [19,20]. The siding previously serving the foundry was taken over by the St Helens Industrial Co-operative Society, again for use as a coal yard [21].

Boundary Road Sidings

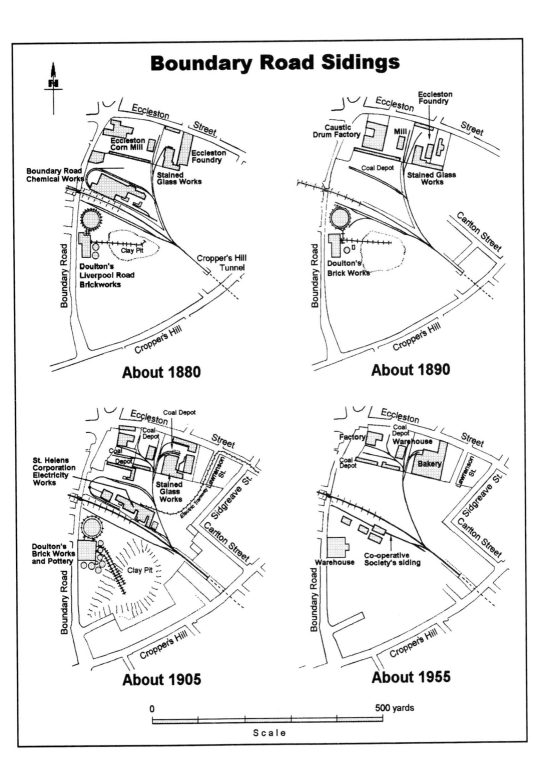

About 1880

About 1890

About 1905

About 1955

0   500 yards

Scale

Lyon's Siding was being used by W.J. Glover and Co Ltd, the wire rope manufacturers, in 1938 and probably earlier. It is not clear if this was to bring in coal to the works or if finished products were brought here by road to be loaded into railway wagons. A note dated 1947 in the Sidings Schedules states that the firm no longer made use of the siding. Presumably it was then relying entirely on motor transport.

The Boundary Road Sidings continued serve a number of coal merchants up to the closure of the Eccleston Branch in 1967. In 1956, in addition to the St Helens Industrial Co-operative Society Ltd, the following firms and individuals were using Lyon's Siding [22].

G.H. Bellis
S.H. Bush
W.J. Caldwell
Farrell and Company
J. Thornton and Company

Lockwood and Leith's Alkali Works and the Corporation Yard and Power Station.

In 1872, James Varley and other partners established the Liverpool and St Helens Alkali Co Ltd on what was apparently a freehold site between Pilkington Brothers' property and the Eccleston Branch railway. The firm became bankrupt in November 1873 and the works was taken over by Lockwood and Leith [9]. The first edition of 25 inch map shows that by 1881 the alkali works had been provided with a connection to the LNWR line and that there was a series of short sidings within the works.

Lockwood and Leith went into receivership in February 1888 [23] and the Eccleston Works was put up for sale on 16th October 1888 [24]. It was subsequently demolished for redevelopment, although one pair of sidings was left in to serve what the 1891 map describes as a coal depot.

The site was acquired in 1891 by St Helens Corporation and part turned into a highways yard [25], the siding then being used for the reception of stone and other building materials brought in by rail. Stabling was built for the horses employed by the Highways Department [26].

A few years later it was decided to use the remainder of the site for a new power station. The Corporation had obtained an Electric Lighting Order in June 1894 [27] and had installed 145Kw of generating plant at a site in Warrington Old Road which was inaugurated in December 1896 [18,28]. With the purchase of the tramways in 1897 and the decision to electrify them [29], increased capacity was needed and a new combined refuse destructor and power station was erected at Boundary Road.

The tramway was extended from Westfield Road along Eccleston Street and Lawrenson Street and into the power station yard. This was in connection with a project to transport compressed night soil from the Parr Manure Depot for use as a cheap fuel, a scheme which was opposed by residents in the neighbourhood of the power station and elsewhere [30]. The idea was dropped, although the use of domestic refuse went ahead. Additional sidings, connecting with those in the Highways Department yard, were provided for the delivery of coal which was also burned at the power station.

The plant consisted initially of four Willans and Robinson 3-crank compound engines coupled to Mather and Platt dynamos [31]. The shed for the new electric trams was situated in the corporation yard, near the power station, although this was only a temporary measure until they could be moved to their permanent depot in Hall Street.

The formal opening by the mayor, Alderman Richard Pilkington, of both the power station and the new electric tramway took place on 3rd August 1899 [29,32]. Extensions to the power station were undertaken in 1901 [33] when an additional 600hp Willans engine coupled to an 830Kw English Electric dynamo was installed. The engine was formally started up on 2nd January 1902 by the mayor, William Windle Pilkington, and named the Windle Pilkington [34].

Subsequently the reciprocating engines and dynamos were replaced by turbo alternators and machines of 1,000, 2,000, 3,000, 5,000 and 6,500Kw were installed [18]. In 1928, instructions were received from the Central Electricity Board to add a 12,500Kw set [18], the extension being completed in 1931 [35].

The power station was taken over by the British Electricity Authority when the industry was nationalised on 1st April 1948. Under subsequent reorganisations it passed to the Central Electricity Authority on 1st May 1955 and to the Central Electricity Generating Board on 1st January 1958. It was converted to oil firing in 1962 [36], when the three wooden cooling towers were demolished [35]. The sidings had already been removed. The Sidings Schedules state that this was ordered on 10th December 1956 and reported to be complete on 17th February 1957.

Gillar's Green Colliery

The first edition of the 6 inch map, surveyed between 1845 and 1847, identifies a Gillar's Green Colliery to the west of the road from Eccleston Four Lane Ends and also a Burrows Lane Colliery a little to the south. Both seem to have been relatively small affairs. Neither appears in the first issue of Mines Lists for 1853-54.

There is no further record of coal mining between 1859, when the extension of the Eccleston Branch was completed, and 1873. In the latter year the Mines Lists show the Gillar's Green Coal Company as sinking pits here. The lease from Samuel Taylor was dated 24th September 1873 and was for a 30 year term [37]. According to the Lists the occupiers were Thomas S. Begbie and William McCandish in 1875 and the West Lancashire Colliery and Fireclay Company from 1876 onwards. The correct title of the latter concern appears to have been the West Lancashire Collieries and Fireclay Works Ltd, which was registered on 31st January 1877 to purchase the Royal Colliery and Firebrick Works at Thatto Heath, lately belonging to Mr John Cross, and also to acquire for £15,000 Gillar's Green Colliery held under lease from Samuel Taylor [38].

It seems likely that operation of the railway between Home Farm Lane and Gillar's Green was taken over by the colliery company as it is recorded that the firm purchased a new locomotive from Fox, Walker and Company of Bristol in 1877. Named GLADYS it was one of that firm's standard six-coupled saddle tanks, with 13 inch cylinders.

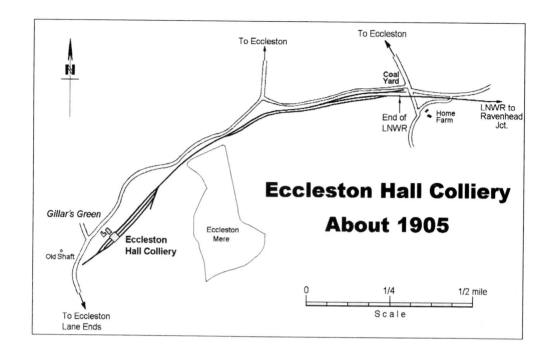

To Eccleston

To Eccleston

N

Coal Yard

End of LNWR

Home Farm

LNWR to Ravenhead Jct.

Eccleston Hall Colliery

About 1905

Gillar's Green

Eccleston Mere

Eccleston Hall Colliery

Old Shaft

0   1/4   1/2 mile

Scale

To Eccleston Lane Ends

The West Lancashire Collieries and Fireclay Works Ltd seems to have been a financial failure. By 1878 the Royal Colliery had, as recounted in an earlier chapter, reverted to John Cross, while Gillar's Green Colliery was the subject of an exhaustive report by Robert Winstanley, a Mining Engineer [37]. This was presumably prepared on behalf of Samuel Taylor in an attempt to dispose of the property.

The plant was put up for auction on 18th and 25th August 1880 [39,40] and included a number of stationary steam engines, a railway weighing machine by Kitchings, an engine shed, steel and wrought iron rails forming the colliery sidings and the colliery railway, about 1 mile in length. The sale must have been postponed as the same items were up for auction again on 24th February 1881 [41].

The colliery itself does not seem to have been sold as the Mines Lists for 1881 show that the landowner, Samuel Taylor, had taken possession. From 1883 to 1886 it appears under the guise of Eccleston Hall Colliery, rather than Gillar's Green, still under Taylor's name. Possibly Samuel Taylor may have attempted to work the colliery himself during this period as there is no indication in the Lists that it was discontinued. He may also have taken over the locomotive GLADYS, perhaps in part payment of debts owing to him by the previous company. There is certainly no mention of the locomotive in any of the sales advertisements, although it later became the property of Holme and King, the Wigan based public works contractors. Its subsequent wanderings are described in our previous volumes [42,43] dealing with Wigan and surrounding districts.

Eccleston Hall Colliery was eventually acquired in February 1889 by W.E.M. Tomlinson, William Rogers and Walter Simpson [44], proprietors of the Worsley Mesnes Colliery Co Ltd. In May 1890 the colliery was reported to be on the point of reopening [45]. The Worsley Mesnes Colliery Company seems to have fared no better than its predecessors. Eccleston Hall closed again on Wednesday 29th May 1895 [46], although the Mines Lists show the firm as occupiers up to and including 1902.

By 1904, William and Thomas Latham had taken over. The Latham brothers were proprietors of the Rose Bridge Colliery at Ince and we have described their activities there and at the East Cannel Pits at Ince in Part 1 of our *Industrial Railways of the Wigan Coalfield* [42]. In 1910, they began to dispose of their mining interests, perhaps because of old age or ill health as William died on 12th November 1910 [47] and Thomas on 26th November 1911 [48].

Eccleston Hall Colliery is shown as abandoned in the Mines List for 1910. The plant, which included two miles of railway and three locomotives, was put up for auction on 16th to 18th August [49,50,51]. The colliery never reopened and the branch line from Hall Farm Lane was taken up .

No reliable information about the locomotives used by the Worsley Mesnes Company or by the Latham brothers has survived. An old employee had recollections of an engine named LYON which had worked here latterly. This may have been during the period that the Worsley Mesnes Company was in occupation, as a locomotive named either LION or LYON has also been mentioned to us at Ellerbeck Colliery, which was also under the control of the Worsley Mesnes directors.

The engine house and other buildings were still in existence in 1918 when Pilkington Brothers Ltd purchased the whole Eccleston Estate for its garden village [52]. Demolition of the engine house was approved in May 1931 [53].

Pilkington Brothers' Garden Village

In the early years of the century, the directors of Pilkington Brothers Ltd began to think in terms of improved housing for the accommodation of its employees. Work started on the Ravenhead Garden Suburb in 1909 but was stopped in September 1915, because of wartime difficulties, before work was complete [54].

Towards the end of the war [55], a more ambitious scheme was drawn up in conjunction with Professor Abercrombie, then a leading figure in town planning matters. The Eccleston Estate of 700 acres was purchased [56] and a plan for 4,000 houses was adopted in February 1919 [54]. A Public Utility Society, Pilkington Garden Village Ltd, was registered in October 1919 and the first sod of the project was cut on 6th November 1919 [54].

A railway system nearly two miles in length was laid down to assist with the construction work [57]. The line started from a small yard at the end of the Eccleston Branch at what later became known as Garden City Siding. From the yard the line made its way over what is now Grange Park Golf Course, reversing twice to gain height, and terminated

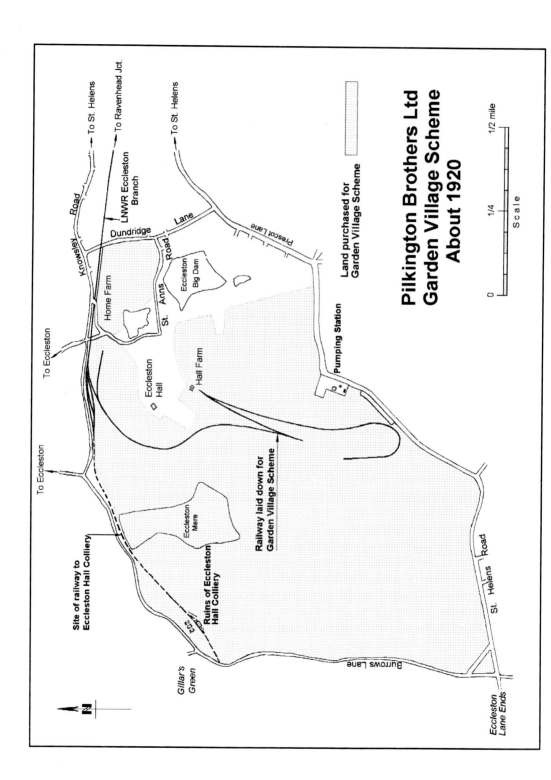

Pilkington Brothers Ltd
Garden Village Scheme
About 1920

Land purchased for
Garden Village Scheme

Scale

0   1/4   1/2 mile

To St. Helens

To Ravenhead Jct.

To St. Helens

LNWR Eccleston
Branch

Knowsley Road

Dundridge Lane

Prescot Lane

St. Anns Road

Home Farm

Eccleston
Big Dam

To Eccleston

Eccleston
Hall

Hall Farm

Pumping Station

To Eccleston

Eccleston
Mere

Railway laid down for
Garden Village Scheme

Site of railway to
Eccleston Hall Colliery

Ruins of Eccleston
Hall Colliery

Gillar's
Green

St. Helens Road

Burrows Lane

Eccleston
Lane Ends

N

192

near the present Eccleston Gardens. Negotiations with the railway company were reported to be approaching completion in May 1919 [58,59] for the connection with the Eccleston Branch, although the Private Sidings Agreement with the LNWR was not signed until 21st January 1921 [60].

As described in Chapter 5, the Greengate Brick and Tile Works was purchased to supply material for the scheme and a four-coupled saddle tank named DAPHNE, built by Peckett and Sons of Bristol in 1899, was obtained second hand from a Gloucestershire quarry to operate on the temporary railway lines on the estate site.

Eccleston Gardens, Broom Road, Seddon Road and Grange Drive, on the south side of the estate, were completed between November 1919 and November 1920 and nine pairs of bungalows on the north side of St Helens Road were ready for occupation between August and October 1920 [54]. Then the whole project was abandoned and Pilkington Garden Village Ltd was wound up in 1922 [54]. Houses in Willow Road and Maple Grove, on which work had started, were completed in 1923.

The locomotive DAPHNE was, as we have seen in an earlier chapter, transferred to Pilkington Brothers' Ravenhead Works. The railway at the Garden Village site was dismantled and the unwanted land leased and later sold off.

The Peckett DAPHNE was obtained second hand to work on Pilkington's Garden Village scheme. It was later transferred to the Ravenhead Works, where it was photographed on 20th July 1952.   *(C.A. Appleton)*

Triplex (Northern) Ltd

Triplex (Northern) Ltd was formed in 1929 as a joint venture between the Triplex Company and Pilkington Brothers to manufacture safety glass for car windscreens. A factory was built on the site previously occupied by the Garden City Sidings and came into production in April 1930 [13,61].

The works was provided with a short internal railway system which connected with the end of the Eccleston Branch. The Private Sidings Agreement between Pilkington Brothers Ltd, Triplex (Northern) Ltd and the London Midland and Scottish Railway was signed on 22nd March 1934 [60], although the connection was probably in use before then.

Additions to the works were made on several occasions before and after the second world war, which involved extensions to the railway sidings. In 1951 it was reported that a small petrol or diesel tractor with flanged wheels was in use for shunting purposes [62], although we have been unable to confirm this.

Triplex (Northern) Ltd became a wholly owned subsidiary of Pilkington Brothers Ltd early in 1965 [13,63]. The factory is still in full production at the time of writing, although rail traffic has long since ceased.

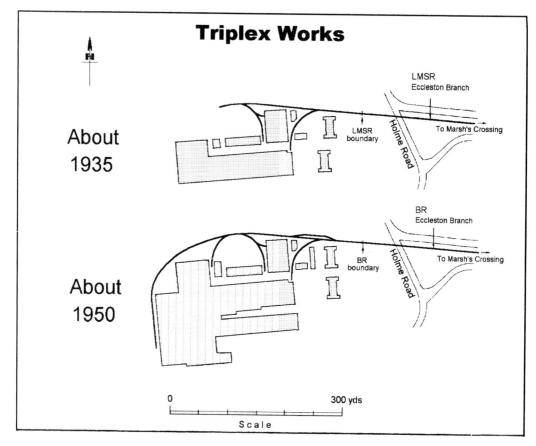

194

LOCOMOTIVE SUMMARY

Gillar's Green Colliery

Gillar's Green Coal Co 1873 to 1874
Thomas Begbie and William McCandish 1875
West Lancashire Collieries and Fireclay Works Co 1876
West Lancashire Collieries and Fireclay Works Co Ltd 1877 to about 1878
Renamed Eccleston Hall Colliery in 1883
Samuel Taylor 1883 to 1886
Tomlinson, Rogers and Simpson 1889 to 1895
William and Thomas Latham 1904 to 1910
Colliery abandoned 1910

GLADYS   0-6-0ST OC   FW   342 1877   13"x20" 3'6"
New to West Lancashire Collieries and Fireclay Works Co Ltd
Possibly taken over by Samuel Taylor
Later with Holme and King Ltd, civil engineering contractors, Wigan and later to Scot
     Lane Colliery Co Ltd

Three locomotive were advertised for sale in 1910 when Latham Brothers gave up the colliery.

Pilkington Garden Village

Pilkington Garden Village Ltd 1919 to 1923

DAPHNE   0-4-0ST OC   P   737 1899   14½"x18" 3'1½"
Class W4
Ex Tytherington Stone Co, Glos, about 1920
To Pilkington Bros Ltd, Ravenhead Works, about 1923

References to Chapter 7

1   16&17 Vic cap cxxxiv; 4th August 1853
2   LRO PDR 595
3   Information supplied to the authors by Mr J.M. Tolson
4   IM&S PB 147/94A
5   StH Intelligencer 5.3.1859
6   StH Intelligencer 26.3.1859
7   StHNews 9.6.1894
8   Royal National Commercial Directory of Lancashire, Isaac Slater, Manchester, 1864

9   A Merseyside Town in the Industrial Revolution St Helens 1750 - 1900, T.C. Barker and J. R. Harris, Frank Cass & Co Ltd, London, 1959
10   Directory of Lancashire, Kelly's Directories Ltd, Manchester, 1898
11   Directory of Lancashire, Kelly's Directories Ltd, Manchester, 1901
12   Letter Ellistown Pipes Ltd to St Helens Library dated 26th April 1979

13 *The Glassmakers Pilkington 1825 - 1975* T.C. Barker, Weidenfeld and Nicolson, London, 1977

14 Pilkington Brothers General Board Minutes 19.2.1863 at IM&S

15 Ibid 15.10.1863

16 Ibid 30.5.1878

17 *StHNews* 28.3.1882

18 *St Helens Commercially Considered*, St Helens Corpn, 1935

19 *Official Handbook of Stations*, Railway Clearing House, London ,1912

20 *Official Handbook of Stations*, Railway Clearing House, London ,1938

21 LNWR Sdgs Diag 178, dated 12.1917

22 *Official Handbook of Stations*, British Transport Commission, London, 1957

23 *StHNews* 25.2.1888

24 *StH Lantern* 4.10.1888

25 *LMerc* 2.7.1891

26 *LMerc* 7.4.1892

27 Electric Lighting Orders Confirmation (No 1) Act, 57 & 58 Vic cap xlix; 3rd July 1894

28 *StHNews* 3.12.18

29 *St Helens Tramways*, E.K. Stretch, St Helens Corpn, 1968

30 *StHNews* 23.10.1897

31 *StHNews* 29.7.1899

32 *StHNews* 5.8.1899

33 *StHNews* 26.7.1901

34 *StHNews* 3.1.1902

35 *StHRep* 24.7.1962

36 *StHRep* 24.12.1963

37 Report by Robert Winstanley, Mining Engineer, of 32 St Ann St, Manchester, 8th July 1880 - Copy in authors' possession

38 *Iron* 17.2.1877

39 *WO* 11.8.1880

40 *WO* 14.8.1880

41 *WO* 9.2.1881

42 *The Industrial Railways of the Wigan Coalfield - Part One*, C.H.A. Townley, F.D. Smith and J.A. Peden, Runpast Publishing, Cheltenham, 1991

43 *The Industrial Railways of the Wigan Coalfield - Part Two*, C.H.A. Townley, F.D. Smith and J.A. Peden, Runpast Publishing, Cheltenham, 1992

44 *StHRep* 19.9.1890

45 *WO* 3.5.1890

46 *WO* 25.5.1895

47 *WO* 17.12.1910

48 *WO* 2.12.1911

49 *MG* 6.8.1910

50 *WO* 2.7.1910

51 *CG* 29.7.1910

52 Pilkington Brothers Ltd General Board Minutes 3.4.1919, at IM&S

53 Ibid 14.5.1931

54 *Pilkington Brothers Garden Village Ventures*, B.R. Penny, January 1975, unpublished typescript - IM&S L 1079

55 Pilkington Brothers Ltd General Board Minutes 11.6.1918 - at IM&S

56 Ibid 9.10.1918

57 Unnumbered plan at IM&S

58 Pilkington Brothers Ltd General Board Minutes 18.3.1919 - at IM&S

59 Ibid 2.5.1919

60 Note on Line Plan of St Helens Railway, LNWR, Rugby, 1871 - at BRPB, Manchester Office.

61 *StHNews* 14.6.1929

62 Information supplied to the authors by Mr C.A. Appleton

63 *StHRep* 20.2.1965

CHAPTER EIGHT

PEASLEY AND SUTTON

We now return to Ravenhead Junction and move eastwards across the railway. Here, in the 1830s, an alkali works was established by Andrew Kurtz. The factory eventually expanded to cover most of the land bounded by the Warrington New Road, the canal and the St Helens to Widnes railway, apart from a small plot occupied by the gas works. After alkali manufacture ceased around 1920 much of the site was used for extensions to the gas works, while Todd Brothers Ltd took over the portion between the canal and Warrington Old Road.

Beyond Warrington New Road, the Hardshaw Brook Alkali Works was set up by the Gamble family in the 1860s. This had sidings connected to the Pocket Nook Branch of the London and North Western Railway, which also served the old established flint glass works of Samuel and Charles Bishop. Both the Hardshaw Brook Works and the Kurtz Works later purchased land to the east of the Pocket Nook Branch partly to dispose of alkali waste and partly for factory extensions.

Kurtz's Sutton Alkali Works

The history of the works goes back to 9th October 1832, when Messrs Darcy and Dierden obtained a plot of land alongside Warrington Old Road, then known as Peasley Cross Lane. Darcy and Dierden failed in 1841 and the works was auctioned in June 1842. It was bought by Andrew Kurtz, who had operated a nearby sulphuric acid plant since May 1839 [1]. Andrew Kurtz died on 31st March 1846 and the property passed to his son, Andrew George Kurtz [1].

The first edition of the 6 inch map, surveyed in 1846 and 1847, shows a siding giving access to the works. This crossed Peasley Cross Lane on the level and connected with Bournes and Robinson's railway to their canal wharf. The sidings were later altered to join the main line from St Helens to Widnes at a point near Ravenhead Junction under an agreement dated 1st December 1852 [2].

From very small beginnings the works expanded rapidly after 1850. Land to the west of Warrington Old Road, which had in part been occupied by Bournes and Robinson's original Sutton Colliery, was acquired. A large canal basin to serve the works was constructed on part of the site while the rest was occupied by new factory buildings.

East of the Pocket Nook Branch, land was purchased from the Bold Estates in 1852 and again in 1859 [1]. This was used for the disposal of waste material from the manufacturing process and over the years extensive spoil banks built up, served by a criss cross of railway lines.

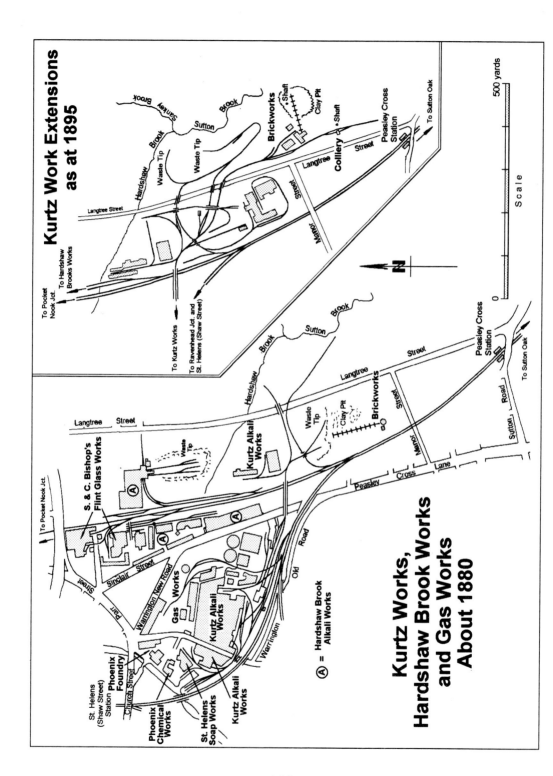

Kurtz Work Extensions as at 1895

Kurtz Works, Hardshaw Brook Works and Gas Works About 1880

Ⓐ = Hardshaw Brook Alkali Works

198

As well as providing tipping space, additional alkali manufacturing plant was erected in the 1870s. In the 1880s an alum plant was added and a brick works was erected at the southern end of the property, east of Langtree Street. For two years, in 1889 and 1890, a small colliery was operated in conjunction with the brick works, but the Mines Lists show that this was abandoned in 1891.

By 1881, when the survey was made for the first edition of the 25 inch map, a complex internal railway network had developed. The canal basin and the western part of the works were joined to the main system by a bridge which crossed Warrington Old Road. Access to the land on both sides of Langtree Street, purchased from the Bold Estates, was gained by means of long viaduct which carried the works line over Warrington New Road and the Pocket Nook Branch. The main exchange sidings with the London and North Western Railway were adjacent to the St Helens to Widnes line near Ravenhead Junction. A second connection was provided with the Pocket Nook Branch to serve the Langtree Street property.

Judging by the extent of the railway system shown on the map, there must have been more than one locomotive in use at that date. Whatever these were, they seem to have been replaced a few years later and no information has survived about them. The new locomotives came from Edward Borrows of the Providence Foundry and were of his distinctive design of four-coupled well tank. The first, named EMILY, with 12 inch cylinders was delivered in 1884. This was followed in 1885 and 1887 by two further well tanks from Borrows, named MARGERY and A.G.K. respectively.

MARGERY before delivery to the Kurtz Works from the Providence Foundry of Edward Borrows in 1885.   *(St Helens Library, Borrows Collection)*

When taken over by the United Alkali Co Ltd in November 1890, the Kurtz Works was by far the largest of the firm's St Helens factories. There seems to have been little further expansion subsequently, except for the construction of a sodium chlorate plant during the first world war [3].

There was one event which made itself felt to the population of St Helens. In the early hours of Friday 12th May 1899, there was a violent explosion in the part of the works making potassium chlorate. Debris was hurled far and wide, demolishing the vitriol chambers and bursting the nearby Corporation gas holder which then caught fire [4]. A locomotive and a wagon which were alongside the potassium chlorate plant were apparently damaged in the blast [5].

The devastation caused by the explosion at the Kurtz Works on 12th May 1899. Some of the damaged rolling stock can be seen in the background. (St Helens Library)

The three locomotives MARGERY, EMILY and A.G.K. were taken over by the United Alkali Company. Subsequently it seems to have been the practice to transfer engines between the St Helens works as the need arose, keeping any which were regarded as spare at the Central Stores at Pocket Nook. By 1919 the three original Kurtz locomotives had moved away. To replace them at the Kurtz Works, the United Alkali Company obtained a four-coupled saddle tank which was given the name NORMAN. Built by the Vulcan Foundry in 1877, this had originally been supplied to J.P. Edwards, a civil engineering contractor, at Chester.

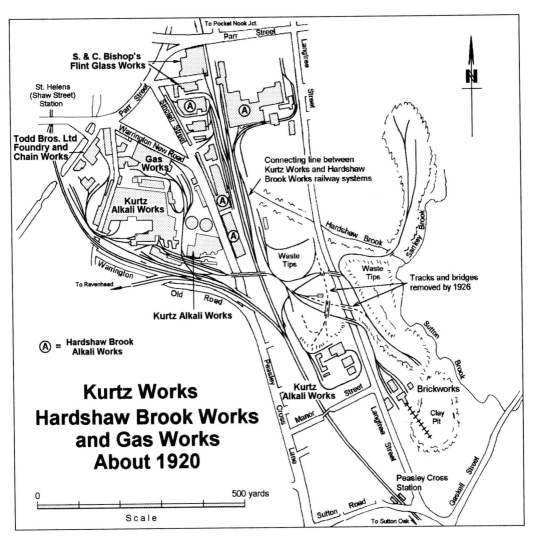

To Pocket Nook Jct.

Parr Street

Langtree Street

S. & C. Bishop's
Flint Glass Works

St. Helens
(Shaw Street)
Station

Smdiai Street

Ⓐ

Ⓐ

Todd Bros. Ltd
Foundry and
Chain Works

Warrington New Road

Gas
Works

Connecting line between
Kurtz Works and Hardshaw
Brook Works railway systems

Kurtz
Alkali Works

Ⓐ

Ⓐ

Hardshaw Brook

Sankey Brook

Warrington

Waste
Tips

Waste
Tips

To Ravenhead

Old Road

Tracks and bridges
removed by 1926

Kurtz Alkali Works

Sutton Brook

Ⓐ = Hardshaw Brook
Alkali Works

Kurtz Works
Hardshaw Brook Works
and Gas Works
About 1920

Peasley Cross Lane

Kurtz
Alkali Works Street

Manor

Brickworks

Clay
Pit

Langtree Street

Gaskell Street

0   500 yards

Peasley Cross
Station

Sutton Road

Scale

To Sutton Oak

An inventory of plant made in June 1919 [3] shows that NORMAN was the only locomotive then at the Kurtz Works. It is also recorded that there were 5950 yards of railway track at the works and that the wagon stock consisted of 14 main line wagons of 8- and 10-ton capacity, 10 8-ton dead buffer wagons for internal use, 2 salt cake tip wagons, 1 10-ton bogie, 3 flat bed wagons, 2 lumber bogies and 16 trams and bogies for the brickworks.

The Kurtz Works closed in 1920 [6], the small portion west of Warrington Old Road including the canal basin having already been sold to Todd Brothers. Only the alum works and the brickworks survived on the part of the site to the east of the Pocket Nook Branch and between 1916 [7] and 1918 [8] these had been connected to the railway system of the neighbouring Hardshaw Brook Works.

The Kurtz and Hardshaw Brook properties, along with the sites of the majority of the other United Alkali works, were purchased by St Helens Corporation on 14th March 1930 with a view to redevelopment for new industries [9]. The Corporation leased the brickworks to Laithwaite and Booth, who traded as T.R. Booth Ltd, initially for 15 years, as from 1st April 1933 [10].

The railway serving the brickworks had originally crossed a bridge over Langtree Street, by now renamed Jackson Street. With the dismantling of most of the former United Alkali Company's railway tracks, the opportunity was taken to alter the line to the brickworks, which now crossed Jackson Street on the level. The connection with the Pocket Nook Branch originally provided for A.G. Kurtz and Company was taken out. The two which had previously served the Hardshaw Brook Works were retained and the line from the brickworks diverted to link up with them.

The four-coupled saddle tank, FRANK, built by Andrew Barclay Sons and Company, which had been used at the Hardshaw Brook Works, was acquired by T.R. Booth Ltd to work traffic to and from the Pocket Nook Branch.

In the post war period, with most of bricks going out by road, FRANK saw little service and was often to be found out of use in a siding near the works. The locomotive was acquired at an unknown date by A. Barton (Engineers) Ltd and advertised for sale in 1950 [11]. It was moved in June 1951 to the Providence Foundry at St Helens Junction, which the firm had taken over from Edward Borrows and Sons. In June 1953, it was noted there in a derelict condition and was later broken up.

FRANK was hired out from time to time after the end of the second world war, for example to Southport Gas Works, to Linacre Gas Works at Liverpool and also possibly to United Glass Bottle Manufacturers Ltd. According to an employee at the brickworks who was interviewed in 1950, it had been moved by rail to and from these locations, but the final transfer to the Providence Foundry must have been by road, as the track near the level crossing over Jackson Street had been lifted by 1949. We have been unable to establish whether the hirings took place before or after the purchase by A. Barton (Engineers) Ltd.

The brickworks subsequently passed to the Kurtz Brick Co Ltd [12] but had closed by 1978 [13]. The alkali tips were cleared away in the 1970s and the material used to fill in old clay pits at Ravenhead [14].

St Helens Gas Works

The St Helens Gas Light Company was established by Act of Parliament on 24th March 1832 [15] and a small works was erected on a site in Warrington Old Road adjacent to the Kurtz Works. The proprietors named in the Act included many prominent figures in local industry such as James Bourne, William Bromilow, William Bromilow Junior, Josias Christopher Gamble, William Pilkington, Thomas Birch Speakman and Lee Watson.

The original company was dissolved in June 1852 and its assets transferred to the St Helens Gas Company [16]. Despite various extensions to the works there were complaints about the poor quality of the gas and the Act of 1869 [17], which created the Borough of St Helens, contained provision for the Corporation to take over the Gas Company. Negotiations to purchase the undertaking started early in 1875 [18] but it was not until 23rd August 1877 that the works was handed over to the Corporation [19] for a sum of £131,600 [20].

An extension scheme started by the old company was completed by the Corporation after the take over [21]. Further extensions, which included a new retort house 183ft long and 16ft wide, together with two coal stores and alterations to the railway tracks, were agreed by the Corporation at the end of 1885 [22,23] and sanctioned by the Local Government Board in March 1886 [24,25,26]. They were completed in 1887 and 1888 [20]. The 72 lbs per yard rails needed for the sidings were supplied by the St Helens Ironworks Company.

A tar distillation plant was installed in 1893 [27] and there was another major expansion in the closing years of the century. Sections 29 and 30 of the St Helens Corporation Act of 1893 [28] authorised the purchase of 6557 sq yds between Warrington Old Road and Warrington New Road. In April 1897 the Borough Council sanctioned a further extension of the retort house, the refurbishment of Nos.1 & 2 gas holders and the installation of new exhausters and other ancillary plant [29,30]. The work was completed towards the end of 1898 [20].

Within a few years more gas making plant was needed and a 10½ acre site at Pocket Nook, formerly occupied by McBryde's chemical works, was purchased in 1901 for a new works [31]. The proposal was rejected by the Local Government Board and instead yet more extensions were undertaken at the Warrington Road Works. Material for new sidings, such as sleepers and rails, were supplied by Todd Brothers [32].

The gas works had no rail connection until the 1860s and one could only be provided then with the permission of A.G. Kurtz, whose property blocked the route to the main line. Instead of joining into the railway system at the Kurtz Works, an independent connection was adopted. This involved crossing several of the Kurtz tracks on the level and was covered by agreements between the Gas Company and Kurtz, dated 25th July 1862 [33] and between the LNWR and Kurtz, in his capacity of landowner, dated 30th June 1864 [2].

With the restricted layout it was not feasible for the LNWR to place loaded coal wagons on the gas works siding nor for the Gas Company to leave empty wagons there to await collection. Instead, arrangements were made for traffic to be exchanged at sidings a short way along the Ravenhead Branch and the gas works locomotive was authorised to cross the main line for this purpose [34].There was no link between the gas works tracks and those of the Kurtz Works before November 1884, when the Corporation gave permission to A.G. Kurtz and Company to build a spur to the gas works line and use it for shunting purposes [35,36].

According to old employees the earliest locomotive used at the gas works was named SEMPER PARATUS and was probably built by Henry Hughes of Loughborough. An engine answering to this description appears in a batch of photographs in the authors' possession, apparently part of a series taken on behalf of Edward Borrows and Sons to illustrate the firm's locomotive buillding and repairing activities.

The Gas and Lighting Committee Minutes make numerous references to repairs and to the purchase of spare parts [37-41]. From these it is clear that until the turn of the century there was only one locomotive at the works. For example, a major overhaul was needed in 1900 which was undertaken by Edward Borrows and Sons and, while this was being carried out, the firm provided an engine for use at the gas works [42]. The boiler required repairs in January 1906 [43] and again in the middle of 1908 [44,45,46].

SEMPER PARATUS, a typical product of Henry Hughes of Loughborough, apparently photographed in the yard of Edward Borrows' Providence Foundry at St Helens Junction, perhaps after it had been repaired there in 1900.   *(J.A. Peden Collection)*

Consideration was given to the purchase of a second locomotive in 1900, although a decision was deferred for a year [42,47]. The tender of Peckett and Sons of Bristol for a four-coupled saddle tank was accepted in June 1901 [48]. The engine, named EX TERRA LUCEM, the motto of St Helens Borough, had arrived at the works by 11th September, when it was inspected by members of the Gas and Lighting Committee [49].

Again the minutes catalogue a series of repairs to the new engine [50-53]. As was the case for what the minutes describe as "the old locomotive" or "the No.1 locomotive", many of these were carried out by Edward Borrows and Sons or later, in 1913 and 1916, by H.W. Johnson and Company. In 1920 EX TERRA LUCEM needed a major overhaul, which was carried out by Peckett and Sons [54,55].

EX TERRA LUCEM marshalled at the rear of a goods train, apparently returning to the Gas Works after an overhaul. Neither the location of the photograph nor the date have been established. *(J.A. Peden Collection)*

The purchase of another new locomotive was discussed in 1918 [56,57] and again deferred for a year. The tender from Andrew Barclay Sons and Company of Kilmarnock was accepted in the middle of 1919 [58,59,60]. VICTORY, a four-coupled saddle tank, was delivered during the following year, after the Committee had agreed to extra costs [54].

With three locomotives now at the works, it was resolved in February 1921 to sell the old locomotive [61]. The minutes do not state who bought it although an old employee, interviewed by one of the authors in 1951, said that it went to a tar works at Rainford. This would corroborate a suggestion that it was purchased by H.W. Johnson and Company, which at that period operated from the works of Leslie Allen and Company at Rainford.

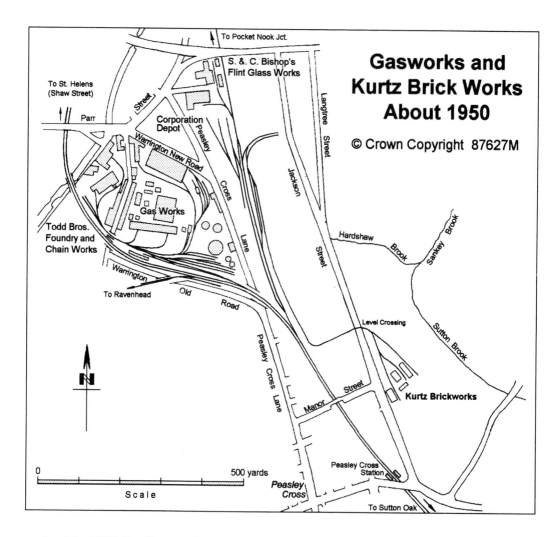

Gasworks and
Kurtz Brick Works
About 1950

© Crown Copyright 87627M

To Pocket Nook Jct.

S. & C. Bishop's
Flint Glass Works

To St. Helens
(Shaw Street)

Parr

Corporation
Depot

Street

Peasley

Warrington New Road

Cross

Lane

Jackson

Langtree Street

Gas Works

Todd Bros.
Foundry and
Chain Works

Hardshaw
Brook

Sankey Brook

Warrington

To Ravenhead

Old

Road

Street

Level Crossing

Sutton Brook

N

Peasley Cross Lane

Manor

Street

Kurtz Brickworks

0

500 yards

Scale

Peasley
Cross

Peasley Cross
Station

To Sutton Oak

In July 1929 the Corporation agreed to purchase, at cost of £6,500, the part of the now disused Kurtz property which lay between the gas works and the main railway line to provide for future extensions [62]. Some work was put in hand in 1930, which included the construction of a new gas holder [63] as well as ancillary buildings such as general stores, workshops and a garage [64]. In April 1929 tenders from Todd Brothers of St Helens and Richard White and Sons of Widnes were accepted for the supply of railway materials [65] needed for alterations to the sidings and in 1932 the locomotive shed was replaced on a new site [66].

A scheme to build a modern carbonising plant on the Kurtz site, with associated coke handling and screening equipment, was authorised in 1934 [67]. The main part of the work was finished by September 1939 [68], with completion of the whole project in the following year [69].

What was essentially a new gas works needed extensive alterations to the railway system formerly serving the Kurtz Works. Most of the existing sidings were removed and replaced by a completely revised layout which required a new junction with the London Midland and Scottish Railway. Negotiations with the railway company were concluded at the end of 1936 [70] and the main line connection was provided under an agreement dated 4th February 1938 [10]. Now that there was ample room to deal with incoming and outgoing wagons, it was no longer neccesary for the gas works locomotives to cross the main line to exchange traffic with the railway company in the sidings at Ravenhead Junction.

The existing locomotive stock was retained. In 1929 or 1930, one of the engines, presumably EX TERRA LUCEM, had been fitted with a new boiler supplied by H.W. Johnson and Company [71]. A tender from Andrew Barclay Sons and Company was accepted in July 1938 for a new boiler for VICTORY [72].

Forty new coal wagons were obtained from the Central Wagon Co Ltd of Wigan in 1936 to replace those that had previously been hired [73]. In addition the gas works owned a number of tank wagons for conveying acid from the by products plant. One had been supplied by Charles Roberts and Co Ltd of Horbury in 1925 [74] and another by the Central Wagon Co Ltd in 1928 [75]. One of the old tank wagons, No. 2, was sold in 1936 [76].

A rather woebegone VICTORY stands out of use at the Gas Works along with a couple of tank wagons on 12th April 1969, after the diesels had taken over.   *(John Tolson)*

Both EX TERRA LUCEM and VICTORY were still in use when the works was taken over by North Western Gas Board on 1st May 1949. EX TERRA LUCEM was transferred to the Board's Warrington Works in 1951 and was broken up there around the end of 1961. In exchange the St Helens Works received an almost new locomotive, JOSEPH POOLE, built by Andrew Barclay Sons and Company of Kilmarnock in the previous year, which was reputedly too heavy for the trackwork at Warrington.

The first diesel locomotive arrived in April 1965 and came from the Board's Linacre Gas Works in Liverpool. It carried the name THE BRADSHAW and had been built by Ruston and Hornsby of Lincoln in 1950. This was followed in 1968 by HODKINSON, from the Marton Gas Works at Blackpool. HODKINSON was a four-coupled machine supplied by the Drewry Car Company in 1950 and built by the Vulcan Foundry. Finally another Ruston and Hornsby locomotive arrived from Bolton Gas Works in 1969. The steam locomotives, which had not seen much service latterly, were both broken up in the same year.

With the introduction of natural gas in the 1970s, the works became redundant. The site was subsequently cleared and is now occupied by a retail park. All three diesel locomotives were sold in February 1974 to Audenshaw Diesel Engines Ltd of Audenshaw, near Manchester, after lying out of use for some time. The siding agreement with British Railways was terminated on 31st August 1970 [10].

Todd Brothers

The firm of Todd Brothers had its origins at the Bridgewater Forge in Watson Street, which was established in 1859 when Richard Pilkington went into partnership with his brother-in-law Hadden William Todd, trading as the St Helens Ironworks Company [77]. In 1864 Richard Pilkington was replaced in the partnership by W.H. Todd's brother Charles and the firm changed its name to Todd Brothers [77].

The Todd Brothers enlarged the scope of their activities by expanding into caustic drum making, iron and steel stock holding and dealing in second hand machinery. A new works was opened in Widnes in 1878 and in 1895 the firm acquired the premises between Warrington Old Road and the canal, previously occupied by the Phoenix Foundry [77]. The foundry had been established by Thomas Williamson about 1865 and, following his failure a few years later, it had been taken over by William Varley and a Mr Riera. It later passed to the firm of Varley and Simpson, which moved to new premises at the Canal Foundry in 1878 and then became bankrupt in the course of the next year [1].

Pilkington Brothers foreclosed on the lease of the St Helens Ironworks in Bridgewater Street in 1897 [78] and Todd Brothers acquired additional property adjacent to the former Phoenix Foundry. Part of the Kurtz Alkali Works east of Warrington Old Road was purchased in 1904 [77]. This was followed in 1908 by the purchase of the soap works [77], established by F.W. Tinker in 1852 [1]. Some years later Kurtz's canal dock was acquired and subsequently filled in [77].

Todd Brothers' premises in Warrington Old Road had a connection to the private railway system of the Kurtz Works. Wagons were taken to and from the main line by the United Alkali Company's locomotives, which also performed what shunting was needed. We understand that, after the Kurtz Works closed in 1920, these duties were taken over by a steam crane owned by Todd Brothers .

LUCY, the four-coupled well tank built by Edward Borrows, was noted in Todd Brothers' yard in September 1934 and was broken up some time later [79]. It came here from the United Alkali Company's Hardshaw Brook Works, presumably after this works closed in 1928. It is not clear if the locomotive was actually used by Todd Brothers or had only been bought for scrap. There is also a note in the Industrial Locomotive Society's list that MARGERY, another four-coupled well tank by Edward Borrows, was purchased from the United Alkali Co Ltd, but we have been unable to confirm this statement.

As we have noted in the previous section, the main Kurtz site between Warrington Old Road and Warrington New Road was taken over by St Helens Corporation in 1929 for new gas making plant. The sidings previously owned by the United Alkali Company became Corporation property and were later entirely remodelled. Todd Brothers' traffic to and from the main line now had to pass over lines belonging to the Corporation and was permitted to do so under an agreement made in 1932 [80].

Over the years there were various changes in the firm. In 1906 Hadden W. Todd, one of the founder members, died and his son Murray Todd was made a partner. Charles Todd retired in 1909, leaving the brothers Arthur and Murray Todd in control. In 1936 Arthur Todd retired and William Hadden Todd, son of Murray, joined the partnership. A private limited company with the title Todd Brothers (St Helens and Widnes) Ltd was formed in 1940 [77]. Shortly after the end of the second world war the name was changed to Todd Steels Ltd and the firm became a subsidiary of British Steel Construction (Birmingham) Ltd [77].

On the railway side, steam cranes continued to carry out the shunting until 1962, when a four-wheeled diesel locomotive was purchased second hand. It had previously been the property of Wirksworth Quarries Ltd, for which firm it had been built by Motor Rail Ltd of Bedford in 1946. Rail traffic at Todd's works appears to have ceased in the late 1960s and the locomotive was sold to Birds Commercial Motors Ltd, Long Marston, Gloucestershire around the end of 1967 or the beginning of 1968.

The chain works was sold to W. Woodcock Sons and Co Ltd in April 1967 [81]. Early in 1976, Todd Steels Ltd was in financial difficulty [82] and went into receivership later that year [83]. The works was closed for a time at the end of 1976 but reopened early in 1977 under the ownership of a new firm Todd - Rixton Steels Ltd [13,84]. The final closure took place before 1988 [85] and most of the site was later cleared to make way for the new road developments which were completed in the early 1990s. Several buildings, now occupied by a number of small firms, still remain in use and Todd Road, which leads to them, serves as a reminder of the former owner.

Hardshaw Brook Chemical Works

We now move across Warrington New Road to where the Hardshaw Brook Alkali Works was located. This had its origins in a small alkali factory established in 1864 by John Lawence Keane and Richard William Sadler [1] on a site to the west of the Pocket Nook Branch. Keane and Company went out of business in 1868 [86] and the works was purchased by J.C. Gamble [1], who set up the Hardshaw Brook Chemical Company to run it.

Gamble had already purchased land on the east side of the Pocket Nook Branch from the Bold Estates at auctions in 1852 and 1859 [1], presumably with the intention of dumping alkali waste from his Gerard's Bridge works. It was now to be used for extensions to the Hardshaw Brook Works, as well as for tipping waste material.

The original works, on the west side of the Pocket Nook Branch, was on a very cramped site and a conventional siding layout would have involved very tight curves. Instead, as is shown on the first edition of the 25 inch map surveyed in 1881, a traverser was provided at the north end of the works which transferred wagons on to the sidings serving the various parts of the factory.

The 25 inch map also shows that new buildings had been erected on the east side of the Pocket Nook Branch while other parts of the land were already occupied by extensive waste tips. These extensions to the works appear to have come into production around 1870 [86] and were served by their own sidings. The connection with the Pocket Nook Branch, which also gave access to the waste dumps, was provided under an agreement between the LNWR and David Gamble dated 24th October 1873 [8].

The Hardshaw Brook Chemical Company was absorbed by the United Alkali Co Ltd, on its formation in November 1890. By 1906, when the survey was carried out for the second edition of the 25 inch map, the traverser in the old works had been removed and replaced by a series of sharply curved sidings. The works locomotive, which had hitherto been confined to the newer part of the works on the east side of the line, was permitted to run over the Pocket Nook Branch to the old works to perform the shunting there under an agreement with the LNWR dated 21st July 1900 [8,87]. Prior to this, wagons had presumably been moved to and from the traverser either by capstan and rope or by horses.

Later maps show that several new buildings had been erected east of the Pocket Nook Branch, probably to increase manufacturing capacity during the first world war. A Siding Diagram dated July 1916 [7] shows that an extra connection was provided with the branch, although the relevant agreement was not signed until 24th January 1918 [8].

As recounted previously, the Hardshaw Brook railway system was linked with that of the Kurtz Works by a short connecting line sometime between 1916 [7] and 1918 [8]. After the closure of the Kurtz Works in 1920 this link appears to have been used by the Hardshaw Brook locomotives to gain access to the Kurtz Brickworks.

The Hardshaw Brook Works survived until 1928 [6], the last of the United Alkali Company's St Helens plants. St Helens Borough Council purchased the site on 14th March 1930 [9] and the agreements in respect of the siding connections were transferred to the Corporation in 1933 [10]. As noted above, those on the east side were retained to provide access to the Kurtz Brickworks. The siding on the west side was used by the Corporation, which demolished the alkali works buildings and replaced them by a store yard.

Derelict land on both sides of Jackson Street was reclaimed after the second world war and the alkali waste dumps of both the Hardshaw Brook and Kurtz Works were cleared away in the 1970s [14]. The area is now occupied by the Jackson Street Industrial Estate.

A maker's photograph of LUCY standing outside Edward Borrow's works at St Helens Junction. The buildings in the background are those of Borrows' Providence Foundry.
(St Helens Library, Borrows Collection)

The first locomotive at the Hardshaw Brook Works seems to have been LUCY, a four-coupled well tank with 10 inch diameter cylinders. This was supplied by Edward Borrows, possibly in the early 1870s and presumably to coincide with the developments on the east side of the Pocket Nook Branch. Walker Brothers of Wigan supplied a new boiler for a 10 inch engine at the Hardshaw Brook Works in 1907 or 1908 [88], which we assume was LUCY.

LUCY was still at Hardshaw Brook when an inventory was made of all United Alkali Company plant in June 1919 [89]. Also here at that date were FRANK, a four-coupled saddle tank which had been obtained from Andrew Barclay Sons and Company of Kilmarnock in 1912, and a 13 inch locomotive named MAY of which no other details are known.

The inventory records 2800 yards of railway sidings at the works and gives the wagon stock as 16 main line spring buffer wagons of 8- and 10-ton capacity, 9 main line tank wagons of 10- and 12-ton capacity, 5 8-ton dumb buffer wagons for internal use, 5 bogies and 167 flat bed 4-wheel wagons for trays, together with 130 trays, whatever they were.

There is a suggestion in the Industrial Railway Society's lists that the Barclays locomotive GREENBANK was transferred to the Hardshaw Brook Works, following the closure of the Greenbank Works in 1921, but we are unable to confirm that.

LUCY, as we have already seen, appeared later in Todd Brothers' yard where it was broken up in 1934 or early 1935 [79]. FRANK was, as recorded earlier, sold to T.R. Booth Ltd for use at the Kurtz Brickworks. We have been unable to discover what happened to MAY.

Samuel and Charles Bishop's Flint Glass Works

To complete the story of the industrial railway sidings south of Parr Street bridge, we turn to the flint glass works of S. & C. Bishop and Company in Frazer Street. This was established in 1833 by Samuel Bishop and passed to his sons, Samuel and Charles Bishop on his death in 1842 [1].

The St Helens Railway Company's line passed close by, but the 1/1056 Town Plan, surveyed in 1849, gives no indication that a siding had been provided to serve the works. However, the first edition of the 25 inch map, surveyed in 1881, shows railway tracks in both parts of the works, north and south of Frazer Street, connecting with the Pocket Nook Branch.

The factory remained virtually unchanged in size throughout its existence and there was little alteration to the sidings within the works. Its railway system was too small to have needed a locomotive. Presumably horses or men were used to move the wagons, perhaps replaced by a road tractor latterly. The sidings remained in use until after the second world war [90] and perhaps up to the closure of the Pocket Nook Branch in 1970.

We have been unable to find out precisely when the works closed. The firm is shown in a directory of 1966 [12] but not in one of 1978 [91].

LOCOMOTIVE SUMMARY

Kurtz Alkali Works

Andrew Kurtz 1839 to 1846
Andrew George Kurtz 1846 to November 1890
United Alkali Co Ltd from November 1890
Works closed 1920

EMILY   0-4-0WT OC   EBS   18 1884   12"
    New to A.G. Kurtz
    In June 1919 at UAC Central Stores at Pocket Nook
    Possibly returned to Kurtz Works
    Scrapped or sold

MARGERY   0-4-0WT OC   EBS   20 1885   10"
    New to A.G. Kurtz. Inventory gives cylinder size as 12"
    In June 1919 at UAC Central Stores at Pocket Nook
    Possibly returned to Kurtz Works
    Scrapped by Todd Bros

A.G.K.   0-4-0WT OC   EBS   22 1887   10"
    New to A.G. Kurtz
    At Gerard's Bridge Works in June 1919

NORMAN   0-4-0ST OC   VF   808 1877   14"x20" 3'3"
    New to J.P. Edwards at Chester
    At Kurtz Works by June 1919
    Scrapped or sold

Kurtz Brickworks

A.G. Kurtz until November 1890
United Alkali Co Ltd November 1890 until about 1928
T.R. Booth Ltd from 1932 to about 1960
Kurtz Brick Co Ltd from about 1960 to mid 1970s
Works closed mid 1970s

Shunting performed by loco from Kurtz Works until about 1920 and by loco from Hardshaw Brook Works between about 1920 and about 1928.

FRANK   0-4-0ST OC   AB   1261 1912   12"x20" 3'2"
    From United Alkali Co Ltd, Hardshaw Brook Works in 1928 to 1931 period
    Hired to Southport Corporation Gas Department
    Hired to Liverpool Gas Co, Linacre Works, August 1946
    Possibly hired to Pilkington Brothers Ltd at Cowley Hill Works
    Possibly hired to United Glass Bottle Manufacturers Ltd
    Sold to A. Barton (Engineers) Ltd at unknown date, possibly about 1945 or earlier
    Moved to Barton's premises at Providence Foundry, St Helens Junction, in June 1951
       and scrapped there after June 1953

St Helens Gas Works

St Helens Gas Light Co March 1832 to June 1852
St Helens Gas Co June 1852 to August 1877
St Helens Corporation August 1877 to 30.4.1949
North Western Gas Board from 1.5.1949
Works closed early 1970s

SEMPER PARATUS   0-4-0ST OC   HH
Sold in 1921, probably to H.W. Johnson and Co, Rainford

EX TERRA LUCEM   0-4-0ST OC   P   894 1901   14"x20"
   Class W4
   New
   To Warrington Gas Works in 1951 and scrapped there about December 1962

VICTORY   0-4-0ST OC   AB   1655 1920   14"x22"   3'5"
   New
   Scrapped on site by Warburton and Sons, September 1969

JOSEPH POOLE   0-4-0ST OC   AB   2295 1950   16"x24"   3'7"
   Ex Warrington Gasworks in 1951
   Scrapped on site by B. Byatt Ltd, of Liverpool, about July 1969

884 THE BRADSHAW   4wDM   RH   299101 1950   88DS class
   Ex Linacre Gasworks, Liverpool, in April 1965
   To Audenshaw Diesel Engines Ltd, Audenshaw, February 1974

HODKINSON   0-4-0DM   DC   2174 1945
                               VF   5271 1945
   Ex Marton Gasworks Blackpool, 1968
   To Audenshaw Diesel Engines Ltd, Audenshaw, February 1974

                    4wDM   RH   435492 1960   88DS class
   Ex Bolton Gasworks 1969
   To Audenshaw Diesel Engines Ltd, Audenshaw, February 1974

Todd Brothers, Warrington Road Works

Todd Brothers 1897 to about 1940
Todd Brothers (St Helens and Widnes) Ltd from about 1940 to about 1946
Todd Steels Ltd from about 1946 to 1977
Todd - Rixton Steels Ltd from 1977 to mid 1980s
Works closed mid 1980s

Steam cranes used for shunting until 1962

                    4wDM   MR   9004 1946
   Ex Wirksworth Quarries Ltd 1962
   To Birds Commercial Motors Ltd, Long Marston, Gloucestershire, about 1.1968

Hardshaw Brook Alkali Works

Hardshaw Brook Chemical Co 1868 to November 1890
United Alakli Co Ltd from November 1890
Works closed 1928

LUCY   0-4-0WT OC   EBS
Here in June 1919
Scrapped by Todd Brothers at its Warrington Road yard late 1935

FRANK   0-4-0ST OC   AB   1261 1912   12"x20" 3'2"
New to Hardshaw Brook Works
To T.R. Booth, Kurtz Brickworks, after 1928

MAY
Here in June 1919 according to plant inventory
Scrapped or sold

References to Chapter 8

1	*A Merseyside Town in the Industrial Revolution St Helens 1750 - 1900*, T.C. Barker and J.R. Harris, Frank Cass & Co Ltd, London, 1959	15	2&3 Wm 4 cap xii; 24th March 1832
		16	15&16 Vic cap lxix; 17th June 1852
		17	32 & 33 Vic cap cxx; 12th July 1869
		18	*StH Standard* 13.2.1875
2	LNWR Sdgs Diag 170, dated 6.1916	19	*StHNews* 31.8.1877
3	CRO DIC/UA11/1/7	20	*StHNews* 29.10.1898
4	*StHNews* 16.5.1899	21	*StHNews* 13.1.1877
5	Plan reproduced in *St Helens-A Pictorial History*, Mary Presland, Philimore, 1995	22	*StHNews* 7.11.1885,
		23	*StHRep* 7.11.1885
		24	*StHNews* 7.2.1885
6	CRO DIC/UA 12/20	25	*StHNews* 7.3.1885
7	LNW Sdgs Diag 166, dated 7.1916	26	*StHNews* 13.3.1886
8	LNW Sdgs Diag 166, dated 9. 1918	27	*StHNews* 6.1.1894 - Review of 1893
9	Conveyance at StHLH ST/4/100/1	28	56 & 57 Vic cap ccxv; 24th August 1893
10	Note on Line Plan of St Helens Railway - Widnes to 8 MP, 2 chains to 1 inch LMSR, Euston, 1925	29	*StHNews* 6.4.1897
		30	*StHNews* 10.4.1897
11	*MM* 18.8.1950	31	*StHNews* 22.11.1901
12	*County Borough of St Helens Directory,* Blair Publications Ltd, Blackpool, 1966	32	*StHNews* 4.4.1902
		33	St Helens Corporation Gas Committee Minutes 23.7.1879
13	*Directory of Manufacturing and Related Industries,* St Helens Metropolitan Borough, 1984	34	Appendix to LNWR Northern Division Working Time Table dated 1905 - at NRM York
14	*StHRep* 27.9.1974	35	*StHNews* 6.12.1884

36	St Helens Corporation Gas and Lighting Committee Minutes 12.11.1884
37	Ibid 10.4.1889
38	Ibid 11.3.1891
39	Ibid 13.7.1892
40	Ibid 10.4.1907
41	Ibid 12.12.1917
42	Ibid 13.6.1900
43	Ibid 10.1.1906
44	Ibid 13.5.1908
45	Ibid 10.6.1908
46	Ibid 8.7.1908
47	Ibid 11.7.1900
48	Ibid 12.6.1901
49	Ibid 11.9.1901
50	Ibid 11.12.1907
51	Ibid 14.10.1908
52	Ibid 14.5.1913
53	Ibid 8.5.1916
54	Ibid 10.3.1920
55	Ibid 14.4.1920
56	Ibid 9.1.1918
57	Ibid 13.2.1918
58	Ibid 11.6.1919
59	Ibid 9.7.1919
60	Ibid 10.9.1919
61	Ibid 9.2.1921
62	Ibid 10.7.1929
63	Ibid 10.12.1930
64	Ibid 7.5.1930
65	Ibid 10.4.1929
66	Ibid 2.6.1932
67	Ibid 14.11.1934
68	Ibid 6.9.1939
69	Ibid 12.6.1940
70	Ibid 9.12.1936
71	Ibid 10.9.1929

72 Ibid 6.7.1938
73 Ibid 8.1.1936
74 Ibid 9.9.1925
75 Ibid 10.10.1928
76 Ibid 14.10.1936
77 *History of Todd Brothers (St Helens and Widnes) Ltd*, Murray Todd, Director and Chairman, no imprint, no date, abt 1948 - StHLH A36.1(P))
78 Pilkington Brothers General Board Minutes 27.10.1896
79 StHLH M/CR/7 Copy letter Edward Borrows to B.D. Stoyel dated 10.9.1934
80 St Helens Corporation Gas and Lighting Committee Minutes 2.6.1932
81 *Haydock Reporter* 20.1.1968
82 *StHRep* 20.2.1976
83 *StHRep* 10.12.1976
84 *StHNews* 8.2.1977
85 *Directory of Manufacturing and Related Industries*, St Helens Metropolitan Borough, 1988
86 *A Directory of the Chemical Works of St Helens 1820 - 1889*, J.D. Turton, C. Kay and P. Meara, Halton Historical Publications No.15
87 LNWR Northern District Working Time Table 1922
88 *The Industrial Railways of the Wigan Coalfield - Part One*, C.H.A. Townley, F.D. Smith and J.A. Peden, Runpast Publishing, Cheltenham, 1992
89 CRO DIC/UA 11/1/6
90 LMSR Plan - Liverpool District No.11, Sheet 16 St Helens, dated May 1947
91 *Manufacturing Trades Directory*, St Helens Metropolitan Borough, 1978

CHAPTER NINE

ST HELENS TOWN CENTRE AND POCKET NOOK

We now move to St Helens town centre and to the district south of Church Street and the present Chalon Way. The second St Helens railway station, opened in 1849 [1], was located at the corner of Salisbury Street and Raven Street, later renamed Church Street. It was served by a short branch which crossed the Ravenhead Arm of the canal over a swing bridge and from here a siding was constructed to provide a rail connection with the St Helens Foundry and several other small works.

The third St Helens station at Shaw Street was opened in 1858 [1], at the same time as the new railway from Ravenhead Junction to Gerard's Bridge and Rainford, and the Raven Street site was given over entirely to goods traffic. When the Huyton and St Helens railway was constructed in the late 1860s, new goods facilities were provided adjacent to the Shaw Street passenger station and the Raven Street premises, together with the approach lines over the canal, were abandoned.

The second part of the chapter decribes the many and varied industrial establishments which were served by the Pocket Nook Branch. Originally known as the Gerard's Bridge Branch, this line was authorised by the St Helens and Runcorn Gap Railway Act of 1830 [2]. It was intended to serve collieries in the neighbourhood of Gerard's Bridge, but construction was delayed for lack of money. The land needed was not purchased until 1836 and in the same year the Haigh Foundry was given the order for the swing bridge over the canal at Pocket Nook [3]. The line was completed in 1837, but only after the Union Plate Glass Company had provided financial support. As late as December 1837, it was still not suitable for use by locomotives [3].

St Helens Foundry

The St Helens Foundry was set up in 1798 on a site to the north of the canal. Its original proprietors were Birkett and Postlethwaite. It was subsequently taken over by a Mr Fletcher and later by members of the Watson family [4]. In August 1819, the foundry was leased by a partnership consisting of Lee Watson of Sutton and John and James Thompson of Wigan [5]. In 1820, the firm was trading as Lee Watson and Company [4] and was busy supplying the needs of local industry. In the 1830s it manufactured much of the equipment needed by the St Helens and Runcorn Gap Railway, including machinery for the inclines and the wagon tipplers at Widnes Dock [3].

Robert Daglish, son of the Robert Daglish of the Haigh Foundry and the Orrell Collieries, joined the firm in 1830. He became managing partner in 1843, after the death of Lee Watson, and the firm later changed its name to Robert Daglish and Company [4].

Robert Daglish was also very much involved in the affairs of the St Helens Railway at this period. From 1st August 1841 until 1st February 1849 he held the contract to operate and maintain the locomotives as well as to keep the track in good order [3]. The locomotives were then housed at the railway company's engine shed at Sutton, in the fork between the lines to Widnes and to St Helens Junction. Repair work was probably carried out here as well, as it was not until 1851 or 1852 that the St Helens Foundry was provided with its own rail connection.

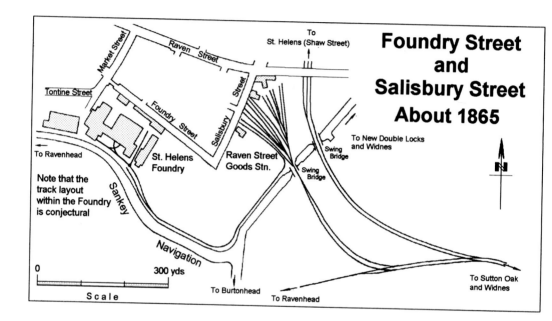

On 18th August 1851, the St Helens Railway Board agreed to construct a branch to the works, subject to Daglish guaranteeing, over a three year period, traffic amounting to ten times the construction cost [3]. The line followed the bank of the canal from the Foundry to the sidings at Raven Street Station [6]. It was diverted in the 1860s to join the Sutton Oak line at a point just south of Raven Street bridge as a consequence of the construction of the Huyton and St Helens railway.

The branch was always regarded as railway company property and worked in turn by the St Helens Railway, the LNWR and the LMSR. In view of the small extent of the internal railway system at the foundry, it seems unlikely that Robert Daglish and Company needed a locomotive of its own.

By 1865 the premises had doubled in size and the company had become one of the leading engineering firms in South Lancashire. Its range of products included horizontal winding engines, pumping engines, bridges for the Lancashire and Yorkshire Railway [4] and coal drops for the new Garston Dock [3].

Locomotive construction does not seem to have featured prominently amongst the firm's activities and there is only fragmentary reference to one engine which appears to have been built at the St Helens Foundry. *The Engineer* of 2nd February 1864 carried an advertisement by the firm for the sale of "a strong six wheeled tender engine by Robert Daglish Junior, quite new" with four coupled wheels 4ft 1in diameter and 15 inch cylinders [7]. The information provided by Baxter [8] about the St Helens Railway locomotive stock suggests that No.13 FORTH was built by Daglish in 1852, but there is nothing to confirm this.

The firm also dealt from time to time in second hand locomotives and stationary engines. For example, it purchased the steam engine used to work the Sutton Incline on the St Helens Railway, when the main line to Widnes was altered in 1849 [3]. This was no doubt refurbished and sold to another customer.

In 1861, Robert Daglish is recorded as purchasing a six-coupled goods locomotive from the LNWR. Built by E.B. Wilson of Leeds in 1846, it had been supplied to the North Eastern Division of the railway as No.37 and had later become No.437 [8]. As described in Part Two, there is a suggestion that Daglish may have resold the engine on to Richard Evans and Sons for use at the Haydock collieries, although this cannot be confirmed.

Some years earlier, in 1844, two locomotives built by Jones and Potts were advertised for sale and potential purchasers were directed to Robert Daglish or to Robin Robinson of Sutton [9]. One was an 0-4-2 with 13in x 20in cylinders, 5ft 0in diameter driving wheels and 3ft 0in diameter trailing wheels. The other, which could be seen at work, may have been either an 0-4-0 or an 0-4-2 and had 12in x 20in cylinders and 5ft 0in coupled wheels.

The advertisement had possibly been placed on behalf of the St Helens and Runcorn Gap Railway, as this was during the period of Robert Daglish's contract to operate the railway. Alternatively, it may be that the two locomotives had some connection with Bournes and Robinson's Sutton Colliery and that Daglish was acting as an intermediary.

There is some evidence to suggest that the latter explanation may be the correct one. It appears that one of the locomotives may have been purchased by the East Lancashire Railway, as that company's minutes of 26th May 1848 record that a bill for £1556 18s 3d had been received from Robert Daglish for repairing what is described as the Broad Oak locomotive [10]. The East Lancashire engine was advertised for sale in January 1853, when it was desribed as having 13in x 20in cylinders and 5ft 0in coupled wheels [10,11].

Robert Daglish died in 1883 [4] and the firm was turned into a limited liability company about 1900 [12]. Despite the attempt by Pilkington Brothers Ltd, mentioned in Chapter 4, to acquire the site in 1918 for postwar expansion of its glass works, the St Helens Foundry continued in operation until the 1930s. Robert Daglish and Co Ltd went into voluntary liquidation and the plant and goodwill were put up for sale on 28th February 1934 [13].

The works never reopened. Some of the buildings were demolished in 1939 [14]. The site was later cleared completely and is now occupied by the Chalon Way car parks.

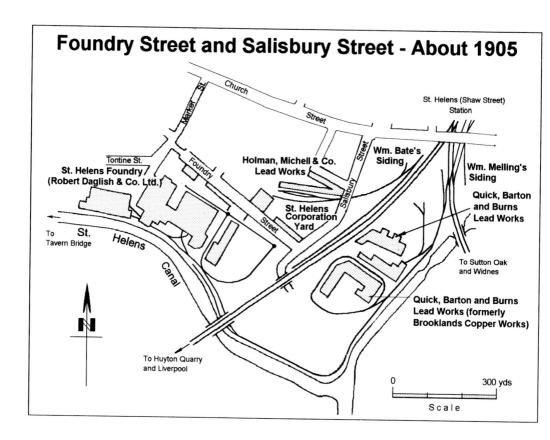

Foundry Street and Salisbury Street - About 1905

Church

Street

St. Helens (Shaw Street) Station

Market St.

Foundry

Tontine St.
St. Helens Foundry
(Robert Daglish & Co. Ltd.)

Holman, Michell & Co.
Lead Works

Salisbury

Wm. Bate's
Siding

Wm. Melling's
Siding

Quick, Barton
and Burns
Lead Works

St. Helens
Corporation
Yard

Street

To
Tavern Bridge

St. Helens

Canal

To Sutton Oak
and Widnes

Quick, Barton and Burns
Lead Works (formerly
Brooklands Copper Works)

To Huyton Quarry
and Liverpool

N

0   300 yds

S c a l e

Quick, Barton and Burns

The branch serving Robert Daglish and Company also provided access to other factories located between the Huyton and St Helens line and the canal. The Brooklands Copper Company established a small works here in the 1860s or early 1870s, which later passed into the hands of W. Roberts and Co Ltd [15]. The works appears to have closed around 1925 [16,17]. Successive 25 inch maps show a single siding connecting with the branch to the St Helens Foundry, which gave access to various parts of the premises by means of turntables.

The St Helens Lead Smelting Company started operations on an adjacent site in the late 1870s [18]. By 1880 the works had been taken over by Quick, Barton and Company [19], later reformed as Quick, Barton and Burns. A single siding, which looped round the site, gave access to the branch to the St Helens Foundry.

The premises were later acquired by Holman, Michell and Co Ltd, the lead fabricators, which moved here from its Salisbury Street premises after the second world war. Rail traffic ceased in the 1950s or 1960s and the area is now occupied by a small trading estate.

Siding serving W. Bates and Co, the Cornwall Lead Works of Holman, Michell and Co and the Corporation Stone Yard

A short siding on the west side of the Huyton line was laid in the 1870s or early 1880s to serve Berner's brickworks on the south side of Raven Street. It was extended across Salisbury Street to provide access to a new works for the manufacture of lead sheet and pipe established by Holman, Rogers and Michell on part of the old Fair Ground. Construction started early in 1882 and the works was in production by the end of the year. [20,21]. By 1888 the firm had changed its name to Holman, Michell and Company [22].

The extension of the siding involved a level crossing over Salisbury Street, application for this being made to St Helens Corporation in November 1881 [20]. Use of the connection with the London and North Western Railway was covered by an agreement dated 24th May 1882 [23].

The site of the brickworks was taken over by William Bates and Company, a firm which appears in directories from 1887 onwards [24,25,26] as builders' merchants. The siding which had previously served the brickworks was now used to bring in materials such as lime, slate and cement.

In May 1888 St Helens Corporation decided to move its highways yard from the gas works to a new location on land leased from Holman, Michell and Company [22]. Extra sidings were provided adjacent to this firm's lead works to unload incoming wagons of stone and other building materials.

The sidings serving Bates' yard were evidently still in use in 1947 as they are shown on a contemporary LMSR diagram of the St Helens area [27]. They appear to have closed a few years afterwards.

William Melling's Siding

One other short private siding remains to be mentioned. This was located on the opposite side of the main railway to that used by Holman, Michell and Company. It connected with the line from St Helens to Sutton Oak and was provided under an agreement dated 12th April 1886 with William Melling [28], who is described in directories from 1887 [24,25,26] as a stone merchant. The premises were later taken over by the North West Timber Company. Like the sidings serving Bates' yard, those here were still apparently in use in 1947 [27].

The Union Plate Glass Works

We now move to Pocket Nook, where the Union Plate Glass Company established its works in 1836. Production started in March 1837 [4], when the first cast of glass took place. The Sankey Navigation ran alongside the works and provided transport for raw materials and probably also for finished products. The Gerard's Bridge Branch of the St Helens Railway, which the firm had helped to finance, also ran close by and the works was provided with a siding at an early date.

A limited liability company was formed in 1864 [4], by which date there had been much development on the site. The 25 inch map surveyed in 1881 shows a threefold increase in the size of the works compared with the 1/1056 Town Plan of 1849 and also that there had been considerable extension to the internal railway system.

In 1884 the Union Plate Glass Company purchased what may have been its first and only locomotive. This came from Fletcher, Jennings and Company of Whitehaven and was one of that firm's patent four-coupled side tank locomotives with 10in x 20in cylinders. Fletcher, Jennings' order book [29] shows that it was begun for stock in January 1880 and despatched to St Helens in April 1884.

In 1891 [30] new plant was erected at Pocket Nook for the production of rolled plate glass. The 25 inch map surveyed in 1891 and 1892 shows that there had also been further extensions and alterations to the works railway system. An additional connection had been provided with the London and North Western Railway at 1152 yards from Peasley Junction to supplement the original one at 1106 yards [31]. Later, the sidings at the north end of the works were extended to link up with the Liverpool, St Helens and South Lancashire line. The connection here was evidently ready for use when the new railway opened for goods traffic on 1st July 1895 [3,32,33].

Cast plate glass manufacture ceased in 1897 or 1898, but rolled plate production continued until the company went into liquidation in 1904 [34]. The premises, as well as 35,500 square yards of coal under the site, were auctioned on 10th May 1905 [35,36] in two lots. There must have been no acceptable offers as both lots were reported to have been withdrawn [37].

On 6th, 7th and 8th June there was an auction sale of the plant. This included the glass making equipment, steam engines and boilers, as well as four canal boats, a large railway transport wagon, coal wagons, 1256 yards of railway material in the casting hall, 5300 yards of "bogie rails", bogies and wagons [38].

There was a further sale of the remaining plant on 13th March 1907 [39] when the Fletcher, Jennings locomotive was included. The advertisement provided the information that it had 10in x 20in cylinders, 3ft 3in diameter driving wheels and a 6ft wheelbase. The boiler, which had a nearly new copper firebox, was pressed to 120 psi. It is not known what happened to the locomotive subsequently, although as suggested later, it may have been taken over by John Forster and Sons Ltd.

The Union Plate Glass Co Ltd was not liquidated until the early 1920s and meanwhile various attempts were made to dispose of the premises. The portion of the site furthest from the canal was sold around 1908 to John Forster and Sons Ltd to provide additional manufacturing capacity for that firm's rapidly expanding glass bottle business. The siding connection at 1152 yards from Peasley Junction was transferred to Forster and Sons, while that at 1106 yards was retained by the Union Plate Glass Company [31]. Another part of the works was sold to H.W. Johnson and some buildings were let to Alfred Barton for use as a cooperage [40-43]

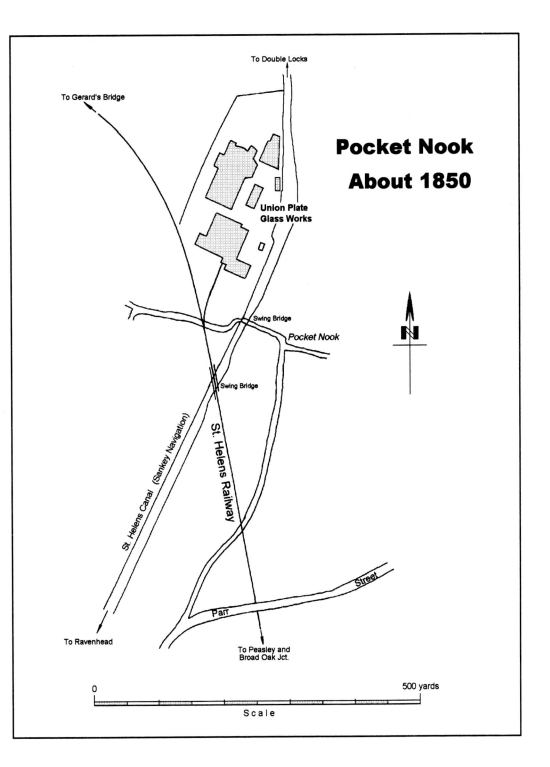

To Double Locks

To Gerard's Bridge

Pocket Nook

About 1850

Union Plate
Glass Works

N

Swing Bridge

Pocket Nook

Swing Bridge

St. Helens Canal (Sankey Navigation)

St. Helens Railway

Street

Parr

To Ravenhead

To Peasley and
Broad Oak Jct.

0   500 yards

Scale

H.W. Johnson and Company

Following the closure of Edward Borrows and Sons' Providence Foundry and its sale in 1912, the locomotive manufacturing and repairing side of the business was taken over by H.W. Johnson and Company. Few facts have emerged about the history of this firm. The first mention we have found is in 1913 [40] after a workshop was established on the Union Glass Works site. This was given up in 1919 or 1920 [41,42] when the company moved to Rainford, where it occupied premises at Leslie Allen and Company's oil works. There was a further move to the Kenyon Iron Works at Sutton Oak in 1926 or 1927. The shops here were vacated in January 1928, when the firm appears to have gone out of business.

During the period that H.W. Johnson and Company was at Pocket Nook, repairs are known to have been carried out on locomotives belonging to the gas works and to Pilkington Brothers Ltd. Similar work was probably undertaken for other firms.

One new locomotive was built in 1913, a four-coupled well tank of Borrows' design, named RAVEN, which went to the Blackwell Colliery Co Ltd in Nottinghamshire. It was presumably constructed at Pocket Nook, as there is no evidence that the firm ever operated from the Providence Foundry. Later, two similar locomotives, named PATIENCE and KELVIN, were supplied to Pilkington Brothers Ltd. Although a start may have been made at Pocket Nook, they do not seem to have been completed until 1921, after H.W. Johnson and Company moved to Rainford.

Ministry of Munitions

There are fragmentary references to the Ministry of Munitions' Central Stores Depot No.34 at Pocket Nook. We have been unable find any firm information about the location of the depot. However the only vacant premises of any size were those on the east side of the Union Glass Works site. It is known that these were sold to a Mr Andrew Mooney in 1916 [41-44] for use as a warehouse and that the agreement in respect of the siding connection at 1106 yards from Peasley Junction was also transferred to him at a later date [45]. The inference is that Mooney leased the premises to the Ministry.

Central Stores Depot No.34 features in advertisements of 1921 [46] and 1922 [47] for disposal of surplus equipment. This included a four-coupled saddle tank with 8in x 14in cylinders, named F. GILL and built by Manning Wardle and Company. It is also known that spare parts were supplied by Peckett and Sons of Bristol to the Ministry of Munitions at Pocket Nook for a locomotive named BARBARA CRIPPS. This was a four-coupled saddle tank built in 1910 for Stephens Silica Brick Company of Kidwelly, which had been acquired by the Ministry of Munitions during the war.

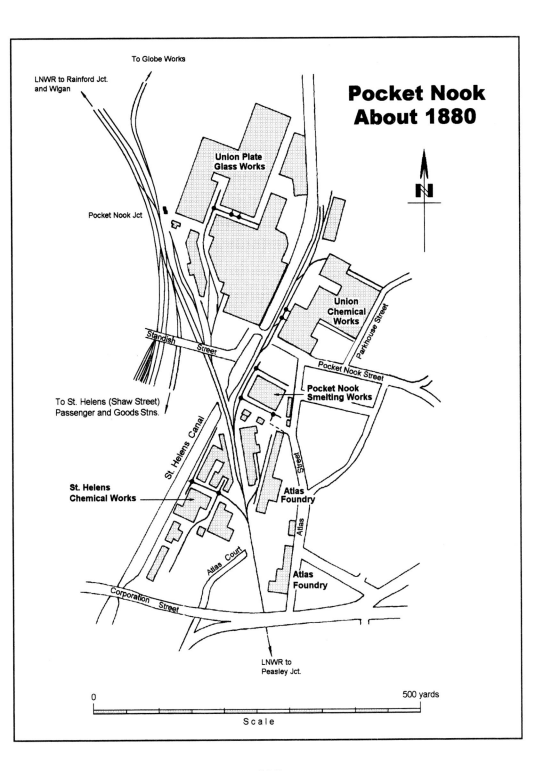

To Globe Works

LNWR to Rainford Jct.
and Wigan

**Pocket Nook
About 1880**

N

**Union Plate
Glass Works**

Pocket Nook Jct

**Union
Chemical
Works**

Parkhouse Street

Standish Street

Pocket Nook Street

To St. Helens (Shaw Street)
Passenger and Goods Stns.

**Pocket Nook
Smelting Works**

St. Helens Canal

**St. Helens
Chemical Works**

**Atlas
Foundry**

Atlas

Street

Atlas Court

**Atlas
Foundry**

Corporation Street

LNWR to
Peasley Jct.

0   500 yards

Scale

Forster's Glass Bottle Works

In 1878 John Forster, who had served his apprenticeship at Robinson and Cooks' Atlas Foundry, went into partnership with his eldest brother, David, at the Navigation Boiler Works in Bridgewater Street, trading as D. & J. Forster. The partnership was dissolved later, when David Forster started his own boiler works at Widnes and John Forster took over sole control of the Bridgewater Street activities [48].

In 1890, when the lease expired and Pilkington Brothers repossessed the Bridgewater Street premises, John Forster moved to a new works at Pocket Nook as a constructional engineer and boiler maker. The 25 inch map, surveyed in 1891 and 1892, shows this as the Navigation Boiler Works on vacant land between Atlas Street and Vernon Street.

A private company, John Forster and Co Ltd, was formed in 1893 [48] and the firm subsequently acquired the rights to manufacture Boucher's patent glass bottle making machine. In 1900 it was decided to set up as bottlemakers and the Atlas Glass Works was built next to the Navigation Boiler Works and facing Barber Street. Forster and Sons Ltd, a private company, was registered on 15th March 1905 to take over this side of the business [48].

Neither the boiler works nor the glass bottle works had a rail connection but it appears that goods may have been carted to the sidings adjacent to the canal which served John Varley and Company's Waterloo Foundry. An LNWR sidings diagram [49] notes that the connection to these sidings also gave access to the yard of Forster and Sons and it is known that at that period the firm occupied a siding on property belonging to St Helens Corporation [42].

The bottle making business expanded rapidly and around 1908, as mentioned earlier, John Forster and Sons Ltd acquired part of Union Plate Glass Company's site [48]. Before the end of 1912, the bottle making plant was in full operation and the firm was using both the London and North Western Railway and the Great Central Railway for the despatch of its products. A London warehouse had been established at Marylebone and an overnight service provided by the GCR enabled goods to be delivered in London next morning [48].

A public company, Forster's Glass Co Ltd, was registered on 15th July 1919 and, according to the firm's history [48], the works was extended in 1920, although in reality this may have not taken place until a few years later. Alfred Barton and Andrew Mooney still occupied part of the Union Glass Works premises in 1920 and 1921 [43], although by 1925 the whole site had been acquired by Forsters [44].

As noted earlier the siding connection to the Union Glass Works at 1152 yards from Peasley Junction was transferred to Forsters soon after the acquisition of the first part of the site. The connection at 1106 yards, taken over by Andrew Mooney, was transferred to Fosters in the 1920s, although the new agreement with the LMSR does not appear to have been signed until 1st May 1937 [50].

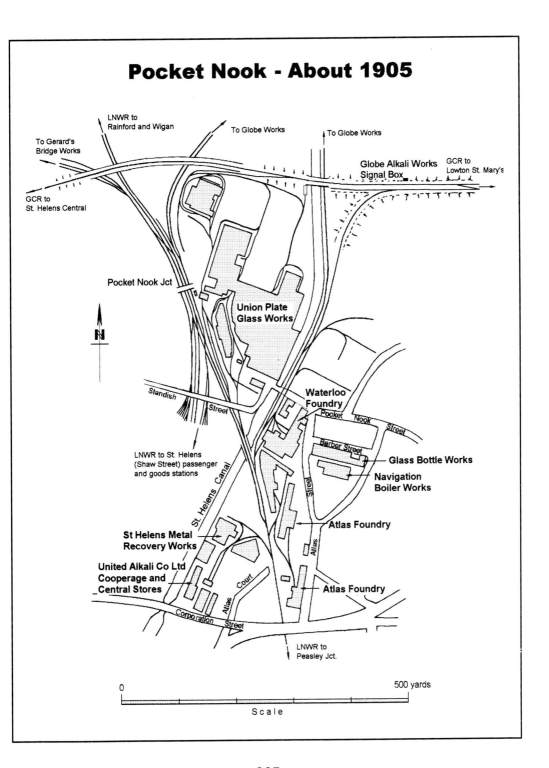

Pocket Nook - About 1905

LNWR to
Rainford and Wigan

To Globe Works

To Globe Works

To Gerard's
Bridge Works

Globe Alkali Works
Signal Box

GCR to
Lowton St. Mary's

GCR to
St. Helens Central

Pocket Nook Jct

Union Plate
Glass Works

N

Standish

Street

Waterloo
Foundry

Pocket Nook Street

Barber Street

Glass Bottle Works

LNWR to St. Helens
(Shaw Street) passenger
and goods stations

St. Helens Canal

Navigation
Boiler Works

Atlas Foundry

Atlas Street

St Helens Metal
Recovery Works

United Alkali Co Ltd
Cooperage and
Central Stores

Atlas Court

Atlas Street

Atlas Foundry

Corporation Street

LNWR to
Peasley Jct.

0

500 yards

Scale

227

The story of the locomotives used by Forster and Sons Ltd after the acquisition of the Union Plate Glass Works has proved difficult to unravel and what has been written in the firm's history [48] has proved to be not entirely correct. Fortunately many of the the boiler inspection reports have survived amongst the firm's archives deposited at the St Helens Local History Library.

The first locomotive which is known to have been here was a four-coupled saddle tank built by Manning Wardle and Company of Leeds in 1883. It had been supplied new to John Mowlem and Company, public works contractors, carrying the name GREENWICH. Its date of arrival at St Helens has not been recorded and it is just possible that Forster and Sons took over the Fletcher, Jennings locomotive from the Union Plate Glass Company as an interim measure. However, we lack firm information about this.

GREENWICH, which may not have carried this name at Forster and Sons, was superseded by PHYLLIS and BAGHDAD, both four-coupled saddle tanks, which were purchased towards the end of the first world war. PHYLLIS was an even older Manning Wardle product, having been built in 1862. When new it had been named FAIRY and had been delivered to Rennie and Company, civil engineering contractors. It had subsequently passed through several owners' hands before coming to St Helens. BAGHDAD had been built by Peckett and Sons of Bristol in 1901 for John Harrison of Levenshulme. It was recorded in boiler inspection reports as being with Forster and Sons in October 1917 and may have arrived somewhat earlier [51].

With the new arrivals, GREENWICH was evidently surplus to requirements and was presumably the locomotive with 8in x 12in cylinders which was advertised for sale by Forster and Sons in August 1917 [52]. The Industrial Locomotive Society's lists suggest that GREENWICH was acquired by the Ministry of Munitions for use at one its sites in the St Helens area and, as F. GILL, it was the engine advertised for sale at CSD No.34 at Pocket Nook in 1921 and 1922 [46,47]. While this seems highly likely, we lack independent confirmation.

In 1925 Forster's Glass Co Ltd purchased a new R2 Class four-coupled saddle tank from Peckett and Sons. Named ATLAS, it was delivered at the end of January or early in February [53,54].

The boiler of BAGHDAD was sent to Peckett and Sons' works for repairs towards the end of 1925 [55]. PHYLLIS was then apparently taken out of service. It does not appear in subsequent boiler inspection reports and was afterwards broken up.

In 1937 the insurance company refused to renew the cover for BAGHDAD as the boiler was worn out [56,57]. The engine was sold to Hough and Sons of Wigan, boiler makers and machinery merchants, and was noted in store at the Ince Wagon Works in 1940. An order was placed with W.G. Bagnall and Company of Stafford for a replacement locomotive in January 1938 [57,58]. Named POCKET NOOK, it was one of that firm's standard four-coupled saddle tanks.

Forster's Glass Co Ltd was taken over by the Rockware Glass Group as from 1st January 1948 [48] but continued to trade under its own name until 1966. Thereafter the Pocket Nook Works was operated by Rockware Glass Ltd [59].

The two locomotives ATLAS and POCKET NOOK were taken over by the new owner and a third engine was purchased about 1949 from Hough and Sons of Wigan. This was a four-coupled saddle tank built by Hawthorn, Leslie and Company of Newcastle in 1921. It had previously been at the Southern Oil Company's works in Trafford Park before being repaired by Hough and Sons at the Ravenhead Brickworks at Upholland. Originally named SCOBRIT, this was changed to HARDSHAW when the locomotive came to St Helens.

ATLAS was broken up around 1959 and POCKET NOOK a year or two later, leaving HARDSHAW and a second hand diesel locomotive to handle the traffic in the works. The diesel, purchased from George Cohen Sons and Co Ltd, machinery merchants of Stanningley near Leeds, arrived in January 1961 and was named POCKET NOOK II. It had been built in 1940 by Robert Stephenson and Hawthorns for the Air Ministry Works Department and had been subsequently used by the Darwen Paper Mill Co Ltd.

Both HARDSHAW and POCKET NOOK II were taken out of service in the middle of 1967. Their replacement was a four-wheeled diesel locomotive with mechanical drive built by F.H. Hibberd and Co Ltd in 1955, which had previously been used by Montague L. Meyer (Northern) Ltd of Widnes.

HARDSHAW, the second hand Hawthorn, Leslie locomotive, at Forster's Glass Works before the diesels took over.   *(W.J. Fletcher)*

The Hibberd shunter was scrapped after the purchase of two further diesel locomotives from the Mersey Docks and Harbour Board in 1973. These had been built in 1958 and one of them was given the name POCKET NOOK I after arrival at St Helens.

In December 1981 it was announced that Rockware was to end its St Helens operations [60] and the works was closed in March 1982. Rail traffic ceased in February and the two remaining diesel locomotives were broken up. The buildings were subsequently demolished and the site redeveloped for the new campus of the College of Technology.

The St Helens Chemical Works, the United Alkali Company's Central Stores, the St Helens Smelting Co Ltd and John Pritchard and Sons Ltd

An alkali works was erected at Pocket Nook on a site between the canal and the railway in 1852 by W.H. Balmain, who had previously been associated with the Patent Alkali Company at Greenbank [4]. Balmain was declared bankrupt in 1865 and the works was taken over by the St Helens Chemical Company [4]. This firm later passed into the hands of the Chadwick family [4] but continued to trade under its original name.

The St Helens Chemical Company was absorbed by the United Alkali Co Ltd in November 1890. The works was on the point of closure, if indeed it had not closed already. It was dismantled during the following year [61].

The northern part of the site was leased to the St Helens Metal Recovery Company, which processed scrap material to separate out non-ferrous metals such as lead, tin, copper, zinc and antimony [62]. Later it specialised in the smelting of antimony. The remainder of the site was redeveloped by the United Alkali Company and new buildings were erected to house a central store, a smithy and workshops and a cooperage to serve the firm's St Helens factories.

The St Helens Chemical Company had a rail connection with the adjacent LNWR line from an early date. The first edition of the 25 inch map surveyed in 1881 shows a series of turntables within the works from which short sidings led to the various buildings. This layout was unsuitable for locomotive working and the wagons must have been either propelled manually or pulled by horses.

The connection with the LNWR was retained to serve both the metal recovery company's premises and the new stores and workshops of the United Alkali Company. Additional sidings were laid in by the latter firm but the layout still appears to have been too restricted to have required the use of anything more than a horse for shunting. Several locomotives are associated with the Central Stores, but these seem to have been those which were surplus to immediate requirements and kept ready to be sent to one or other of the firm's St Helens works when the need arose. It is also possible that engines from the various factories may have been overhauled in the adjacent workshops.

In June 1919, when an inventory of all United Alkali plant was made, there were two locomotives at the Central Stores, EMILY and MARGERY [63]. They were recorded, perhaps incorrectly, as having 12in and 13in cylinders respectively and are evidently the two four-coupled well tanks built by Borrows for A.G. Kurtz in 1884 and 1885.

The Central Stores closed in 1923 [64] and we have no information about the disposal of any locomotives which were still on hand. Some of the buildings remain at the time of writing and are used by a number of small firms while another part of the site is occupied by St Helens Glass Ltd.

Early in the twentieth century, the St Helens Metal Recovery Company was bought out by a Mr C.H. Nevill, who formed the St Helens Smelting Company to take over the works. As recounted earlier, the old Ravenhead Copper Works was purchased in 1913 and much of the firm's business was transferred there. Although the Pocket Nook Works was kept in operation during the first world war, it closed soon afterwards.

The metal recovery works was purchased in 1919 or 1920 [42,43] by John Pritchard and Sons Ltd and converted to an iron foundry. The siding connection with the Pocket Nook Branch was retained. John Pritchard and Sons Ltd was still in existence at Atlas Court in 1966 [65] when the firm was described as general engineers and iron founders. The works subsequently closed and the buildings are now occupied by various small firms.

The Union Chemical Works

In the early 1850s, Llewellyn William Evans, late manager of the St Helens Foundry of Robert Daglish and Company, built the Union Chemical Works alongside the St Helens Canal, on the east side of the railway. In 1854, James McBryde was taken into the partnership. He became sole owner when Evans sold out in 1873 and later reformed the firm as James McBryde and Co Ltd [4]. The works was taken over by the United Alkali Co Ltd on its formation in November 1890 and closed in 1894 [64]. It had largely been dismantled by 1899 [66].

A St Helens Railway plan dated 1863 [67] shows that the sidings serving the works consisted of a pair of tracks running along the canal bank, merging to form a single line connection with the Pocket Nook Branch immediately to the south of the swing bridge. Turntables gave access to short lengths of track within the works. The same layout appears on the first edition of the 25 inch map, surveyed in 1881. By the time that the survey was made in 1891 and 1892 for the revision of the 25 inch map, these tracks had been extended, presumably by the United Alkali Company, to link up with the railway system at the Globe Works.

The construction of the Liverpool, St Helens and South Lancashire Railway in the mid 1890s led to further changes to the rail layout. A spur was built from the new railway to join the link line from the Globe Works. This spur, which was primarily intended to give access to the Globe Works, was evidently complete when the Liverpool, St Helens and South Lancashire Railway opened for goods traffic on 1st July 1895 [3,32,33].

231

Around 1900, St Helens Borough Council purchased the site of the Union Chemical Works, with the intention of building a new gas works. A proposal was submitted to the Local Government Loan Board in 1901 [68], but was evidently turned down. The site remained largely undeveloped until after the second world war, apart from the construction of a gasholder. It is now used by British Gas plc as a repair base .

Rights to use the sidings leading to the Union Chemical Works passed to the Corporation with the purchase of the site. In July 1905, the Great Central Railway, which had absorbed the Liverpool, St Helens and South Lancashire Railway, approached the Borough Council seeking terms on which it could make use of the sidings to reach the Globe Chemical Works and John Varley and Company's Waterloo Foundry [69,70]. In the event, the railway company decided that it only required access to the Waterloo Foundry and did not need to make use of the link line to the Globe Works [71], which was apparently worked by the United Alkali Company's locomotive [72]. John Varley and Company were charged four shillings for each wagon left on Corporation property [73].

One of the sidings on Corporation property was let out to the Worsley Mesnes Colliery Co Ltd for use as a coal depot, although this was vacated towards the end of the first world war [41,42]. Around 1915 or 1916, the Corporation leased a parcel of land to British Petroleum Ltd which established an oil storage depot on the site [41]. The depot passed to Shell Marketing Co Ltd in 1920 [74] and later to Shell Mex Ltd [44,75]. A second oil storage depot was built by the Anglo American Oil Co Ltd in the 1920s [44,75]. Both seem to have closed during the second world war or shortly afterwards and are not shown in the *Railway Clearing House Handbook* for 1956 [76].

The Pocket Nook Smelting Works

The sidings along the canal bank also gave access to the Pocket Nook Copper Smelting Works. This had been established in 1851 by Alexander Robertson Arrott, lately manager of Union Plate Glass Works. James Radley, the colliery proprietor, had taken over by 1859, apparently trading later as the Pocket Nook Smelting Company [4,77].

The works was advertised for sale by auction on 7th February 1888 [78]. It was taken over to manufacture sulphate of copper, probably by William B. Marshall and Son [79]. The venture was unsuccessful and the the newly erected plant was auctioned on 28th July 1892 [80]. The site was purchased by John Varley and Company and its subsequent history is described later in the chapter.

The Atlas Foundry

A small foundry was established in Bridge Street in 1841 by Thomas Robinson and his uncle John Cook [4]. The firm, later known as Robinson and Cooks [81], soon needed bigger premises and the much larger Atlas Foundry, alongside the Pocket Nook Branch opposite to the St Helens Chemical Company's works, was erected around 1850. The date of 1847 given by Barker and Harris [4] for the move is probably a little too early, as the works is not shown on the 1/1056 Town Plan, surveyed in 1849.

The Atlas Foundry doubled in size during the next decade as the demand for its equipment for the chemical industry grew and in 1861 the firm opened a second factory at Widnes to supply the alkali works which were beginning to be established there [4]. Thomas Robinson devoted most of his time to the Widnes works, leaving Joseph and Thomas, John Cook's two sons, in charge at St Helens [4]. Other members of the Robinson and Cook families joined the firm and in November 1884 the partnership consisted of Thomas Robinson, Samuel Robinson, Joseph Cook, William Joseph Cook, John Joseph Cook and Benjamin Brown [81].

In the early years of the present century the firm decided to concentrate its activities at Widnes and the Widnes Foundry Co Ltd was formed, possibly in 1905, to take over the works there. The Atlas Foundry at St Helens was closed in 1907 [82]. The premises and plant were put up for sale on 2nd and 16th December 1908 [83,84] and were purchased by John Varley and Company. We continue the history of the site below.

The Atlas Foundry had a rail connection to the Pocket Nook Branch which gave access to a very limited series of tracks within the works yard. It seems unlikely that a locomotive was required during the period that the premises were occupied by Robinson and Cooks.

John Varley and Company's Waterloo and Atlas Foundries

The Varleys had been prominent in the foundry business in St Helens since the early part of the nineteenth century and, for a time, several different works were operated independently by different branches of the family.

John Varley's business was established in 1837 in Waterloo Street on the site later occupied by the Technical College [85], although prior to that he seems to have been involved in another foundry in Water Street owned by Henry Varley [4]. By 1857, the partners in John Varley and Company were James and Jesse Varley and at the end of February that year Jesse left the firm to set up business on his own [86]. Later the firm passed into the hands of James's sons, James and Henry [87]. Subsequent entries in directories show John Varley and Company at the Waterloo Foundry in Waterloo Street [24,88-91]. As we have seen in Chapter 7, the firm also occupied a foundry at Boundary Road between 1866 and 1878.

Jesse Varley was at the Brookfield Foundry in Foundry Street in 1864 [88]. Following his death, his executors carried on the business and are shown at the Brookfield Foundry in 1871 [92] and 1876 [90], the address being given as St Mary Street in the latter entry. The firm must have closed down soon afterwards and does not appear in a directory for 1883-84 [91].

John Varley and Company, as we have already mentioned, moved to Pocket Nook where the firm purchased the site of the copper smelting works and erected a much enlarged Waterloo Foundry. In 1908 the adjoining Atlas Foundry, previously owned by Robinson and Cooks, was taken over.

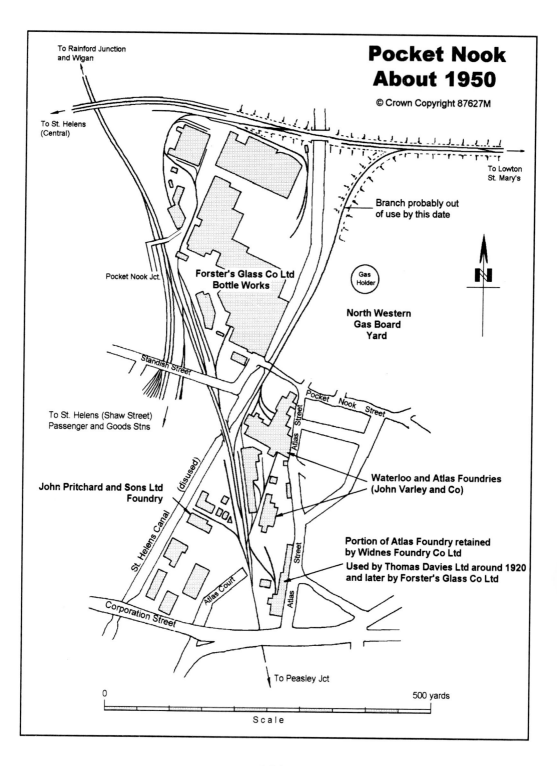

Pocket Nook About 1950

© Crown Copyright 87627M

To Rainford Junction and Wigan

To St. Helens (Central)

Branch probably out of use by this date

To Lowton St. Mary's

Pocket Nook Jct.

Forster's Glass Co Ltd Bottle Works

Gas Holder

North Western Gas Board Yard

N

Standish Street

To St. Helens (Shaw Street) Passenger and Goods Stns

Pocket Nook Street

Atlas Street

St. Helens Canal (disused)

John Pritchard and Sons Ltd Foundry

Waterloo and Atlas Foundries (John Varley and Co)

Portion of Atlas Foundry retained by Widnes Foundry Co Ltd

Used by Thomas Davies Ltd around 1920 and later by Forster's Glass Co Ltd

Atlas Court

Atlas Street

Corporation Street

To Peasley Jct

0   500 yards

Scale

234

Both the Waterloo Foundry and the Atlas Foundry had a number of small sidings which led to various parts of the works and each had its own separate connection with the Pocket Nook Branch. There was no internal rail link between the two premises and the firm had permission, under an agreement of 8th December 1915, for its steam crane to travel over 150 yards or so of the Pocket Nook Branch between the two works [49].

John Varley and Sons became John Varley (Ironfounders) Ltd in the late 1970s [60,93] and at that time the firm was advertising that it could produce small and medium castings between 1 kg and 15 tonnes in weight [93]. The Waterloo and Atlas Foundries closed a few years later. Only the derelict sites remain at the time of writing.

Steam cranes continued to be used for shunting until around 1950, when the firm purchased a rather elderly four-coupled saddle tank from the Kingsbury yard of George Cohen Sons and Co Ltd, the machinery merchants.

Varley's ancient Hunslet hard at work in August 1951. (C.A. Appleton)

The locomotive had been built by the Hunslet Engine Company of Leeds in 1879 and fitted with a new boiler from the same firm in 1924. It had been previously used at the Cliffe Hill granite quarries in Leicestershire. The engine performed a useful job at Varleys for a further ten years or so. Rail traffic had ceased at the works by the time that the Pocket Nook Branch closed on 4th May 1970 and the locomotive was broken up on site by Todd Brothers.

Thomas Davies Ltd

A portion of the Atlas Foundry, at the southern end of the site, was not included in the sale to Thomas Varley and Company and was retained by Robinson and Cooks Ltd for use as an office and a warehouse [40,41,42]. To avoid passing over tracks belonging to John Varley and Company a separate connection was provided to the Pocket Nook Branch, but it is unlikely that a locomotive was used in view of the restricted size of the sidings.

These premises were leased to Thomas Davies Ltd, probably in 1918. This firm, which had its headquarters in Widnes, specialised in the supply of railway material and evidently needed additional space. Thomas Davies Ltd purchased a four-coupled saddle tank from the Stoke on Trent firm of Kerr, Stuart and Company and the manufacturer's records [29] show that it was despatched to the Atlas Ironworks at St Helens in July 1918.

It seems unlikely that the firm intended to make use of the engine at St Helens. It may have been bought as a speculative venture, but there is another tentative explanation. In the period immediately after the first world war, the railway system at the British Insulated and Helsby Cable Company's works at Prescot was rebuilt and extended. It is possible that the work was undertaken by Thomas Davies Ltd and, although we have no documentary evidence to support this, it is perhaps no coincidence that the locomotive became the property of the cable company in 1920.

The part of the Atlas Ironworks premises occupied by Thomas Davies Ltd was vacated about 1921 [43,44]. It was then leased by the Widnes Foundry Co Ltd, as successors of Robinson and Cooks, to P.F. Delaney, trading as Andrew Mooney [44]. By 1930 [75] it had become the property of Mooneys Ltd and is marked on the 25 inch map, revised in 1926, as "Hardshaw Works".

An LMSR Plan of 1947 [27] shows that the premises had by then changed hands again and were occupied by Forster's Glass Co Ltd. The siding serving the works possibly survived until the 1960s or 1970s. A number of small firms now occupy those buildings which remain.

LOCOMOTIVE SUMMARY

Union Plate Glass Works

Union Plate Glass Company 1836 to 1864
Union Plate Glass Co Ltd from 1864
Works closed 1904
Part sold to John Forster and Sons Ltd about 1908
Part sold to H.W. Johnson and Co about 1913
Part sold to Andrew Mooney in 1916 and possibly used by Ministry of Munitions as
    Central Stores Depot No.34
Whole site taken over by Forster's Glass Co Ltd in early 1920s

	0-4-0T	OC	FJ	175	1884	10"x20"	3'3"

New to Union Plate Glass Co, April 1884
Advertised for sale 13.3.1907
Scrapped or sold

Ministry of Munitions Central Stores Depot No.34 Pocket Nook

F. GILL	0-4-0ST	OC	MW			8"x14"	

Advertised for sale in 1921 and 1922
Possibly MW 887 of 1883, ex John Forster and Sons Ltd

BARBARA CRIPPS	0-4-0ST	OC	P	1247	1910

Ex Stephens Silica Brick Co, Kidwelly
Spares to Ministry of Munitions at Pocket Nook
To Blackmountain Silica Co Ltd, via C. Williams

Forster's Glass Bottle Works

John Forster and Sons Ltd until July 1919
Took over part of Union Glass Works about 1908
Forster's Glass Co Ltd from July 1919
Took over whole of Union Glass Works site in early 1920s
Subsidiary of Rockware Group from 1.1.1947
Rockware Glass Ltd from 1966
Works closed March 1982

GREENWICH	0-4-0ST	OC	MW	887	1883	8"x14"	2'8"

Class D
New to John Mowlem and Co, public works contractors
Advertised for sale by John Forster and Sons Ltd, August 1917
Believed to have been purchased by Ministry of Munitions

PHYLLIS   0-4-0ST OC   MW   68   1862   9½"x14"   2'9"
   Class E
New to Rennie and Co, public works contractors, at Neath as FAIRY
Later with Logan and Hemingway at Rotherham. Then to Mountsorrel Granite Co,
   Loughborough as PHYLLIS. Then possibly with Holme and King.
Purchased by John Forster and Sons in about 1917
Scrapped in 1925 or a year or two later

BAGHDAD   0-4-0ST OC   P   914   1901   10"x14"   2'6"
   Class M4
Ex John Harrison Ltd, Levenshulme, before October 1917
To Hough and Sons, Wigan, in about 1939

ATLAS   0-4-0ST OC   P   1680   1925   12"x18"
   Class R2
   New
   Scrapped in about 1959

POCKET NOOK   0-4-0ST OC   WB   2592   1939   13"x18"   3'0½"
   New
   Scrapped in 1962

HARDSHAW   0-4-0ST OC. HL   3491   1921   14"x22"   3'6"
   Ex Southern Oil Co, via Hough and Sons, in about 1949
   Scrapped on site by A. Lowe in June 1966

POCKET NOOK II   0-4-0DM   RSH   6991   1940
   Ex Cohen in January 1961, previously Darwen Paper Mill Co Ltd
   Scrapped in about May 1967

        4wDM   FH   3769   1955
   Ex Montague L. Meyer (Northern) Ltd, Widnes 1967
   Scrapped or sold in about 1974

400/703   0-6-0DM   HC   D1038 1958   200HP
   Named POCKET NOOK I
   Ex Mersey Docks and Harbour Co in about May 1973
   Scrapped in about June 1982

400/704   0-6-0DM   HC   D1039 1958   200HP
Ex Mersey Docks and Harbour Co in about September 1973
   Scrapped in about June 1982

United Alkali Co Ltd, Central Stores

On part of site of St Helens Chemical Company's works
Stores closed 1923

Apparently spare locomotives were kept here for the United Alkali Company's St Helens group of works. Locomotives may also have been sent here for repair.

In July 1919 the following two locomotives were recorded at the Central Stores :

EMILY	12"
MARGERY	13"

Atlas and Waterloo Foundries

Atlas Foundry
    Robinson and Cooks from about 1850 to 1908
    James Varley and Co from 1908 to late 1970s
    James Varley (Ironfounders) Ltd from late 1970s
    Works closed in 1980s

Waterloo Foundry
    On site of Pocket Nook Smelting Works
    James Varley and Co from about 1892 to late 1970s
    James Varley (Ironfounders) Ltd from late 1970s
    Works closed in 1980

0-4-0ST OC   HE   215 1879

Ex Cliffe Hill Granite Co Ltd, via G. Cohen Sons and Co Ltd, Kingsbury, in about 1949
Scrapped on site by Todd Bros (St Helens and Widnes) Ltd, in July 1960

Before 1949 steam cranes were used for shunting

Thomas Davies Ltd

Occupied part of Atlas Ironworks site from about 1918 to about 1921

0-4-0ST OC   KS   3107 1918   12"x16"

New to Thomas Davies Ltd, Atlas Ironworks, St Helens, July 1918
To British Insulated and Helsby Cables Ltd, Prescot, 1920

References to Chapter 9

1   *The St Helens Railway*, J.M. Tolson, Oakwood Press, 1983
2   11 Geo 4 cap lxi; 29th May 1830
3   Information supplied to the authors by Mr J.M. Tolson
4   *A Merseyside Town in the Industrial Revolution   St Helens 1750 - 1900*, T.C. Barker and J.R. Harris, Frank Cass & Co Ltd, London, 1959
5   WRO DDX/Ta 16/6
6   LRO PDR 799
7   *The Engineer* 19.2.1864
8   British Locomotive Catalogue 1825 - 1923" - Vol 2A LNWR, ed David Baxter Moorland Publishing Co, Ashbourne, 1978
9   *Herepath* 20.7.1844
10 Early Locomotives of L&YR, E. Craven, in *Journal of the Stephenson Locomotive Society*, No XXXVIII, July 1962
11 *Railway Times* 10.1.1853
12 *Directory of Lancashire*, Kelly's Directories Ltd, 1901
13 *StHNews* 9.2.1934
14 Photograph at StHLH
15 *Liverpool and District Trades Directory*, Town and County Directories Ltd, 1908
16 *Liverpool and District Trades Directory*, Town and County Directories Ltd, 1924
17 *Liverpool and District Trades Directory*, Town and County Directories Ltd, 1925
18 *Mineral Statistics* for 1879
19 *Mineral Statistics* for 1880
20 *StHNews* 19.11.1881
21 StHNews 30.12.1882 Retrospect for 1882
22 StHNews 18.5.1888
23 LNWR Sdgs Diag 167, dated 12.1916
24 *Directory of St Helens, Widnes and Surrounding Districts*, Sutton and Co, Manchester, 1887
25 *Directory of St Helens*, Slater's Directory Ltd, Manchester, 1895
26 *Directory of Lancashire*, Kelly's Directories Ltd, 1905
27 LMSR Plan, Liverpool District No.11, Sheet 16 St Helens, dated May 1947
28 LNWR Sdgs Diag 168, dated 12.1916
29 At National Railway Museum, York
30 *MG* 25.3.1905
31 LNWR Sdg Diag 162, dated 12.1916
32 *StHNews* 2.7.1895
33 *StHNews* 6.7.1895
34 *The Glassmakers   Pilkington 1826 - 1976*, T.C. Barker, Weidenfeld and Nicolson, London, 1977
35 *StHNews* 22.4.1905
36 *MG* 6.5.1905
37 *StHNews* 12.5.1905
38 *MG* 7.5.1905
39 *MG* 2.3.1907
40 Rate Book Hardshaw Ward, 1913/14, at StHLH
41 Ibid 1916/17
42 Ibid 1918/19
43 Ibid 1920/21
44 Ibid 1925/26
45 LMSR Sdg Diag 162A, dated 3.1926
46 *Surplus* 1.9.1921
47 *Surplus* 2.10.1922
48 *A History of Forster's Glass Co Ltd*, no author, no pub, nd, abt 1969, StHLH A 37.8
49 LNW Sdgs Diag 163, dated 9.1916
50 Endorsement on LMSR Sdg Diag 162A, dated 3.1926
51 Letter Vulcan Boiler Insurance Co to Forster and Sons 23rd Oct 1917, StHLH FO/4/5/253
52 *MM* 24.8.1917
53 Report Vulcan Boiler Insurance Co to Forster's Glass Co Ltd 6th Jan 1925, StHLH FO/4/5/253
54 Letter Vulcan Boiler Insurance Co to Forster's Glass Co Ltd 17th Feb 1925, StHLH FO/4/5/253

55   Letter Vulcan Boiler Insurance Co to Forster's Glass Co Ltd 9th Sept 1925, StHLH FO/4/5/253

56   Letter Vulcan Boiler Insurance Co to Forster's Glass Co Ltd 12th Nov 1937, StHLH FO/4/5/253

57   Letter Forster's Glass Co Ltd to Vulcan Boiler Insurance Co 6th Jan 1938, StHLH FO/4/5/253

58   Letter Vulcan Boiler Insurance Co to Forster's Glass Co Ltd 29th Mar 1938, StHLH FO/4/5/253

59   *Manufacturing Trades Directory*, St Helens Metropolitan Borough Council, 1978

60   *Post and Chronicle* 1.12.1981

61   *StHNews* 18.9.1891

62   *A History of Antimony Smelting in St Helens*, Peter Hampson, Typescript, 1994, at StHLH A 36.1 HAM (P)

63   CRO DIC/UA 10/7

64   CRO DIC/UA 12/20

65   *County Borough of St Helens Directory*, Blair Publications Ltd, Blackpool,1966

66   *StHNews* 25.3.1899

67   St Helens Rly Engineers Office Plan dated Apl 28th 1863, StHLH Rolled Plan 611C

68   *StHNews* 22.11.1901

69   St Helens Corporation Gas and Lighting Committee Minutes 10.7.1905

70   Ibid 13.9.1905

71   Ibid 11.7.1906

72   Ibid 8.7.1908

73   Ibid 12.12.1906

74   Ibid 10.3.1920

75   Rate Book Hardshaw Ward, 1930/31, at StHLH

76   *Official Handbook of Stations*, British Transport Commission (Railway Clearing House), London, 1956

77   *A Directory of the Chemical Works of St Helens 1820 - 1889*, J.D. Turton, C. Kay and P. Meara, Halton Historical Publications No.15

78   *StH Lantern* Feb 1888

79   *Royal National Commercial Directory of St Helens and District*, Isaac Slater, Manchester, 1891

80   *MG* 23.7.1892

81   LRO DDX 1041/2/2

82   *A History of the Chemical Industry in Widnes*, D.W.F. Hardie, Imperial Chemical Industries Ltd, Widnes, 1950

83   *MG* 7.11.1908

84   *WEx* 7.11.1908

85   *StHNews* 20.2.1979

86   *LG* 6.3.1857

87   *StHRep* 29.8.1902

88   *Royal National Commercial Directory of Lancashire*, Isaac Slater, Manchester, 1864

89   *Royal National Commercial Directory of Lancashire*, Isaac Slater, Manchester, 1869

90   *Directory of Warrington, Wigan, St Helens etc*, John Worall, Oldham, 1876

91   *Directory of Warrington, Widnes, St Helens and Earlestown*, Isaac Slater, Manchester, 1883-84

92   *Directory and Historical Sketches of St Helens and District*, P. Mannex and Co, Preston, 1871

93   *St Helens Directory of Manufacturing and Related Industries*, St Helens Metropolitan Borough, 1984

94   Advertising brochure, nd, abt 1980, a' StHLH A36.1(P)

CHAPTER TEN

AROUND GERARD'S BRIDGE

From Pocket Nook we move northwards to the area around Gerard's Bridge. Industrial development dates from the opening of the Sankey Navigation, which reached the terminal basin here in 1759. As elsewhere around St Helens, coal mines were sunk to supply the Liverpool market and the Cheshire salt workings, now both accessible by water borne transport.

The Liverpool and Manchester Railway, as originally proposed in 1824 [1], would have passed near to Gerard's Bridge and would have competed with the navigation for the coal trade. However, the route finally adopted passed to the south of St Helens and it was not until the late 1830s that the collieries around Gerard's Bridge were provided with a rail connection.

The 1830 Act [2], under which the St Helens and Runcorn Gap Railway was incorporated, authorised a branch from Peasley Cross to Gerard's Bridge and Rushy Park but construction was delayed by a shortage of money. As we have seen in a previous chapter, work on the line did not start until 1836 or 1837 and then only with the financial assistance of the Union Plate Glass Company [3].

The line to Gerard's Bridge was probably opened for traffic at the end of 1837, at the same time as the section from Peasley Junction to the Union Plate Glass Works [3], although no official record of the event has been found. It was certainly in use by December 1839 when Speakman, Caldwell and Company was recorded as one of the five firms sending coal over the St Helens Railway [4]. No work was carried out on the extension beyond Gerard's Bridge to the Rushy Park Colliery.

There were several projects in the 1840s and 1850s which would have served Gerard's Bridge and surrounding districts. In 1845 the Liverpool and Manchester Railway was granted powers for a line from Sutton to Rainford [5,6]. A year later the Grand Junction Railway was authorised to construct a line from Huyton to join the Rainford line near Gerard's Bridge [7,8]. In both cases the powers were allowed to lapse. A St Helens Railway scheme in 1845 for a branch to Eccleston Four Lane Ends was also dropped [9].

The St Helens and Rainford projects were revived in 1851 [10] and again in 1852 [11]. The latter line, proposed by the St Helens Railway Company, was authorised by Parliament in 1853 [12] and opened to traffic in 1858. The Lancashire Union Railways Company's line from Gerard's Bridge Junction to Wigan was brought into use in 1869 and the railway network was completed in July 1895, when the Liverpool, St Helens and South Lancashire Railway was opened for freight traffic.

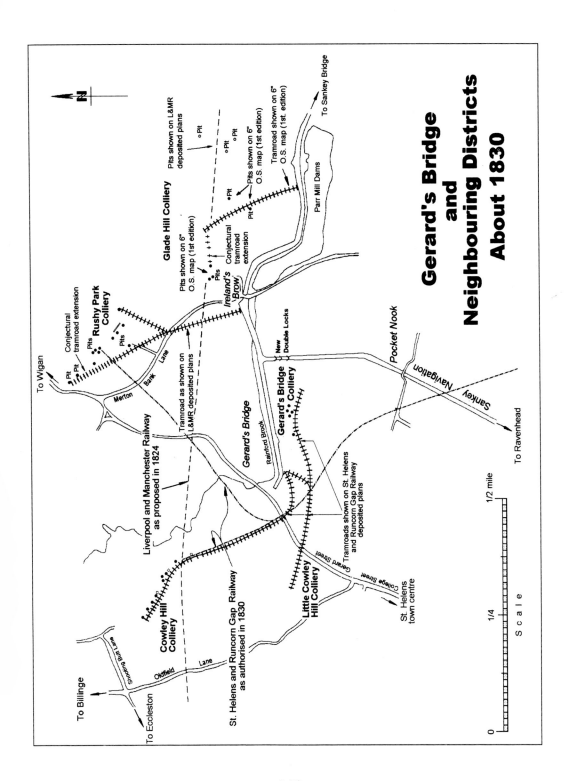

Gerard's Bridge
and
Neighbouring Districts
About 1830

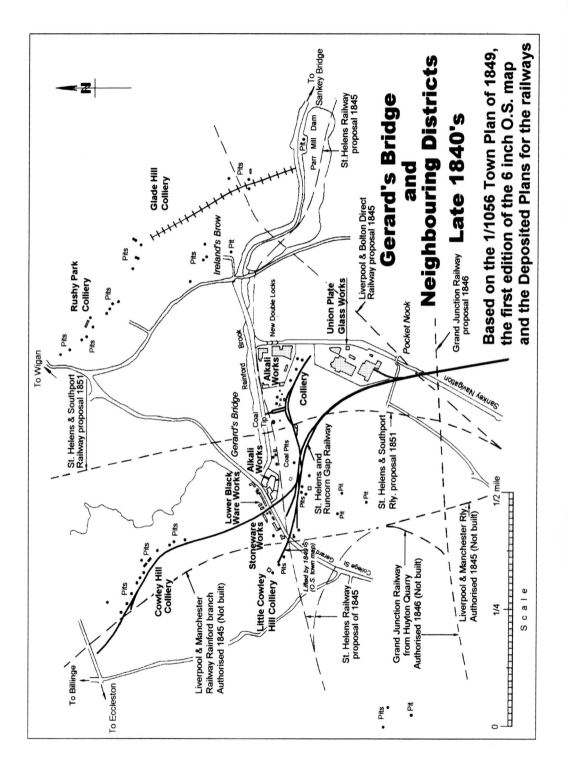

Gerard's Bridge
and
Neighbouring Districts
Late 1840's

Based on the 1/1056 Town Plan of 1849,
the first edition of the 6 inch O.S. map
and the Deposited Plans for the railways

N

To Wigan

To Billinge

To Eccleston

St. Helens & Southport Railway proposal 1851

Rushy Park Colliery

Pits

Pits

Pits

Pits

Pits

Glade Hill Colliery

Pits

Ireland's Brow

Pit

Pits

Pit

Parr Mill Dam

St.Helens Railway proposal 1845

To Sankey Bridge

Liverpool & Bolton Direct Railway proposal 1845

Union Plate Glass Works

Grand Junction Railway proposal 1846

Pocket Nook

Sankey Navigation

New Double Locks

Rainford Brook

Gerard's Bridge

Alkali Works

Colliery

Coal

Tip

Coal Pits

St. Helens and Runcorn Gap Railway

St. Helens & Southport Rly. proposal 1851

Pit

Pit

Pit

Lower Black Ware Works

Alkali Works

Stoneware Works

Little Cowley Hill Colliery

Lifted by 1849-5 (O.S. town map)

Gerard St.

College St.

St. Helens Railway proposal of 1845

Grand Junction Railway from Huyton Quarry Authorised 1846 (Not built)

Liverpool & Manchester Rly. Authorised 1845 (Not built)

Cowley Hill Colliery

Pits

Pits

Pits

Pits

Pits

Liverpool & Manchester Railway Rainford branch Authorised 1845 (Not built)

Pit

Pit

Pits

Scale

0   1/4   1/2 mile

244

Our exploration commences with the collieries and their associated tramroads as they existed in the 1820s and 1830s. Later in the century alkali manufacture replaced coal mining as the chief industry of the district and by 1865 the last pit had closed. Since 1873, the scene has been dominated by the plate glass factory which Pilkington Brothers established on a 120 acre site at Cowley Hill.

Glade Hill Colliery

Glade Hill Colliery was in existence in the early 1820s [1] and by 1840 was being worked by the Glade Hill Coal Company in which James Muspratt, Robert Daglish Junior, John Speakman and William Bromilow were partners. James Muspratt and William Bromilow retired on 8th February 1840 [13] leaving the firm in the hands of Daglish and Speakman.

The colliery was taken over a few years later by John and Thomas Johnson, who were also involved with the nearby Laffak Colliery which we deal with in Part Two. John and Thomas Johnson remained in occupation at Glade Hill until 1861, after which the colliery disappears from the Mines Lists.

Glade Hill was never served by the main line railway system. The bulk of its output appears have been sent away by canal and the pits were connected to a wharf opposite Parr Mill Dam by a series of short tramroads. These are shown on the first edition of the 6 inch map, surveyed in 1845 and 1846, and on the Parr Tithe Map of 1843 [14]. Although the lines do not appear on the Deposited Plans for the Liverpol and Manchester Railway of 1824 [1] there is reason to believe that they had been constructed much earlier than the 1840s. The tramroad presumably remained in use until the colliery closed around 1860.

Mining was resumed at Glade Hill in the early years of the present century by William Hilton of Orrell, but only on a very small scale. Typical figures shown in the Mines Lists for the total number of employees range from 7 to 14. Work ceased in 1919.

Rushy Park Colliery

Rushy Park Colliery was located to the west of Glade Hill. It was probably this mine which is mentioned by Barker and Harris as being leased to the Rushy Park Coal Company, a partnership consisting of Cheshire salt proprietors and Liverpool merchants, in 1801 [4]. It was connected by a tramroad, which was in existence as early as 1824 [1], to a wharf on the canal near the bridge at Islands Brow, known at that date at Ireland's Brow.

By 1825 the colliery was being worked by Whitley, Bromilow and Caldwell [15] and by 1834 it had passed to the firm of Bromilow and Sothern [16]. It seems to have closed in the 1840s and is not recorded in the first issue of Mines Lists dated 1853-54.

Gerard's Bridge, Cowley Hill and Little Cowley Hill Collieries

We now turn to three collieries which started out as separate concerns but later came under common ownership.

Gerard's Bridge Colliery consisted of two groups of pits. One group was located near the Double Locks, where the Ravenhead and Gerard's Bridge branches of the Sankey Navigation diverged, and was sufficiently close to the canal for coal to be loaded directly into barges. The other group was nearer to Gerard's Lane, the present College Street, and was connected to the canal by a short tramroad [17].

Cowley Hill Colliery was on the higher ground north of Gerard's Lane and consisted of a string of shallow pits and at least one drift. These extended almost to Shooting Butt Lane, a continuation of the present Windle City and long since obliterated by Pilkington Brothers' Cowley Hill Works. The Deposited Plans of November 1824' for the Liverpool and Manchester Railway [1], and of November 1829, for the St Helens and Runcorn Gap Railway [17], show a tramroad which ran past most of the pits and terminated at a loading point on the canal in the vicinity of Gerard's Bridge Colliery.

Little Cowley Hill Colliery was also located on the north side of College Street, roughly in the position of the present day Cowley Street. As shown on the plans of 1829 [17], it was linked to the canal at a point near the terminal basin by a tramroad.

Gerard's Bridge Colliery had been the property of the West family since the end of the eighteenth century [4] and it is shown in the occupation of Thomas West and Company in both 1825 [15] and in 1834 [16]. Cowley Hill Colliery was evidently opened out by members the Speakman family. The firm o

f Charles Speakman and Company, in which John Sothern was also a partner, was reported to be sinking new pits here in 1821 [4], although some parts of the colliery may have been older. The early history of Little Cowley Hill does not seem to have survived, but it is known that in 1834 [16] and 1837 [18] it was being worked by Thomas Hamer Rigby.

Although Thomas West and Company and Thomas Speakman and Company were nominally separate concerns, they were in fact controlled by the same partners, who also owned a salt works at Anderton, near Northwich. In the 1830s the partners were William Anthony Augustin West, Thomas Birch Speakman, Edward Speakman and Thomas Caldwell. Following the retirement of W.A.A. West in March 1833 [19], James Underhill West and James Mackay joined the partnership [20]. In the late 1830s, both firms were dissolved and the partnership reformed as Speakman, Caldwell and Company [4,21]. As well as taking over Gerard's Bridge and Cowley Hill Collieries, the new concern appears to have acquired Little Cowley Hill Colliery [22].

The St Helens and Runcorn Gap Railway Act of 1830 [2] authorised spurs to Gerard's Bridge, Cowley Hill and Little Cowley Hill Collieries, following the routes of the tramroads. However, it seems unlikely that the railway company constructed its own tracks much beyond the point where they intersected the tramroads on the south side of Gerard's Lane, leaving the colliery companies to convert the tramroads to standard gauge lines at their own expense. The conversion had been completed by November

1844, when Deposited Plans were prepared for a railway from St Helens to Southport [23], and may have been undertaken a few years earlier.

Following the death of the surviving partner in the firm of Speakman, Caldwell and Company, the Gerard's Bridge, Cowley Hill and Little Cowley Hill Collieries were put up for sale at the beginning of 1848. The advertisement [22] stated that they had been established upwards of thirty years and that they were in full operation. They were subsequently taken over by the firm of Caldwell and Thompson [24]. William Thompson died on 4th July 1856 [25] and the partnership was reformed once again under the title of Caldwell and M'Cormach. The collieries were offered for sale as a going concern on 12th October 1864 when it was stated that, in addition to the sidings to the St Helens Railway, there were two pier heads on the canal [26].

In the event there was no further mining at Gerard's Bridge, apart from a brief period from 1872 to 1874 when the Mines Lists record that Willliam Middlehurst was working here. Presumably this was a pillar robbing operation or something similar. The Gerard's Bridge Pumping Engine was taken over by Pilkington Brothers and Bromilow, Haddock and Company and operated on a joint basis [4]. It became the responsibility of St Helens Collieries Ltd, following the merger of the Pilkington and Bromilow and Haddock colliery interests in 1876.

The Mines Lists suggest that there was a brief period from 1872 to 1874 when coal was again being worked at Gerard's Bridge by William Middlehurst. The 1/1056 Town Plan of St Helens, surveyed in this district in 1849, records the changes to the railway layout which had taken place since the conversion of the tramroads. The centre of railway operations was at the terminus of the St Helens Railway, where the single line from Peasley Cross widened into double track. From this loop a single track led to Cowley Hill Colliery, crossing Gerard's Lane on the level and passing close to the earthenware works established by Richard Lightfoot in the early years of the century. A siding leading off the loop gave access to the part of Gerard's Bridge Colliery nearest to College Street, where four shafts are marked.

From the opposite end of the loop, a single track served the other part of Gerard's Bridge Colliery, nearest to the Double Locks, where there were six shafts. Midway along this line there was a short loop, with turntables giving access to a tip on the canal. Also marked is a small building with a track leading into it, which has the appearance of being an engine shed. Did Speakman, Caldwell and Company and its predecessors have a locomotive of their own ? We have found nothing in the records.

No railway is shown serving Little Cowley Hill Colliery and the implication is that the pits here had ceased production shortly after their acquisition by Caldwell and Thompson. However, a line leading to Little Cowley Hill is marked on Deposited Plans for the St Helens and Southport Railway prepared in November 1851 [10] and those for the St Helens Railway's branch to Rainford, dated November 1852 [11].

The construction of the Rainford Branch of the St Helens Railway brought about alterations to the sidings at Gerard's Bridge Colliery. A new line was built from Pocket Nook Junction to provide access to those pits nearest to the Double Locks, while it appears that the pits closest to College Street were served by a siding from Pocket Nook Junction which followed the earlier alignment.

Gerard's Bridge Alkali Works

A small works to manufacture alum was established by Edward Rawlinson and Joseph Edwards in 1829 [27] on the south side of the canal near the Gerard's Bridge terminus . Edwards retired in October 1830 [4]. Rawlinson added an alkali plant [27] but was declared bankrupt on 3rd August 1833 [4].

The factory was auctioned on 7th January 1836 when it was bought by a partnership consisting of Joseph and James Crosfield and Josias Christopher Gamble [4]. The Crosfields withdrew from the Gerard's Bridge works around 1843 and by 1844 it was under the control of J.C. Gamble and his son David [4].

Evidently the works relied entirely on canal and road transport at this time. No rail connection is shown on the 1/1056 Town Plan, surveyed in 1849, although the branch to Cowley Hill Colliery passed nearby.

Considerable expansion took place over the next two decades and it was during this period that sidings were laid in to serve the works. There had been major changes to the railway layout in the area following the construction of the line from St Helens to Rainford, opened for traffic in 1858. This intersected the course of the original Gerard's Bridge Branch at what became Pocket Nook Junction and the siding connection leading to the alkali works joined the Rainford line just north of the junction.

There was more expansion in the 1870s. The Earthenware Works of Lightfoot and Company and the Lower Blackware Works of Lightfoot Brothers, on the north side of College Street, were put up for auction on 22nd July 1875 [28]. The Earthenware Works was purchased by J.C. Gamble and Son to provide space to expand its manufacturing capacity. To provide access between the old and new parts of the works, the level crossing over College Street, which had once served Cowley Hill Colliery, was brought back into use. The Lower Blackware Works seems to have continued in production as a pottery but was up for sale again on 18th February 1878 [29]. When a survey was made in 1891 and 1892 for a revision of the 25 inch map, the site had been cleared.

The firm of J.C. Gamble and Son was absorbed into the United Alkali Co Ltd on its formation in November 1890. Some ten years later the works on the north side of College Street, on the earthenware factory site, was closed and the level crossing taken out. Its buildings were subsequently demolished and the site incorporated into Pilkington Brothers' Cowley Hill complex. The main works continued in production until 1922 [30] and was sold in 1930 to St Helens Borough Council. The site was later turned into a recreation ground.

We have records of only one locomotive used at the Gerard's Bridge Works. In June 1919, when an inventory [31] was made of all United Alkali plant, the four-coupled well tank A.G.K. built by Borrows in 1887 was working here. There were also seven main line spring buffer wagons,three 8-ton dumb buffer wagons, presumably for internal use, and one main line tank wagon. The railway system comprised 760 yards of sidings.

A.G.K. had originally been owned by A.G. Kurtz and Company and had been used at this firm's alkali works in Warrington New Road, which was also taken over by the United Alkali Company. Before A.G.K. was transferred from the Kurtz Works; it is possible that one of the locomotives attributed to the Hardshaw Brook Works, also a Gamble family concern, was used at Gerard's Bridge.

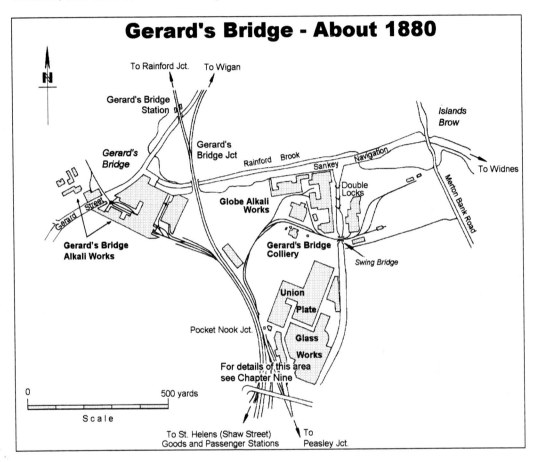

Gerard's Bridge - About 1880

The Globe Alkali Works

The Globe Works had its origins in a small factory which was erected by James Muspratt and Josias Christopher Gamble on land near the Double Locks, leased from Greenalls in 1828 [4]. Muspratt opened his own works at Newton le Willows in 1831 [4] and the works at Double Locks was taken over in March 1836 by the partnership of Joseph and James Crosfield and J.C. Gamble which had earlier the same year purchased the Gerard's Bridge Works [4]. Gamble left the partnership in 1845 [4] to devote the whole of his time to the Gerard's Bridge Works, while the Crosfield brothers took over control of the Globe Works [4].

In the twenty years between 1845 and 1864 the Globe Works increased fourfold in size [4]. The whole of the land between the colliery and the canal was leased as from the 29th September 1848 from Gilbert Greenall [32]. Then, on 1st November 1860, land on the east of canal was taken on lease [32].

The Globe Works had no railway connection when the 1/1056 Town Plan was surveyed in 1849. Later several sidings were provided which joined into those which gave access to the Gerard's Bridge Pumping Pit. The earliest agreement with the LNWR about the use of the main line connection that we have been able to trace is dated 31st August 1866 [33]. Permission to build a swing bridge over the canal to carry the railway to the eastern part of the works was granted under Section 9 of the St Helens Canal and Railway Transfer Act of 1864 [34].

In 1879 the works was sold by Crosfield Brothers to the Globe Alkali Co Ltd [4]. This firm had been formed in the same year [34] under the auspices of Wigg Brothers and Steel of Runcorn [27].

Up to this time, the land occupied by the railway lines from the LNWR boundary to the pumping station and the Globe Works was owned by Sir Gilbert Greenall who presumably levied some form of toll in respect of traffic which was worked over it. As from 1st November 1879 [32], this land was leased by the Globe Alkali Company from Sir Gilbert, which effectively gave the firm free use of the tracks. It was perhaps this which gave rise to the remarks in Pilkington Brothers' minutes [36] when the partners heard that the works had been taken over. "The rails [at the pumping station] belong to us and are on our land. Will propose to sell them [Globe Alkali Company] the rails at present price and pay them a trifle for handling our [coal] traffic to the engine house."

The Globe Alkali Company was taken over by the United Alkali Co Ltd on its formation in November 1890. As described in Chapter 9, a line was built to connect with the sidings at the Union Chemical Works at Pocket Nook and later a connection was made with the Liverpool, St Helens and South Lancashire Railway by this route.

Nothing is known about the earliest locomotive which was used at the Globe Works except that it was advertised for sale in May 1882 [37] when it was stated to have 8½ inch diameter cylinders. It had been made redundant by a new four-coupled saddle tank named GLOBE which had been purchased from the Hunslet Engine Company of Leeds in 1880. There seems to have been no spare engine as, when GLOBE needed repairs in 1888, the Globe Alkali Company advertised that it needed to hire a four-coupled locomotive for three or four weeks [38]. After the takeover by the United Alkali Company, engines were no doubt brought in from other works in the St Helens area when GLOBE was out of action.

In June 1919, when the inventory was made of UAC plant [31], GLOBE was still the only locomotive here. The inventory records that there were 2400 yards of sidings at the works and the rolling stock comprised fourteen main line spring buffer wagons of 8- and 10-ton capacity, seven 8-ton dumb buffer wagons for internal use and one trolley.

The works closed in 1924 [35] and the site was later taken over by St Helens Corporation. The fate of GLOBE has not been recorded.

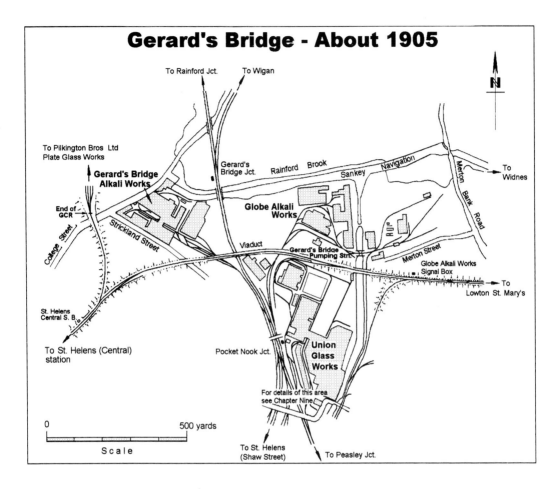

Gerard's Bridge - About 1905

To Rainford Jct.

To Wigan

N

To Pilkington Bros Ltd
Plate Glass Works

Gerard's Bridge Jct.

Rainford Brook

Sankey Navigation

Merton Bank Road

To Widnes

Gerard's Bridge Alkali Works

End of GCR

Strickland Street

College Street

Globe Alkali Works

Viaduct

Gerard's Bridge Pumping Stn.

Merton Street

Globe Alkali Works Signal Box

To Lowton St. Mary's

St. Helens Central S. B.

To St. Helens (Central) station

Pocket Nook Jct.

Union Glass Works

For details of this area see Chapter Nine

0   500 yards
Scale

To St. Helens (Shaw Street)

To Peasley Jct.

Pilkington Brothers' Cowley Hill Works

1873 to 1892

In the early 1870s Pilkington Brothers decided to branch out into the manufacture of plate glass and a site at Cowley Hill was chosen for a new factory. The works took three years to build and the first glass was cast on 14th July 1876 [39]. Grinding began on 9th August, when the steam engine driving the plant was started up at 7.30 am [40].

Edward Borrows seems to have played a large part in designing the layout of the railway system for the new works [41,42]. The scheme included a siding to hold four wagons for Lightfoot's Lower Blackware Works [43,44], although as these premises were sold in February 1878 [45] it is not certain that this was completed. He also supplied some of the glass making equipment, such as pot carriages, smoothing and grinding benches and polishing weights [46,47], as well as much of the railway material. Turntables and pointwork were ordered at the end of 1875 [46,48,49,50] together with 4,000 chairs at 5/6d per cwt.

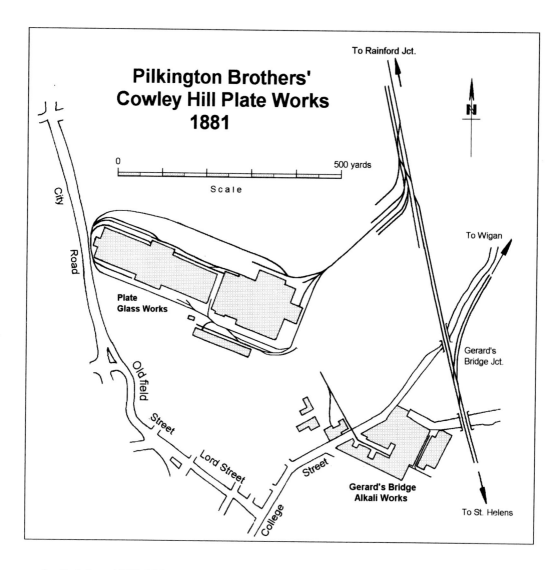

Pilkington Brothers'
Cowley Hill Plate Works
1881

To Rainford Jct.

N

0 ⊢————————————————⊣ 500 yards
Scale

City

Road

Plate
Glass Works

To Wigan

Old field

Street

Gerard's
Bridge Jct.

Lord Street

Street

College

Gerard's Bridge
Alkali Works

To St. Helens

In October 1875 300 yards of rail for lines in the Casting Hall were ordered from Borrows at £8.5s. per ton and from Todd at £7.12s.6d per ton [42]. These were presumably for the broad gauge tracks used to convey glass plates to the grinding and polishing rooms [51]. Another railway was installed to take rough cast glass to the annealing kilns [52].

Despite delays in completion of the work, for which Borrows was duly reprimanded by the partners, the connections with the LNWR Rainford Branch were completed in 1875 [53] at a cost of £1,000 and the main part of the internal railway system was ready for use in the summer of 1876 [47,51,54,55]. In September 1876 [56] some work still remained to be completed and further work was carried out in 1877 for which Borrows drew up the plans and supplied the rails [57,58].

Some doubt exists about the first locomotive to be used at the Plate Works. In 1874 two four-coupled well tanks were ordered from Borrows at a cost of £1325 each, with delivery in 6 months [59]. There were delays, for which Borrows was again reprimanded [60,61,62], and the first of the engines, SUTTON, was not completed until the autumn of 1875 [63]. WINDLE followed in August 1876 [64].

SUTTON seems to have been intended for the Sheet Works, although it may have worked initially at the Plate Works. This is to some extent confirmed by the authorisation in March 1876 [55,65,66], before WINDLE had been completed, of the erection of a temporary shed, located near the grinding and smoothing houses, to accommodate the Plate Works locomotive. WINDLE may have been delivered to Plate Works, thus releasing SUTTON for the Sheet Works.

The need for a stronger locomotive for the Plate Works was identified in 1882 in order to take more wagons up a steep incline on the railway system [67] and in November it was decided to obtain quotations for a 16 inch cylinder four-coupled engine [68]. Most firms refused to tender or quoted deliveries of 12 to 18 months. Only Hawthorns of Newcastle offerred a short delivery of 3 months and a price of £1350. Edward Borrows was then approached and quoted £1689 for a 16 inch locomotive and £1328 for a 14 inch one, strongly recommending the latter [69].

A decision was made to order the 14 inch engine from Borrows [69] and a further engine of the same type was ordered in July 1883. RAINFORD, intended for the Plate Works, was delivered in 1883, with KNOWSLEY following in 1884. The partners were unable to decide straight away whether KNOWSLEY should be charged to the Sheet Works or the Plate Works [70] and it may have been regarded as being available at either works. WINDLE was apparently transferred to the Sheet Works at this time.

In 1891, there were only two locomotives permanently allocated to the Plate Works [71], presumably RAINFORD and KNOWSLEY, although we cannot be sure. Another new engine, ROBY, was completed by Borrows at the beginning of 1892 [72]. This was later associated with the Plate Works, but we have been unable to ascertain if it went there immediately. There were still only two locomotives permanently allocated to the Plate Works in 1895 [73].

A few pieces of information have survived about the wagon stock at the Plate Works during this period. In 1876 it was noted that a number of sand wagons would be required for the traffic from the Dock at Widnes, as well as for 'jobbing' around the works [74]. In March 1880, four of the worst wagons belonging to the colliery were transferred to the Plate Works for use as ballast wagons [75]. The Widnes traffic appears to have been grit, dredged from the River Mersey, which was used in the glass grinding process at the works. From 1881 onwards at least some of the sand needed for glass making was brought in by rail from the firm's own sandfield at Rainford. By the beginning of 1891 Pilkington Brothers possessed 50 sand wagons. As around 12 were under repair at any one time, these were insufficient and a further ten or twelve were ordered [76].

1892 to 1914

The Cowley Hill Works was extended and modernised in the closing years of the nineteenth century. Electrically driven machinery was introduced, a new casting hall and new annealing kilns were built in 1896 and 1897 [39] and a chemical works was erected near the exchange sidings with the LNWR [77].

During the period from 1903 to 1914, £620,000 was spent on further expansion of the glass making plant, which included a new factory block to the north of the original works, and also on ancillary facilities [39]. In 1909 [78,79,80] land at Islands Valley and Islands Brow was purchased to provide a site for disposing of sand from the grinding and polishing processes, supplementing the tips which were already in use on the Cowley Hill site. The new tips were on the east side of the London and North Western Railway and the waste material was conveyed as a slurry in a pipeline over the railway. There were negotiations in 1920 to purchase a further 43 acres at Haresfinch, probably for the same purpose [81].

In 1912 it was necessary to enlarge the power plant at a total cost of £42,000. A 4,500 Kw turbo generator from Parsons costing £16,248 was ordered to supplement the earlier gas engines. The new power station was completed just in time to be officially started up by King George V on his visit to the works on 8th July 1913 [39,82].

A major alteration to the railway system took place at the end of the century. Under powers obtained in 1897 [83] the Liverpool, St Helens and South Lancashire Railway was authorised to build a short branch across College Street into the Cowley Hill Works. The necessary alterations to Pilkington Brothers' lines were were put in hand in December 1899 [84] and the connection was in use by May of the next year [85]. The exchange sidings were extended at a cost of £300 towards the end of 1902 [86].

Plans were drawn up around 1910 to improve the transfer of wagons to and from the London and North Western Railway. It was intended to replace the existing dead end sidings with a gridiron of twelve through roads, the eight nearest the main line being for inwards traffic and the remaining four for outwards traffic [87]. Although the scheme was still under consideration in 1912, it was eventually dropped.

Within the works itself there were considerable alterations to the track layout to accommodate the factory extensions [88 to 91]. A new locomotive shed was provided in the Spring of 1911 [92,93].

Construction of the Windle Sand Wash at the north end of the site, adjacent to Washway Lane, was started in 1913 [94] and the plant came into operation on 13th May 1914 [95]. It was connected to the main works railway system by a single track line which commenced at the site of the old brickworks, previously dismantled around 1904 [96].

Initially the Sand Wash processed sand brought by narrow gauge railway from William Pilkington's estate in Windle and, when that supply was exhausted, it continued in operation to deal with sand from other sources. It was under the control of the Plate Works, although some sand was also sent to the Sheet Works [95].

254

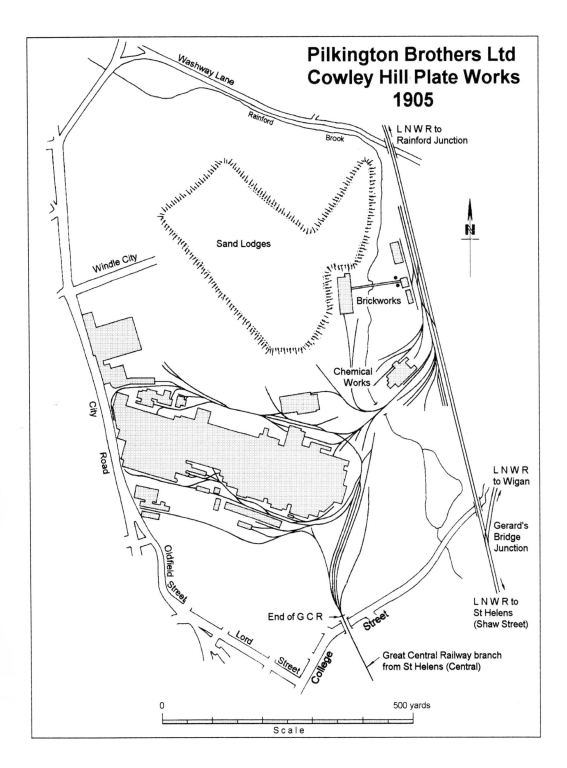

Pilkington Brothers Ltd
Cowley Hill Plate Works
1905

Washway Lane

Rainford Brook

L N W R to
Rainford Junction

N

Sand Lodges

Brickworks

Windle City

Chemical
Works

City Road

L N W R
to Wigan

Gerard's
Bridge
Junction

Oldfield Street

End of G C R

Street

College

Lord Street

L N W R to
St Helens
(Shaw Street)

Great Central Railway branch
from St Helens (Central)

0   500 yards

S c a l e

The extended railway system and the extra traffic from factory developments required more locomotives. Quotations were sought in 1902 for the first of these, which was named EDENHURST. This came from Edward Borrows at a cost of £1,350 in spite of Chapman and Furneaux quoting a lower price of £1,320 [97]. Another engine for the Plate Works was agreed with Borrows in April 1908 at a cost of £1,350 [98]. It was delivered later in the same year and was named BRIARS HEY.

The arrival of BRIARS HEY brought the total at the Plate Works to four working locomotives and one spare [99], the others presumably being RAINFORD, KNOWSLEY, ROBY and EDENHURST. A sixth engine, HOLLIES, was delivered by Borrows in 1910 and a new boiler for KNOWSLEY was ordered, at a cost of £320, in October 1914 [100].

By 1908 70 wagons were employed carrying river sand from Widnes, each wagon doing three trips per week. This was insufficient and 20 more wagons were put on the traffic. It was also noted that the loading facilities at Widnes were considered to be inadequate [101].

ROBY in a much modified condition, photographed at Pilkington Brothers' Plate Works in the early 1950s. It had been fitted a few years earlier with new frames supplied by the Worsley Mesnes Iron Co Ltd and was later to undergo several other rebuildings which are described in the Locomotive Summary.
(C.A. Appleton)

In 1909 eight 15-ton wagons were allocated to the Plate Works for sand traffic to replace the same number of 10-ton wagons [102]. A year later the possibility of using 20-ton wagons for sand was under discussion [103], presumably for the traffic from Old Mill Lane, where similar wagons were already carrying sand to the Sheet Works [104]. A new steam crane was purchased in 1912 [105]. In 1913, consideration was given to breaking up some of the oldest rubbish wagons, which were reaching the end of their useful lives [106].

BRIARS HEY, with a wagon of plate glass and two empties, tackles an incline at the north end of the Plate Works. The buildings on the left are part of the 1910 - 14 extensions. Raw materials were taken in on a high level over the bridge in the background. Finished glass came out over the low level lines. *(J.A. Peden)*

1914 to 1939

During the first world war, part of the works operated as a National Projectile Factory. Production of casings for high explosive shells started in 1915 and eventually 5,000 were being turned out each week. Another part of the works was loaned to the Ministry of Munitions for the reception of shells from factories in Lancashire and North Wales [107].

When peace returned, many of the glass making processes were updated as new methods of production were developed [39], although few extra buildings were needed. The only major change to the railway layout was the provision of four extra sidings, each to hold twenty wagons, authorised in September 1919 at a cost of £2,300 [105,108].

There were, however, two additional locomotives. ROSEBANK, a four-coupled saddle tank came in 1919 from Kerr, Stuart and Company of Stoke on Trent and was generally similar to the three engines bought at around the same time for the Sheet Works and for Ravenhead Colliery. KELVIN, which arrived at the Plate Works in February 1922 after a short period at the Sheet Works [105], was a return to the traditional Borrows design of four-coupled well tank. Edward Borrows and Sons had closed down in 1912, but the locomotive side of the business had been taken over by H.W. Johnson and Company, which completed KELVIN at its Rainford works in 1921.

KNOWSLEY was transferred to the Ravenhead Works at an unknown date, presumably after the new locomotives arrived. It was broken up at Ravenhead in 1936 [109]. Other contemporary items of railway information were that the purchase of a steam travelling crane was authorised in September 1919 at a cost of £1,125 [105,108], followed by another in January 1926 [105]. A spare locomotive boiler, presumably for a 15 inch Borrows engine, was ordered in November 1920 at a cost of £1,550 [110]. In 1926 and 1927 31 wagons for internal use were purchased second hand, replacing 42 existing wagons which were broken up [105]. The goliath crane, which became such a prominent feature of the Cowley Hill scene, was commisioned at the end of 1924 or early in 1925 [105]. Located on the old waste tips at the north end of the works, its purpose was to transfer large pieces of plate glass between railway wagons and the storage area.

ROSEBANK, the Kerr, Stuart Moss Bay Class locomotive of 1919, photographed in July 1950, with the Haresfinch sand lodges prominent in the background   (C.A. Appleton)

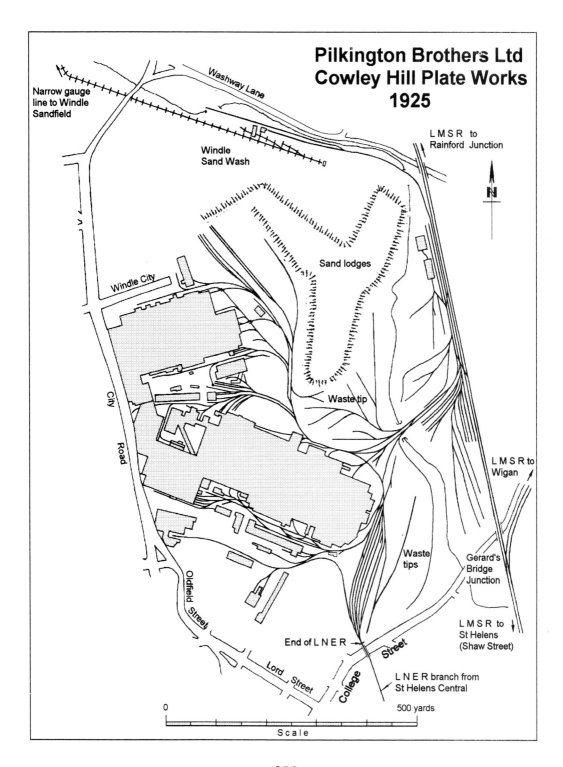

Pilkington Brothers Ltd
Cowley Hill Plate Works
1925

Narrow gauge line to Windle Sandfield

Washway Lane

Windle Sand Wash

LMSR to Rainford Junction

N

Sand lodges

Windle City

City Road

Waste tip

LMSR to Wigan

Oldfield Street

Waste tips

Gerard's Bridge Junction

LMSR to St Helens (Shaw Street)

End of LNER

Street

College

Lord Street

LNER branch from St Helens Central

0   500 yards

Scale

1939 to 1960

As in 1914 to 1918, certain work associated with the war effort was undertaken at the Plate Works during the period from 1939 to 1945. Glass production also remained at a high level, largely because of the need to replace windows destroyed by bombing. In the post war period demand for glass continued to rise both at home and in the export market. The high level of production was reflected in the intensive use of the works railways. In February 1958 four or five engines were in daily operation out of a total stock of six steam and two diesel locomotives. There were 17 miles of track and an operating staff of twenty men [111].

There had been some changes to the locomotive stock. RAINFORD had been scrapped in 1941 as the result of an accident [112] and had been replaced by PROGRESS, obtained second hand from Hough and Company of Wigan in 1942. PROGRESS was a four-coupled saddle tank built by Andrew Barclay Sons and Company of Kilmarnock in 1919 and had previously been at the Winstanley Collieries, near Wigan.

Another four-coupled saddle tank, REX, had been purchased from Hough and Company in 1947. It was a relatively new engine, having been built by Hawthorn, Leslie and Company of Newcastle on Tyne in 1937 for Pemberton Colliery, where it was named BESS. It is said that, on arrival at the Plate Works, the powers that be thought this sounded like a dog's name, so they gave it the regal title of REX !

HOLLIES had disappeared in 1944 at the start of a programme to rebuild the Borrows well tanks, which involved interchange of parts including the boilers. The hybrid locomotives kept the name associated with the boiler and carried plates recording the changes which had taken place.

The boiler from KELVIN was fitted to the chassis of HOLLIES in 1944, the engine then being known as KELVIN, while the frames of KELVIN were fitted to the boiler of EDENHURST in 1949 to make up the new EDENHURST. To complicate the task of the historian, two new frames were obtained from the Worsley Mesnes Iron Co Ltd of Wigan around 1950 for use in the reconstructions. The full story, as far as it is known, is recorded in the Locomotive Summary at the end of the chapter.

The first diesel electric locomotive, named CITY ROAD, arrived in January 1957 from the Yorkshire Engine Company, followed by DONCASTER in August 1957, COWLEY HILL in June 1958 and CROSSLEY in December 1958. CROSSLEY did not stay long very long, as it was transferred to the Ravenhead Works in June 1959. Two further diesel electric locomotives, ST ASAPH and QUEENBOROUGH, arrived from the Yorkshire Engine Company in March and April 1960 respectively. By the end of the year use of steam locomotives at Cowley Hill had ceased.

The first to go had been PROGRESS, which had been transferred to the Ravenhead Works about 1953. EDENHURST was withdrawn from service in February 1958 [113]. It was broken up, along with KELVIN and ROSEBANK, in August of that year. ROBY and BRIARS HEY were scrapped in October 1960 [113]. REX is reputed to have been transferred to the Sheet Works some time in 1960 and scrapped there in the same year.

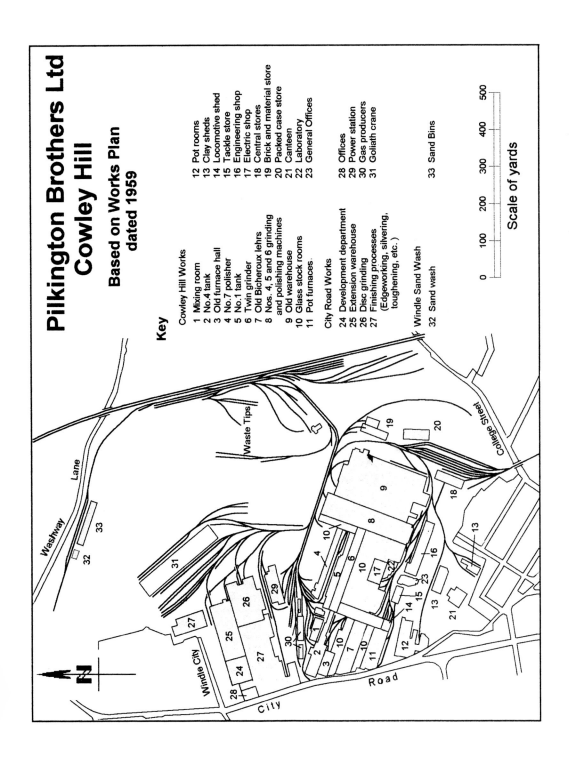

Pilkington Brothers Ltd
Cowley Hill

Based on Works Plan dated 1959

Key

Cowley Hill Works

1 Mixing room
2 No.4 tank
3 Old furnace hall
4 No.7 polisher
5 No.1 tank
6 Twin grinder
7 Old Bicheroux lehrs
8 Nos. 4, 5 and 6 grinding and polishing machines
9 Old warehouse
10 Glass stock rooms
11 Pot furnaces.

12 Pot rooms
13 Clay sheds
14 Locomotive shed
15 Tackle store
16 Engineering shop
17 Electric shop
18 Central stores
19 Brick and material store
20 Packed case store
21 Canteen
22 Laboratory
23 General Offices

City Road Works

24 Development department
25 Extension warehouse
26 Disc grinding
27 Finishing processes (Edgeworking, silvering, toughening, etc.)

28 Offices
29 Power station
30 Gas producers
31 Goliath crane

Windle Sand Wash

32 Sand wash

33 Sand Bins

Scale of yards
0 100 200 300 400 500

The Windle Sand Wash, which was still dealing with sand brought by road from workings in the area north and north west of St Helens, acquired its own diesel locomotive in 1956. This seems to have been the result of changes to the organisational structure of Pilkington Brothers Ltd, which placed the supply of sand under a separate management unit.

The 1956 locomotive was an 88 HP diesel mechanical machine, built by Ruston and Hornsby of Lincoln and named STRETTON. The Industrial Railway Society lists record several exchanges of locomotives with the Old Mill Lane Sidings at Rainford, which are given in the Locomotive Summary at the end of the chapter. Use of the Windle Sand Wash seems to have ceased in the early 1970s and STRETTON, the last locomotive to be used there, was sold for scrap about 1972.

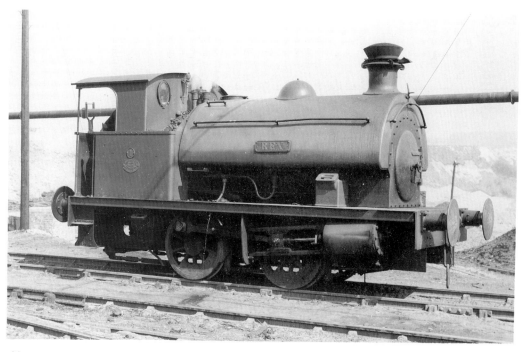

Above :

REX, obtained second hand in 1947, seen here in May 1956 after it had been transferred from Cowley Hill to the Sheet Works.

(Industrial Railway Society, Bernard Mettam Collection)

On the opposite page, two views at Cowley Hill Works when steam was still supreme :

Top - A busy scene in the British Rail exchange sidings alongside the Rainford Branch, probably taken in the 1950s. *(Pilkington Brothers Archives at IM&S)*

Bottom - The engine shed at Cowley Hill Works, photographed on 26th November 1949, with ROBY, BRIARS HEY and REX in steam. *(C.A. Appleton)*

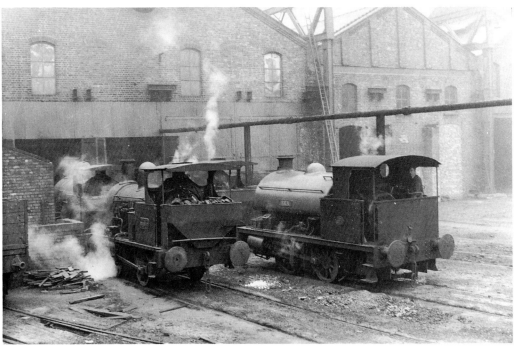

1960 to 1996

The Plate Works, known from 1953 as the City Road Works [39], was the setting for the development of the revolutionary new float glass process. Experimental work had started in the early 1950s [39] and the first production unit was set up in 1957. Saleable glass was not made until January 1959 [39] and then very quickly three other float lines were installed in existing buildings. The last plate glass tank was shut down on 17th November 1961 [114].

In the early 1970s a large new building was erected on the site of the old waste banks to provide space for more float glass production plant [115]. As a consequence changes had to be made to the railway layout, which by now was very much reduced in size.

Freight traffic on the former Great Central Railway had ceased in January 1965 and the exchange sidings at the south side of the City Road site had been removed. Less traffic was being handled through the former London and North Western sidings, partly as a result of the increasing use of road transport for the finished glass and partly because of the change over from coal to oil as the fuel for the production process.

CITY ROAD, the first of the Yorkshire Engine Company's diesel electric locomotives to work at Cowley Hill. Between 1956 and 1960, six of these 200 HP machines were purchased, replacing the stock of steam locomotives. *(E. Richards)*

Pilkington Brothers Ltd had negotiated a long term contract with Shell Mex and B P Ltd for the supply of 300,000 tons of oil per year. Two special unloading facilities were provided, one for the City Road Works and the other for the Sheet Works and the new Greengate Works. That for the City Road Works was situated alongside the British Rail line and was formally opened on 15th October 1968 by Dr Lawrence Pilkington [3,116]. It dealt with some 25 block trains of 100-ton tankers each month from the refineries at Stanlow and Heysham.The wagons were placed in position by the British Railways locomotives which worked the trains.

Most of the internal railway system closed at the end of March 1984 and three of the diesel lcomotives had been disposed of by the autumn of 1985. CITY ROAD was sold to Marcroft Engineering Ltd at Coalville, DONCASTER went to the Sandtoft Transport Centre near Doncaster for preservation and QUEENBOROUGH to the Llangollen Railway, also for preservation. Rail traffic ceased entirely a little later and the two remaining locomotives, COWLEY HILL and ST ASAPH, were noted out of use in 1986. It is assumed that they were subsequently broken for scrap.

An aerial view of Cowley Hill Works, looking south east, probably in the 1930s. The older part of the works is to the right, with the 1910-14 extensions nearer the camera, on the right. The light coloured patch of ground in the top left is the sand lodge, where waste material from the polishing process was deposited. The LNER line from Lowton to St Helens is just visible, running across the top right of the picture, with the derelict buildings of the Gerard's Bridge Alkali Works in front of it. *(Pilkington Brothers Archives at IM&S)*

LOCOMOTIVE SUMMARY

Gerard's Bridge Alkali Works

Crosfield and Gamble until about 1843
J.C. Gamble and Son 1843 to November 1890
United Alkali Co Ltd from November 1890
Works closed 1922

A.G.K.	0-4-0WT OC	EBS	22	1887	10"

New to A.G. Kurtz and Sons
Transferred to Gerard's Bridge Works by United Alkali Co Ltd
At Gerard's Bridge Works in 1919
Scrapped or sold

Globe Alkali Works

Muspratt and Gamble until mid 1830s
Crosfield and Gamble 1836 to 1845
Crosfield Brothers 1845 to 1879
Globe Alkali Co Ltd 1879 to November 1890
United Alkali Co Ltd from November 1890
Works closed 1924

	Tank loco				8½"

Advertised for sale, May 1882

GLOBE	0-4-0ST OC	HE	241	1880	13"

New
At Globe Works in 1919
Scrapped or sold

Cowley Hill Glass Works

Pilkington Brothers 1873 to 1894
Pilkington Brothers Ltd from 1894
Pilkington Brothers plc from 1981
Pilkington plc from 1987

SUTTON	0-4-0WT OC	EBS	4	1876	13"x20"	3'6"

It is not known whether this engine was initially delivered to the Sheet Works or the Plate Works at Cowley Hill, probably the former.

WINDLE	0-4-0WT OC	EBS	5	1876	13"x20"	3'6"

It is not known whether this engine was delivered to the Sheet Works or to the Plate Works at Cowley Hill, probably the latter. It was later at the Sheet Works.

RAINFORD	0-4-0WT OC	EBS		15	1883	14½"x20"	3'6"

RAINFORD   0-4-0WT OC   EBS   15   1883   14½"x20"   3'6"
New
Scrapped at Plate Works in 1941 after accident

KNOWSLEY   0-4-0WT OC   EBS   19   1884   15"x20"   3'6"
New
Transferred to Ravenhead Works and scrapped there in October 1936

ROBY   0-4-0WT OC   EBS   33   1892   14½"x20"   3'6"
New
For later history see below

EDENHURST   0-4-0WT OC   EBS   44   1902   14½"x20"   3'6"
New
For later history see below

BRIARS HEY   0-4-0WT OC   EBS   52   1908   14½"x20"   3'6"
New
For later history see below

HOLLIES   0-4-0WT OC   EBS   55   1910   14½"x20"   3'6"
New
For later history see below

No. 3 ROSEBANK   0-4-0ST OC   KS   4026   1919   15"x20"   3'6"
New
Scrapped at Plate Works October 1958

KELVIN   0-4-0WT OC   HWJ   58   1921
New to Sheet Works and transferred to Plate Works in February 1922
For later history see below

FRANK   0-4-0ST OC   AB   1261   1912
According to Industrial Railway Society records, hired from T.R. Booth in 1941

No. 2 PROGRESS   0-4-0ST OC   AB   1465   1916   14"x22"   3'5"
Purchased in 1942 from Hough and Sons Ltd, dealers, Wigan. Previously Winstanley
     Collieries Co Ltd
To Ravenhead Works in about 1953 and scrapped there early 1959

No. 1 REX   0-4-0ST OC   HL   3933   1937   14"x22"   3'6"
Purchased in 1947 from Hough and Sons Ltd, dealers, Wigan. Previously Pemberton
     Colliery Co Ltd, BESS
Transferred to Sheet Works in 1960 and scrapped there in same year

CITY ROAD	0-4-0DE	YE	2626 1956	200HP

New,delivered 29,1.1957
To Marcroft Engineering Ltd, Thornbrough Works, Coalville by 8.3.1985

DONCASTER	0-4-0DE	YE	2654 1957	200HP

New, delivered 13.8.1957
To Sandtoft Transport Centre, Sandtoft, near Doncaster by September 1985

COWLEY HILL	0-4-0DE	YE	2687 1958	200HP

New, delivered 2.6.1958
Scrapped or sold about 1986

CROSSLEY	0-4-0DE	YE	2730 1958	200HP

New, delivered 22.12.1958
To Ravenhead Works in about June 1959

ST ASAPH	0-4-0DE	YE	2781 1960	200HP

New, delivered 10.3.1960
Scrapped or sold in about 1986

QUEENBOROUGH	0-4-0DE	YE	2782 1960	200HP

New, delivered 7.4.1960
To Llangollen Steam Railway Society by 6.7.1985

Windle Sand Wash

Pilkington Brothers Ltd
Opened in 1914 and worked by locomotives from Cowley Hill Works until about 1956
Own locomotive stock until closed in early 1970s

STRETTON	4wDM	RH	408492 1956	Class 88DS

New
To Mill Lane Sand Wash in about 1964 and returned in about 1967
To Lowton Metals Ltd, Haydock, in about 1972

	0-4-0DM	HC	D622 1942	

Hired from T.W. Ward Ltd in 1965 and 1966. Formerly ROF Wilford, Notts

THE SCHOLES	4wDM	RH	299104 1950	Class 88DS

Ex Mill Lane Sand Wash in about 1967
Scrapped Oct 1969

The rebuilding of the well tanks at Pilkington Brothers Ltd's Cowley Hill Works

Between 1942 and 1957 there was an interchange of boilers and other parts between the surviving well tanks. Each reconstructed locomotive took the name of the engine to which the boiler had previously been fitted. Some engines changed boilers several times and thus also changed names several times. The following is believed to be a complete record based on the observations of the authors and their colleagues.

ROBY (I)
New in 1892
Frames used in reconstruction of EDENHURST (II), July 1942

ROBY (II)
ROBY boiler fitted to reconstructed frame of EDENHURST (I) January 1942
This information recorded on maker's plate
Frames of EDENHURST (I) broken up, probably late in 1950

ROBY (III)
Rebuilt 1950 with new frames supplied by Worsley Mesnes Iron Works
Plate altered to read "Reconditioned 1950"

ROBY (IV)
Rebuilt December 1954 with frames of HOLLIES (I), previously on KELVIN (II)
Plate altered to read "ROBY boiler on HOLLIES frame"

ROBY (V)
Rebuilt October 1957 ROBY with frames of EDENHURST (III) frames previously on
    KELVIN (II)
Plate altered to read "ROBY boiler fitted to EDENHURST frame October 1957"
Scrapped at end of 1960

EDENHURST (I)
New 1902
Frames used in reconstruction of ROBY (II) Jan 1942

EDENHURST (II)

New boiler fitted to reconstructed frame of ROBY (I) July 1942
This information recorded on maker's plate

EDENHURST (III)
Rebuilt with frames of KELVIN (I), March 1949
Plate altered to read "EDENHURST boiler fitted to frames of KELVIN"
Overhauled in 1951 without interchange of parts and "Overhaul 1951" stamped on
    plate
Scrapped at end of 1958

BRIARS HEY (I)
New 1908
Reconstructed chassis and new copper firebox completed April 1943. Put into service
    July 1943.

BRIARS HEY (II)
   Fitted with new frames from Worsley Mesnes Ironworks about 1950
   Maker's plate still reads Borows 52 of 1908

BRIARS HEY (III)
   Rebuilt Feb 1954 with frame of ROBY (III)
   Plate altered to read "BRIARS HEY boiler reconditioned by Messrs Hough and Sons
      fitted to reconditioned frame of locomotive ROBY"
   Scrapped late 1960

HOLLIES
   New 1910
   Boiler scrapped in 1944 and frames used on KELVIN (II) in 1947

KELVIN (I)
   New 1921
   Overhauled in 1944, with new cylinders, but retained original boiler and frames
   Plate altered to read "Reconstructed 1944"

KELVIN (II)
   KELVIN boiler fitted to HOLLIES (I) frame in 1947
   Maker's plate altered to record this
   Rebuilt in 1951 without interchange of parts and plate altered to read "Reconstructed
      1951"

KELVIN (III)
   Rebuilt December 1953 with boiler reconditioned by Hough and Sons and with frames
      of BRIARS HEY (II)
   Plate altered to read "KELVIN boiler on BRIARS HEY frames"
   Scrapped at end of 1958

The story of the interchange of frames is as follows

ROBY (I) to EDENHURST (II) in July 1942 and scrapped after 1949

EDENHURST (I) to ROBY (II) in January 1942 and scrapped after 1950

HOLLIES (I) to KELVIN (II) in 1947 and then to ROBY (IV) in December 1954

KELVIN (I) to EDENHURST (III) in March 1949 and then to ROBY (V) in October 1957

BRIARS HEY (I) scrapped after 1950

New Worsley Mesnes frame to ROBY (III) in 1950 and then to BRIARS HEY (III) in
   January 1954 with boiler reconditioned by Hough

New Worsley Mesnes frame to BRIARS HEY (II) in about 1950 and then to KELVIN (III)
   December 1953 with boiler reconditioned by Hough

References to Chapter 10

1	LRO PDR 132
2	11 Geo 4 cap lxi; 29th May 1830
3	Information supplied to the authors by Mr J.M. Tolson
4	*A Merseyside Town in the Industrial Revolution - St Helens 1750-1900*, T.C. Barker and J.R. Harris, Frank Cass & Co Ltd, London, 1959
5	8&9 Vic cap cxxiii; 21st July 1845
6	LRO PDR 407,
7	9&10 Vic cap cclxi; 17th July 1846
8	LRO PDR 424
9	LRO PDR 465
10	LRO PDR 572
11	LRO PDR 595
12	16&17 Vic cap cxxxiv; 4th August 1853
13	*LG* 4.2.1842
14	LRO DRL 1/62
15	*History, Directory and Gazetteer of the County Palatine of Lancaster*, Edward Baines, Liverpool, 1824 and 1825
16	*National Commercial Directory for the Counties of Chester, Cumberland, Durham and Lancaster*, James Pigot and Son, Manchester, 1834
17	LRO PDR 188
18	*Wigan Gazette* 1.9.1837
19	*LG* 8.4.1834
20	*LG* 7.8.1835
21	*Royal National Commercial Directory and Topography of the County of Lancaster*, Isaac Slater, Manchester, 1848
22	*BC* 15.1.1848
23	LRO PDR 424
24	*Royal National Classified Commercial Directory and Topography of the County of Lancaster*, Isaac Slater, Manchester, 1851
25	*BC* 19.7.1856
26	*WO* 7.10.1864
27	*A Directory of the Chemical Works of St Helens 1820-1889*, J.D. Turton, C. Kay and P. Meara, Halton Historical Publications No.15
28	*WO* 16.7.1875
29	*StH and Prescot Reporter* 2.2.1878
30	CRO DIC UA 12/20
31	CRO DIC UA 11/1/10
32	Recited in Conveyance Imperial Chemical Industries Ltd to St Helens Corpn, StHLH ST/4/100/1
33	LNWR Sdgs Diag 161 dated 10.1916
34	27&28 Vic cap ccxcvi; 29th June 1864
35	CRO DIC/UA 16/40
36	Pilkington Brothers General Board Minutes 13.11.1879, at IM&S
37	*The Engineer* 12.5.1882
38	*The Engineer* 9.11.1888
39	*The Glassmakers - Pilkington 1826 - 1976*, T.C. Barker, Weidenfeld and Nicolson, London, 1977
40	Pilkington Brothers Plate Board Minutes 15.8.1876, at IM&S
41	Ibid 22.9.1875
42	Ibid 1.10.1875
43	Ibid 14.10.1875
44	Ibid 21.10.1875
45	*StH and Prescot Reporter* 2.2.1878
46	Pilkington Brothers Plate Board Minutes 8.9.1875
47	Ibid 27.4.1876
48	Ibid 13.8.1875
49	Ibid 12.11.1875
50	Ibid 21.8.1875
51	Ibid 30.6.1876
52	Ibid 6.7.1876
53	Ibid 9.5.1875
54	Ibid 21.3.1876
55	Ibid 14.6.1876
56	Ibid 7.9.1876
57	Ibid 3.10.1877

#	Reference		#	Reference
58	Pilkington Brothers General Board Minutes 28.3.1877		91	Ibid 14.4.1910
59	Pilkington Brothers Plate Board Minutes 13.11.1874		92	Ibid 5.8.1910
60	Ibid 11.6.1875		93	Ibid 25.9.1910
61	Ibid 18.6.1875		94	Pilkington Brothers General Board Minutes 27.3.1913
62	Ibid 24.6.1875		95	Pilkington Brothers Plate Board Minutes 10.5.1914
63	Ibid 24.8.1875		96	Pilkington Brothers General Board Minutes 13.9.1904
64	Ibid 4.8.1876		97	Pilkington Brothers Plate Board Minutes 14.3.1902
65	Ibid 2.3.1876		98	Pilkington Brothers General Board Minutes 7.4.1908
66	Ibid 15.3.1876		99	Pilkington Brothers Plate Board Minutes 22.5.1908
67	Ibid 22.6.1882		100	Ibid 29.10.1914
68	Ibid 2.11.1882		101	Ibid 13.4.1908
69	Ibid 10.11.1882		102	Ibid 14.10.1909
70	Ibid 25.9.1884		103	Ibid 8.3.1910
71	Pilkington Brothers General Board Minutes 13.1.1891		104	Pilkington Brothers General Board Minutes 7.3.1905
72	Ibid 29.12.1891		105	Cowley Hill Works Capital Requisitions 1912 to 1926, at IM&S PB 657
73	Ibid 22.1.1895		106	Pilkington Brothers General Board Minutes 1.4.1913
74	Pilkington Brothers Plate Board Minutes 11.10.1876		107	IM&S PB 1/1080
75	Ibid 4.3.1880		108	Pilkington Brothers General Board Minutes 2.9.1919
76	Ibid 8.1.1891		109	Letter E.M.S. Wood to F.D. Smith dated 21.5.1956
77	Ibid 19.3.1896		110	Pilkington Brothers Ltd Cowley Hill Subsidiary Board Mins 19.11.1920
78	Pilkington Brothers General Board Minutes 23.2.1909		111	*StHRep* 11.2.1958 - Article on Cross and Borrows locomotives
79	Ibid 13.5.1909		112	*The St Helens Well Tanks*, B. Roberts, in *Journal of the Stephenson Locomotive Society*, December 1950
80	Ibid 10.8.1909		113	Letter E.M.S. Wood to B. Roberts dated 27.11.1961
81	Ibid 18.3.1920		114	*StHRep* 18.11.1961
82	Ibid 17.9.1912		115	*StHNews* 11.11.1969
83	60&61 Vic cap cxi; 15th July 1897		116	*StHRep* 19.10.1968
84	Pilkington Brothers Plate Board Minutes 29.12.1899			
85	Ibid 24.5.1900			
86	Ibid 25.9.1902			
87	Uncatalogued plan at IM&S, Sidings at Gerard's Bridge as amended 10th January 1912			
88	Pilkington Brothers Plate Board Minutes 13.12.1905			
89	Ibid 25.11.1909			
90	Ibid 7.4.1910			